Praise for *Acedia & me*

"Norris traverses theology, psychology, and personal experience in blunt, scholarly and surprisingly funny prose. . . . *Acedia & me* radiates. . . . [It] has an unsparing beauty, like a Georgia O'Keeffe painting of bleached bones, and flashes of unexpected humor."
—*USA Today*

"[W]rite she does, clearing a path to clarity for the rest of us. A deeply personal narrative, *Acedia & me* shows how the numbing repetitions of everyday life, whether in a monastery or a house in rural South Dakota, can lead to a sense of hopelessness. . . . And gently, with no fanfare, she preaches the practicality of love—he̶l̶i̶. . . t demon, however insidious, can comp. . . *O, the Oprah Magazine*

"Meditative . . . Ta. . . rary writings of Joan Didion and Saul. . . me, among them St. Thomas Aquinas. . . vagrius Ponticus. But it is in those mon. . . words, her own story, that the reader experiences the real spiritual awakening."
—*San Francisco Chronicle*

"This is an intensely personal memoir . . . Norris moves gracefully back and forth in time, landing on the final years of [her husband, David's] life. . . . *Acedia & me* is also a loving homage to the art of etymology at the hands of a fine and generous poet. . . . Ancient language with contemporary relevance. Norris is at her best when she shares the many brilliant touch points between theology and her life. In *Acedia & me* she also makes the connection with the larger world. . . . Read it gently and carefully, and not without humility."
—*The Portland Oregonian*

"A moving memoir and an etymological explication of acedia."
—*The Atlantic*

"In a book that is scholarly and deeply personal, Norris writes about the acedia she experienced in various seasons of her life, her husband's battle with depression, and the implications for a society that grows 'more reluctant to care about anything past our perceived needs.'"
—*The Miami Herald*

"Norris movingly describes her bouts with a nameless detachment as an adolescent, later with a familiar affliction that could arise out of nowhere and spiral down into apathy and despair. When she narrates actual events—her husband's suicide attempt, her fortieth high school reunion, her husband's death from cancer—and her responses to them, she writes with clarity, honesty, and rigor."
—*The Boston Globe*

continued . . .

"Part memoir and part history of religious thought, *Acedia & me* is a thought-provoking book, bringing you deep into Norris's life and thoughts. . . . An excellent book, both on a memoir level and that as a philosophical discourse."
—*Sacramento Book Review*

"A poet's reflection on acedia—a kind of spiritual malaise that's been around for eons—and how it tested her faith and marriage. Full of wisdom and comfort."
—*Good Housekeeping*

"[*Acedia & me*] takes Norris into terrain that will be new for her fans and appealing for her novitiates. . . . With or without the safety net of divine love, Norris makes a compelling case that a life of self-mastery is the preferred route from here to the grave."
—*The San Diego Union-Tribune*

"Norris's meditative memoir-meets-philosophy lecture is just the means to explore this elusive concept. . . . She has an unusual ability to draw on the imagery of the Psalms and the solace of her own Christian beliefs without proselytizing. She leaves it to us to define what comprises our spiritual practice. . . . Norris's intellect allowed her to take the measure of acedia; her faith empowers her to fight it off. Sloth is kept at bay, and we, her readers, are the better for it."
—*The Seattle Times*

"Norris's far-ranging intellectual curiosity, gentle humor, and honesty about her own doubts and missteps make it a welcoming read for people of diverse spiritual experience."
—*Sojourners*

"Norris's prodigious study shows us that acedia's reach is both wide-ranging and profound."
—*Los Angeles Times*

"Readers walk with [Norris] through life in a small town in South Dakota, a difficult but deeply loving marriage; her husband's bouts with alcoholism and severe illness and finally his death; her widowhood; and her dialogue with ancient and modern writers who have grappled seriously with life's ultimate issues. It is a bracing and enlightening journey."
—*America*

"A masterpiece of a book: part memoir, part history about a little-known but much-suffered malady."
—*Spirituality & Health*

"A touching narrative about the heartaches [Norris has] confronted in her own life . . . Norris writes beautifully, poetically, opening up for discussion an affliction that no doubt plagues many, few of whom could even put a name to their condition. . . . This work will resonate with all who've fought this fight—and they are legion."
—*Rocky Mountain News*

"This astonishingly revealing memoir is crafted around three subtly woven narratives . . . This profound, provocative book deserves a wide readership. . . . Self-diagnosis is a long and difficult process, requiring patience and thoughtful searching, as Norris's extraordinary odyssey with acedia bears witness."
—*St. Louis Post-Dispatch*

"Kathleen Norris has accomplished the impossible again. Who else but this much-loved author, poet, and Benedictine oblate could resurrect a Latin word from its oak-gall-ink-and-vellum grave? . . . *Acedia & me* is the most intimate work to date by the author. . . . The result of Norris's decades-long meditation on acedia is peaceful, graceful prose, amplified by word histories and gentle humor."
—*Christianity Today*

"Norris, a superb storyteller, careful synthesizer, and brilliant interpreter, presents the 'peculiar history' of the history of acedia and chronicles her own battles with this particular 'soul-sickness.' Her personal stories are truly moving and instructive but the most arresting and resonant aspect of this engrossing extrapolation is Norris's theory of social acedia as the explanation of our inaction in the face of so much violence and injustice. . . . Fascinating . . . Reading this strongly argued, paradigm-altering work may be the first strike against the demon it portrays."
—*Booklist* (starred review)

"In this penetrating theological memoir, Norris details her relationship with acedia, a slothful, soul-weary indifference long recognized by monastics. . . . Filled with gorgeous prose, generous quotations from Christian thinkers across the centuries and fascinating etymological detours, this discomfiting book provides not just spiritual hope but a much-needed kick in the rear."
—*Publishers Weekly* (starred review)

Praise for *Amazing Grace*
A *NEW YORK TIMES* NOTABLE BOOK

"An engaging meditation on the language of faith."
—*The New York Times Book Review*

"[Norris] combines an impressive understanding of theology with personal experience, making her essays read like letters from a highly literate friend."
—*People*

continued . . .

Praise for *The Cloister Walk*

A *NEW YORK TIMES* NOTABLE BOOK

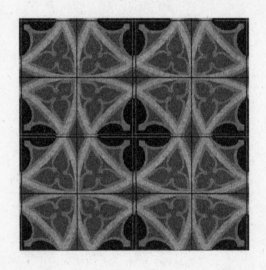

RIVERHEAD BOOKS

New York

Acedia & me

A MARRIAGE, MONKS, AND

A WRITER'S LIFE

KATHLEEN NORRIS

RIVERHEAD BOOKS
Published by the Penguin Group
Penguin Group (USA) Inc.
375 Hudson Street, New York, New York 10014, USA
Penguin Group (Canada), 90 Eglinton Avenue East, Suite 700, Toronto, Ontario M4P 2Y3, Canada
(a division of Pearson Penguin Canada Inc.)
Penguin Books Ltd., 80 Strand, London WC2R 0RL, England
Penguin Group Ireland, 25 St. Stephen's Green, Dublin 2, Ireland (a division of Penguin Books Ltd.)
Penguin Group (Australia), 250 Camberwell Road, Camberwell, Victoria 3124, Australia
(a division of Pearson Australia Group Pty. Ltd.)
Penguin Books India Pvt. Ltd., 11 Community Centre, Panchsheel Park, New Delhi—110 017, India
Penguin Group (NZ), 67 Apollo Drive, Rosedale, North Shore 0632, New Zealand
(a division of Pearson New Zealand Ltd.)
Penguin Books (South Africa) (Pty.) Ltd., 24 Sturdee Avenue, Rosebank, Johannesburg 2196, South Africa

Penguin Books Ltd., Registered Offices: 80 Strand, London WC2R 0RL, England

The publisher does not have any control over and does not assume any responsibility for author or third-party
websites or their content.

First Riverhead hardcover edition: September 2008
First Riverhead trade paperback edition: March 2010
Riverhead trade paperback ISBN: 978-1-59448-438-4

The Library of Congress has catalogued the Riverhead hardcover edition as follows:

Norris, Kathleen, date.
Acedia & me : a marriage, monks, and a writer's life / Kathleen Norris.
p.   cm.
Includes bibliographical references.
ISBN 978-1-59448-996-9
1. Acedia.   2. Melancholy—Religious aspects—Christianity.
3. Sadness—Religious aspects—Christianity.   4. Apathy—Religious aspects—Christianity.
5. Monastic and religious life.   6. Norris, Kathleen.   I. Title.   II. Title: Acedia and me
BT732.4.N67   2008   2008010150
818"5403—dc22
[B]

PRINTED IN THE UNITED STATES OF AMERICA

10 9 8 7 6 5 4 3 2 1

Penguin is committed to publishing works of quality and integrity. In that spirit, we are proud to offer this
book to our readers; however, the story, the experiences, and the words are the author's alone.

In loving memory of

David Joseph Dwyer

1946–2003

The ancient word *acedia*, which in Greek simply means the absence or lack of care, has proved anything but simple when it comes to finding adequate expression in English. Modern writers tend to leave the term untranslated, or employ the later Latin *accidie*. A few examples from dictionaries may help the reader comprehend the broad range of meaning of the word, as it is currently understood.

accidie
heedlessness, torpor ... *[a] non-caring state*
—*Oxford English Dictionary,* 2nd edition, 1989

acedia
a- + kedos care, anxiety, grief + *ia, iea*—more at HATE
1. the deadly sin of sloth
2. spiritual torpor and apathy
—*Webster's Third New International Dictionary
of the English Language,* unabridged, 1976

acedia
a mental syndrome, the chief features of which are listlessness, carelessness, apathy, and melancholia
—Online Medical Dictionary, 2000

CONTENTS

Author's Note   xiii

I. SOMEWHERE   *1*

II. TEDIUM   *7*

III. FROM EIGHT BAD THOUGHTS TO SEVEN SINS   *20*

IV. PSYCHE, SOUL, AND MUSE   *48*

V. UP AND DOWN   *65*

VI. GIVE ME A WORD   *87*

VII. ACEDIA'S PROGRESS   *112*

VIII. ACEDIA'S DECLINE   *133*

IX. A SILENT DESPAIR   *153*

X. THE QUOTIDIAN MYSTERIES   *178*

XI. THE "NOON" OF MIDLIFE   *199*

XII. DAY BY DAY *223*

XIII. AND TO THE END ARRIVING *238*

XIV. A WIDOW'S UNEASY AFTERWORD *257*

XV. ACEDIA: A COMMONPLACE BOOK *287*

Acknowledgments *330*

Selected Bibliography *332*

AUTHOR'S NOTE

Several themes are threaded throughout this book: the much-maligned doctrine of sin; the question of whether acedia may be equated with depression; the implications of believing that human beings are made in the image of God; the psychological insights to be found in monastic literature and practice; and the meaning of marriage and motherhood. My hope is that each time I raise these subjects, I am enhancing the reader's understanding of them.

Some passages in *Acedia & Me* come from an address I wrote at the invitation of the Sisters of the Holy Cross, who asked me to talk to college women about how traditional monastic wisdom might be of use to them today. Working on this talk (eventually published as a chapbook, *The Quotidian Mysteries: Laundry, Liturgy, and "Women's Work"*) convinced me that I needed to write a longer meditation on the subject of acedia. The word and the concept have fascinated me since I first encountered them, many years ago, in a monastery library.

The words "Abba" and "Amma" were titles of respect employed by the early monastics of Egypt, Syria, Palestine, and Asia Minor to designate elders ("Fathers" and "Mothers") who had attained wisdom in the spiritual life and could offer good counsel.

The demon of *acedia*—also called the noonday demon—is the one that causes the most serious trouble of all. He presses his attack upon the monk about the fourth hour and besieges the soul until the eighth hour. First of all he makes it seem that the sun barely moves, if at all, and that the day is fifty hours long. Then he constrains the monk to look constantly out the windows, to walk outside the cell, to gaze carefully at the sun to determine how far it stands from the ninth hour [or lunchtime], to look this way and now that to see if perhaps [one of the brethren appears from his cell]. Then too he instills in the heart of the monk a hatred for the place, a hatred for his very life itself, a hatred for manual labor. He leads him to reflect that charity has departed from among the brethren, that there is no one to give encouragement. Should there be someone at this period who happens to offend him in some way or other, this too the demon uses to contribute further to his hatred. This demon drives him along to desire other sites where he can more easily procure life's necessities, more readily find work and make a real success of himself. He goes on to suggest that, after all, it is not the place that is the basis of pleasing the Lord. God is to be adored everywhere. He joins to these reflections the memory of his dear ones and of his former way of life. He depicts life stretching out for a long period of time, and brings before the mind's eye the toil of the ascetic struggle and, as the saying has it, leaves no leaf unturned to induce the monk to forsake his cell and drop out of the fight. No other demon follows close upon the heels of this one (when he is defeated) but only a state of deep peace and inexpressible joy arise out of this struggle.

Evagrius Ponticus (345–399), *The Praktikos*

I. *Somewhere*

One of the best stories I know is found in *The Institutes* by John Cassian, a monk who was born in the fourth century. Cassian speaks of Abba Paul, who, like many desert monks, wove baskets as he prayed, and subsisted on food from his garden and a few date palms. Unlike monks who lived closer to cities and could sell their baskets there, Paul

> could not do any other work to support himself because his dwelling was separated from towns and from habitable land by a seven days' journey through the desert . . . and transportation cost more than he could get for the work that he did. He used to collect palm fronds and always exact a day's labor from himself just as if this were his means of support. And when his cave was filled with a whole year's work, he would burn up what he had so carefully toiled over each year.

Does Abba Paul epitomize the dutiful monk who recognizes that the prayers he recites during his labors are of more value than anything he can make? Or is he the patron saint of performance art, methodically destroying the baskets he has woven to demonstrate that the process of making them is more important than the product? Paul's daily labors may have been designed to foster humility, but the annual burning had another, greater purpose. Cassian notes that it aided the monk in "purging his heart, firming his thoughts, persevering in his cell, and conquering and driving out acedia."

Acedia may be an unfamiliar term to those not well versed in monastic history or medieval literature. But that does not mean it has no relevance for contemporary readers. The word has a peculiar history, and as timelines on the *Oxford English Dictionary* website reveal, it has gone in and out of favor over the years. References to *accyde* cluster in the fourteenth century, then disappear until 1891; *accidie* appears in 1607, and then not again until 1922, in a citation from William R. Inge's *Outspoken Essays*. Reflecting on the cultural shock that followed the Great War, particularly in Europe, he writes that "human nature has not been changed by civilisation," and discerns "acedia . . . at the bottom of the diseases from which we are suffering." In the 1933 *OED*, *accidie* was confidently declared obsolete, with references dating from 1520 and 1730. But by the mid–twentieth century, as "civilized" people were contending with the genocidal horror of two world wars, *accidie* was back in use. A four-volume supplement to the *OED* published between 1972 and 1986 instructs, "Delete Obs.," and the current 1989 edition includes references from 1936 and 1950. Languages have a life and a wisdom of their own, and the reemergence of the word suggests to me that *acedia* is the lexicon's version of a mole, working on us while hidden from view. It may even be that the word has a significance that stands in inverse proportion to its obscurity.

The scholar Andrew Crislip writes that "the very persistence of the term 'acedia' betrays the fact that none of the modern or medieval glosses adequately conveys the semantic range of the monastic term." He cites a French monk, Placide Deseille, who describes the word as "so pregnant with meaning that it frustrates every attempt to translate it." I believe that such standard dictionary definitions of *acedia* as "apathy," "boredom," or "torpor" do not begin to cover it, and while we may find it convenient to regard it as a more primitive word for what we now term depression, the truth is much more complex. Having experienced both conditions, I think it likely that much of the restless boredom, frantic escapism, commitment phobia, and enervating despair that plagues us today is the ancient demon of acedia in modern dress. The boundaries between depression and acedia are notoriously fluid; at the risk of oversimplifying, I would suggest that while depression is an illness treatable by counseling and medication, acedia is a vice that is best countered by spiritual practice and the discipline of prayer. Christian teachings concerning acedia are a source of strength and encouragement to me, and I hope to explore its vocabulary in such a manner that benefits readers, whatever their religious faith or lack of it.

At its Greek root, the word *acedia* means the absence of care. The person afflicted by acedia refuses to care or is incapable of doing so. When life becomes too challenging and engagement with others too demanding, acedia offers a kind of spiritual morphine: you know the pain is there, yet can't rouse yourself to give a damn. That it hurts to care is borne out in etymology, for *care* derives from an Indo-European word meaning "to cry out," as in a lament. Caring is not passive, but an assertion that no matter how strained and messy our relationships can be, it is worth something to be present, with others, doing our small part. Care is also required for the daily routines that acedia would have us suppress or deny as meaningless repetition or too much bother.

Why care? I can answer that only by relating my personal history with acedia, telling stories from my infancy, childhood, and adolescence, and from a marriage that flourished for nearly thirty years until my husband died, after a lengthy illness, in 2003. In a sense I have been writing this story all my life. But I can also say that it began more than twenty years ago, when I first encountered the word *acedia* in *The Praktikos*, a book by the fourth-century Christian monk Evagrius Ponticus. Across a distance of sixteen hundred years he spoke clearly of the inner devastation caused by the demon of acedia when it "[made] it seem that the sun barely moves, if at all, and that the day is fifty hours long." Boredom tempts him "to look constantly out the windows, to walk outside the cell, to gaze carefully at the sun to determine [the lunch hour]." But Evagrius soon discovers that this seemingly innocuous activity has an alarming and ugly effect, for having stirred up a restlessness that he is unable to shake, the demon taunts him with the thought that his efforts at prayer and contemplation are futile. Life then looms like a prison sentence, day after day of nothingness.

As I read this I felt a weight lift from my soul, for I had just discovered an accurate description of something that had plagued me for years but that I had never been able to name. As any reader of fairy tales can tell you, not knowing the true name of your enemy, be it a troll, a demon, or an "issue," puts you at a great disadvantage, and learning the name can help to set you free. "He's describing half my life," I thought to myself. To discover an ancient monk's account of acedia that so closely matched an experience I'd had at the age of fifteen did seem a fairy-tale moment. To find my deliverer not a knight in shining armor but a gnarled desert dweller, as stern as they come, only bolstered my conviction that God is a true comedian.

I did laugh then, and also later, when I encountered another passage from Evagrius, recognizing myself in the description of a listless monk who

> when he reads . . . yawns plenty and easily falls into sleep. He rubs his eyes and stretches his arms. His eyes wander from the book. He stares at the wall and then goes back to his reading for a little. He then wastes his time hanging on to the end of words, counts the pages, ascertains how the book is made, finds fault with the writing and the design. Finally he just shuts it and uses it as a pillow. Then he falls into a sleep not too deep, because hunger wakes his soul up and he begins to concern himself with that.

The desert monks termed acedia "the noonday demon" because the temptation usually struck during the heat of the day, when the monk was hungry and fatigued, and susceptible to the suggestion that his commitment to a life of prayer was not worth the effort. Acedia has long been considered a peculiarly monastic affliction, and for good reason. It is risky business to train oneself ("training" being a root meaning of *asceticism*) to embrace a daily routine that mirrors eternity in its changelessness, deliberately removing distractions from one's life in order to enter into a deeper relationship with God. Under these circumstances acedia's assault is not merely an occupational hazard—it is a given. It is also an interfaith phenomenon. When I asked two Zen Buddhist monks how they defined the boredom that is endemic to monastic life, one replied that as her community was founded by an Anglican, they call it acedia. The other was unfamiliar with the Greek term, but readily identified torpor as one of the Five Hindrances to Prayer.

We might well ask if these crazy monks don't have it coming: if your goal is to "pray without ceasing," aren't you asking for trouble? Is this a reasonable goal, or even a good one? Henri Nouwen tells us that "the literal translation of the words 'pray always' is 'come to rest.' The Greek word for rest," he adds, "is 'hesychia,' and 'hesychasm' is a term which refers to the spirituality of the desert." The "rest" that the monk is seeking is not an easy one, and as Nouwen writes, it "has little to do with the absence of conflict or pain. It is a rest in God in the midst of a very intense daily struggle." Acedia is the monk's temptation because, in a demanding life of prayer, it offers the ease of indifference. Yet I have come to believe that acedia can strike anyone whose work requires self-motivation and solitude, anyone who remains married "for better for worse," anyone who is determined to stay true to a commitment that is sorely tested in everyday life. When I complained to a Benedictine friend that for me, acedia was no longer a noontime demon but seemed like a twenty-four-hour proposition, he replied, "Well, we are speaking of cosmic time. And it is always noon somewhere."

II. *Tedium*

The Music Building

During my sophomore year of high school in Honolulu, my scholarship job was to work the milk machine in the school cafeteria. The manufacturer's name, set in large, raised letters, was Norris, and some students amused themselves by making off-color remarks about breast milk as I filled their glasses. Keeping busy, wiping up spills, I tried to ignore them. But just the thought of lunch gave me tension headaches, and I was glad to transfer to the job of noontime receptionist in the music building.

Montague Hall sat in a cool, shaded part of the campus, far from the noise and harsh fluorescence of the cafeteria. My desk was in an open-air corridor, just off the pleasant courtyard through which one entered the building, and my duties were minimal: answer the phone, which seldom rang, and perform whatever secretarial jobs had been left for me. I had time on my hands, accompanied by the sound of birds and the practice of other students. A violinist doing scales. A pianist working on a sonata. I looked forward to this quiet, solitary pause in the middle of my day. I read. I pondered.

The only thing I missed about the cafeteria was the sticky rice with gravy, and inari sushi, an egg-sized portion of vinegary rice wrapped in fried soybean curd. I was happy not to be tempted, as I had lately decided that I needed to lose a few pounds. My mother was still packing my lunches but agreed to let me try a meal substitute called Metrecal, cookies laced with vitamins and minerals, which I washed down with a no-calorie soft drink. In the early 1960s, diet food left a strong chemical aftertaste, and my dense little wafers, dry as cardboard, were no exception. Chocolate flavoring did little to disguise the bitterness. This food was comically austere fare for my paradisical surroundings: trade winds wafting in the archways, leaf shadows dancing through latticed stone, birdsong and Bach.

One day during my lunchtime reverie, a thought slithered into my Eden, pulling a string of thoughts, each one worse than the one before. I became intensely aware of time, in a new and comfortless way. My mother's solicitude was no longer reason for gratitude but a grim reminder that she would not always be there. Who would care for me when she was gone? The obvious answer, that it was time for me to learn to care for myself, induced only anxiety. I took for granted so much that my parents did for me, and those daily tasks loomed large when I considered that one day I would have to do them on my own. How in the world would I manage? Whatever would I do? Suddenly, the future seemed oppressive, even monstrous. Deeply discouraged, but unable to explain why I should feel defeated before I had even begun to live as an adult, I felt foolish and alone.

The bracing thought of adulthood as opportunity, as terra incognita that I might be glad to explore, was swept away by a burgeoning sense of helplessness, self-pity, and terror. The present moment had become unbearable, and I could conceive of the future only as more of the same, an appalling, interminable progression of empty days to fill. I thought that the hour would never end, and I was eager to go to class again, and be among my fellow students. I hoped that the intensity of these troubling thoughts would dissipate once I got busy with schoolwork. That fragile hope became a survival strategy, and I repressed this odd and unsavory episode as an aberration.

This bleak mood returned occasionally during college in Vermont and in my postcollege years in New York City, and while it disrupted my life in minor ways, it never lasted long. By my mid-thirties I was settled with my husband in my maternal grandparents' former home in a tiny South Dakota town. The isolation of western South Dakota was such that I began frequenting monasteries for intellectual stimulation as well as guidance in coping with the religious questions that had lately assumed an unexpected importance in my life. As I discovered the early monastic writers, I readily latched on to Evagrius with his description of the demon acedia, which "depicts life stretching out for a long period of time, and brings before the mind's eye the toil of the ascetic struggle and, as the saying has it, leaves no leaf unturned to induce the monk to forsake his cell and drop out of the fight."

As a teenager, I had not conceived of myself as having an ascetic struggle. I did what was expected of me in getting through the school day, and used each night to finish my homework and practice my flute. I was driven by fear of failure to the former; my musician parents got after me if I neglected the latter. Looking back, however, I can see that in adolescence my life had a rigid and rigorous form, not unlike a monastic *horarium*. All that was missing were the prayers, except for the few that I said before exams, and communal utterances that I rushed through without much comprehension at church on Sundays. I enjoyed worship as a welcome refuge where I could sing, listen to stirring language, and envision life as more than the sum of its parts, but these glimpses of beauty soon faded in the daily slog. On school days I rose very early to catch a bus that drove through Navy housing, picking up private school students destined for Honolulu. After school I often went downtown to the state library to do research, then waited impatiently for the city bus that would take me on the long drive back to Pearl Harbor.

After supper I would settle in my second-story bedroom. It was hot and stuffy, as narrow as a cell, but I was grateful for the privacy it afforded. Until I was in my early teens, I shared a room with my two younger sisters. The other "cell" in which I resided was the cocoon of adolescence. I was both proud and shy, deeply afraid of ridicule and failure. This made me reluctant to expose and share myself, and leery of taking on the challenges appropriate to the young. I often spurned my classmates in favor of older company, as if by doing so I could fast-forward into adulthood. Acedia, feeding on a willing withdrawal from the pains and joys of ordinary life, was my enemy even then. But I had never heard of it, and I had little idea of how it would thrive in the rich soil I had provided.

Rumpelstiltskin

My sour noontime experience had introduced a nagging sense that life might not be everything it was cracked up to be. What if it was all a sham, a daily round without much purpose? Since I couldn't articulate how I felt, I kept this peculiar thought to myself. In a sense I hid it from myself as well, adopting an edgy bravado for my public persona. But this tactic only reinforced my apprehension that I was stranded on a nightmare bridge: rickety, swaying in the wind, a mere thread spanning a chasm. The good moments in life—and there were many, with my family, with friends, with books, and playing flute in a citywide youth symphony—seemed feeble attempts to forestall the coming disaster. The chasm remained, and at any moment, I could stumble and fall into it. I would not have easily admitted thinking in such stark terms, and to all appearances I was an industrious high school student, adeptly managing a busy schedule and enjoying eclectic cultural pursuits. I adored Bob Dylan, Frank Sinatra, and the Bach cello suites; Ingmar Bergman's *The Silence* and Richard Lester's *A Hard Day's Night*. While I happily devoured the James Bond novels and Terry Southern's *Candy*, I also gladly plunged into the readings for my advanced literature class: *Crime and Punishment, The Fall*, and Bertrand Russell's *A History of Western Philosophy*, which inspired me to form a short-lived but devoted Heraclitus Fan Club.

During my junior year of high school, once I had completed the minimum requirements for math and science and could choose an elective, I enrolled in a psychology course. With hindsight I can see that I was searching, in both philosophy and psychology, for an explanation of my malaise. But philosophy proved too abstract to be of use, and while what psychologists termed depression often followed on the heels of my soul-sickness, it did not seem to be its cause. Like the girl in "Rumpelstiltskin," I had to spin the story of my life without knowing the baleful name that could help set me free. This is not surprising, given that for many years the topic of acedia was the province of scholars of monasticism or medieval theology. It was not until after Vatican II, which directed religious orders to take a fresh look at their foundational literature, that the sayings of the early monks and the writings of Evagrius and Cassian became more readily available in English.

I knew none of this at fifteen. I did not know that what happened to me that day in Honolulu was a classic experience of the demon, or bad thought, of acedia, as described by Evagrius many centuries before. I did not know that it had been identified and accurately named. Most important, I did not recognize it as a temptation, something that I could resist. I was not aware that even as I maintained a busy and productive life, sloth, acedia's handmaid, had a firm grip on me. For I had become aware that it was possible to reject time, as well as embrace it. If I wanted to, I could live just barely, refusing the gift of each day.

Repetition

The difficult thing about days is that they must be repeated. It may be, as we read in the Second Letter to Peter, that with the Lord, one day is like a thousand years, and a thousand years are like a day. What we perceive as slowness is merely the Lord's patience. But like many children of the middle class, I was schooled in a particular kind of impatience that devalues such chores as cooking, cleaning, and taking out the garbage. An unspoken premise of my education was that it would enable me to employ someone else to perform these tasks. If the heady world of ideas tempted me to despise repetition, it also taught me to value the future over the present moment. The immediate future for which I was meticulously preparing, of course, was college. From the eighth grade on, my classmates and I were urged to endeavor to become "well rounded" so as to be more attractive to college admissions officers. As the dean politely reminded me every year, when I met with her to assess my program of study, I was deficient in that regard, harboring a virulent case of "math anxiety." But rather than attempt to become less lopsided, I rebelled, enrolling in both art and music courses. The dean disapproved, but my parents backed me up, and I won that battle. In the long run, though, the preparatory nature of my schooling had its effect. I had learned that the present is but a prelude to something more important.

I was a moody adolescent, unathletic, the last to be picked for any team sport. Perversely, I turned my shyness into pride and wore my role of campus oddball like armor. Eventually I found a small group of friends with whom I shared similar interests, and who were also socially inept. I could reveal myself in their company, in the safe environs of the art studio, English class, or the office of the school literary magazine. Under my senior photo in the yearbook, where my classmates cited Kahlil Gibran or the Beach Boys, I placed a quotation from Søren Kierkegaard: "When a man dares declare, 'I am eternity's free citizen,' necessity cannot imprison him, except in voluntary confinement." In way over my head, I had misread this statement as a manifesto of the airy freedom I aspired to. The significance of "voluntary confinement" escaped me, and I sensed none of the grit of Kierkegaard's insight, that true freedom develops out of discipline and a healthy respect for necessity. I was a bratty kid who didn't want to make her bed.

"Why bother?" I would ask my mother in a witheringly superior tone. "I'll just have to unmake it again at night." To me, the act was stupid repetition; to my mother, it was a meaningful expression of hospitality to oneself, and a humble acknowledgment of our creaturely need to make and remake our daily environments. "You will feel better," she said, "if you come home to an orderly room." She was far wiser than I, but I didn't comprehend that for many years. Neither of us could see that I was on my way to becoming a cerebral disaster zone.

Reading Sylvia Plath's *The Bell Jar,* I identified uncomfortably with her protagonist, Esther, and cringed at her rationale for not washing her hair for three weeks: "The reason I hadn't washed my clothes or my hair was because it seemed so silly. I saw the days of the year stretching ahead like a series of bright, white boxes. . . . I could see day after day glaring ahead of me like a white, broad, infinitely desolate avenue. It seemed so silly to wash one day when I would only have to wash again the next. It made me tired just to think of it. I wanted to do everything once and for all and be through with it."

One of the first symptoms of both acedia and depression is the inability to address the body's basic daily needs. It is also a refusal of repetition. Showering, shampooing, brushing the teeth, taking a multivitamin, going for a daily walk, as unremarkable as they seem, are acts of self-respect. They enhance the ability to take pleasure in oneself, and in the world. But the notion of pleasure is alien to acedia, and one becomes weary thinking about doing anything at all. It is too much to ask, one decides, sinking back on the sofa. This indolence exacts a high price. Esther's desire to "do everything once and for all and be through with it" has all the distorted reasoning of insanity. It is a call to suicide.

Spinning Gold into Straw

Repetition is at the heart of learning to play any musical instrument, and while I knew that practicing scales and fingering exercises on my flute was intended to provide a foundation for more advanced work, I was easily bored, and often skipped to playing what I enjoyed. I mystified my long-suffering teacher by excelling at the Bach flute sonatas when I had done miserably with work she considered much easier. I had an affinity for the Bach, and enjoyed it more. As she pointed out to me, with exasperation, and on more than one occasion, I liked to play, rather than to practice, and that marked me as an amateur.

If I was slow to appreciate the role of repetition in my learning to play the flute, I also resisted acknowledging its value in learning to live my life. My father used to say that if he ever wrote a self-help book, he would call it *Overcoming Peace of Mind*. His little joke packs a punch for me, because it reminds me that I all too readily spin my gold into straw until my precious equilibrium and sense of well-being give way to restlessness and dissatisfaction. Unfortunately, this process takes hold precisely when I most need rest and relaxation, and I succumb to an anxious acedia.

It begins as a deceptively slight shift in thought, or rather—in a process much commented on by the desert monks—a quick succession of thoughts that distract me from my right mind. I've been working too long and need a break; maybe I should read a mystery novel to clear my head. I tell myself that I'm too weary to concentrate. I tell myself that it is a matter of respecting my limitations, and of being good to myself. If I manage to read one book, and then return to my other obligations, no harm is done. But often, one book does not satisfy me. My "rest" has only made me more restless, and as I finish one book, I am tempted to pick up another. If I don't check myself, I can slip into a state both anxious and lethargic, in which I trudge through four or five paperbacks a day, for three or four days running. I am consuming books rather than reading them.

I may have begun with a well-written novel, but soon I am ingesting whatever I can get my hands on. Morbidly conscious of the time I am wasting, I race feverishly through a book so preposterous and badly written that it nauseates me. If I pick up a more serious book, something that might bring me to my senses, I am likely to plow through it as thoughtlessly as if it were a genre thriller. I have become like the child I once knew who emerged one morning from a noisy, chaotic Sunday-school classroom to inform the adults who had heard the commotion and had come to investigate, "We're being bad, and we don't know how to stop." In this new, repulsive world I now inhabit—and indeed, have created for myself—I sleep fitfully with the light on, waking at frequent intervals to read the same sentences over and over. My days are not lived so much as wasted in compulsive reading. I stop answering the phone and getting the mail, ignoring everything but the next page, the next book in the pile.

The contemporary maxim "Listen to your body" is useless to me when all I want to do is lie down, turn pages, and ignore that ringing phone. I may in fact need bodily refreshment, yet that is exactly what acedia will prevent. My lying for hours on the sofa, book in hand, is a sad parody of leisure. I have reached the state Søren Kierkegaard described in *Either/Or*: "I do not care for anything. I do not care to ride, for the exercise is too violent. I do not care to walk, walking is too strenuous. I do not care to lie down, for I should either have to remain lying, and I do not care to do that, or I should have to get up again, and I do not care to do that either. *Summa summarum:* I do not care at all."

It amazes me how quickly acedia can deaden what has long been a pleasure for me, and with what facility despair will replace the joy I once found in the act of reading. But my dilemma is less literary than spiritual. If my torpor is left unchecked, I lose the ability to savor not only reading, but life itself. I develop a loathing for fresh food, letting salad greens and strawberries languish in the refrigerator while I fill up on popcorn. As Chaucer notes in "The Parson's Tale," acedia "wastes, and it allows things to spoil." Although reading has led me into this dreary state, the books are not to blame. I have been reading for all the wrong reasons, rejecting life as it is in favor of a world of neat conclusions. While I would distinguish this onslaught of acedia from episodes of depression I have experienced, there are also correspondences. William Styron, in *Darkness Visible*, describes a state in which the mind feels "like one of those outmoded small-town telephone exchanges, being gradually inundated by floodwaters: one by one, the normal circuits began to drown, causing some of the functions of the body and nearly all of those of instinct and intellect to slowly disconnect." As the telephone rings, and my mother begins to leave me a message, I am too heavy with weariness to answer. I do not know why I am unable to respond to that dear voice, and why this should trouble me so little. If I were depressed, I suspect that I would feel more pain. But safe within my carapace of sloth, I sluggishly acknowledge that even though I do love my mother, it is easy to act as if I did not.

In Maurice Sendak's *Pierre*, a child responds to all parental inquiries by saying "I don't care." When he encounters a lion who offers to eat him, and responds with his habitual "I don't care," the lion pounces and devours him. The book is a perfect exposition of acedia: happily, when the lion is shaken upside down, Pierre emerges, laughing because he is not dead, and because life is worth living. If only I could so easily free myself from the lion of acedia! Often I can. But if I become too weary, I can care for so little that it becomes hard to care even whether I live or die. I need help to learn to see again, and to reclaim my life through ordinary acts: washing my hair, as well as the dishes in the sink, and walking out of doors to enjoy the breeze on my neck. I may attempt to regain my ability to concentrate by taking on a good book of poetry. And I certainly will answer that ringing phone. Even if it is someone calling over a trivial or annoying matter, our conversation will have the salutary effect of reconnecting me with another. When I stop running from my life, I can return to living it, willing to be present again, in the present moment. But this means embracing those routine and repetitive activities that I tend to scorn.

Spinning Straw into Gold

Repetition is at the heart of monastic life, which is one reason my attraction to it seemed odd at first. Morning, noon, and evening, monks return to church to pray the psalms. When they have gone through the entire cycle of one hundred fifty psalms, a process that takes three or four weeks, they begin again, day after day, year after year. In a similar way, a community reads through major portions of the Bible. Every Advent, one hears Isaiah, and during Easter, the Acts of the Apostles and Revelation. An elderly monk, disparaging the romantic image of monastic life once said to me, "People don't realize how much of it is just plain tedium."

But it is tedium with a purpose. To support themselves, the first Christian monks spent their days weaving palm branches into baskets and ropes they could sell. And as they worked, they prayed. The steady rhythm of the work helped the monks memorize the psalms and the Gospels, which was a necessity in the fourth-century desert, as books were expensive and rare. But the monks also regarded this repetitive work and prayer as their way to God, hoping that over time the "straw" of mundane tasks could become the "gold" of ceaseless prayer. Cassian's story of Abba Paul reveals this hope as firmly established in the real world of unrelenting and seemingly fruitless toil. Because Paul lived at such a remove from civilization that he could not even distract himself with the notion of selling his baskets, he was forced to admit that he was engaged, day in and day out, in useless activity. As soon as he had filled his cave with baskets, he would have only to burn them and begin again. The tale is a wry comment on the futility of all human effort, and on mortality itself. There is no denying that we, like Paul's baskets, will one day be nothing but ashes. Our work is bound to be forgotten. But monks still tell Paul's story because they take heart from his perseverance and bold humility in the face of acedia. His steadfast labor at both work and prayer reminds us that even if what we do seems worthless, it is worth doing.

The notion that repetition can be life-enhancing was not something I found in the literature that had made its way onto my high school reading lists: Sartre's *No Exit,* Camus's *The Stranger,* Ionesco's *The Bald Soprano.* Resigning myself to the notion that straw can be nothing but straw, and that ennui is an inevitable, if not preferable, emotional state, I resolved to live a life superior to that of people still entranced by the false promises of religion or the inanities of popular culture. What I most needed to know as a young woman who, like many of her peers, suffered from occasional bouts of despondency, was effectively hidden from me by the confluence of a determinedly fashionable literary education and a typically deficient religious one, which excluded much mention of spiritual experience. The notion that monastic wisdom might be of use to me was unthinkable. It took me years to discover in the curious history of acedia a key to understanding myself and my work as a writer.

III. *From Eight Bad Thoughts to Seven Sins*

Is Acedia Depression?

To examine acedia is to come face-to-face with a crucial question: Is acedia sin or sickness? It is an easy temptation to equate acedia and depression. The medical historian Bill Bynum, writing in *The Lancet*, notes that "there is an often repeated trajectory in medical history, from sin through crime and vice, ending in disease. . . . By the late 19th century, psychiatrists defined acedia as a mental condition of sadness, mental confusion and apathy, bitterness of spirit, loss of liveliness, and utter despair. [Now] psychiatrists medicalize it, Catholic priests theologise it, and management consultants denigrate it to 'laziness.'" All of this is true, insofar as it goes, but it is not the whole story.

In *The Sin of Sloth*, the scholar Siegfried Wenzel provides a useful survey of acedia's history. He observes that for Evagrius, it was a thought, or a temptation, resulting from "a combination of an external agent and a disposition in human nature," one of the eight bad thoughts that plagued a monk, while John Cassian discerned in acedia a stubborn sadness that could lead the monk into a far worse state of distress. In the sixth century, John Climacus equated tedium with despondency, and spoke of it as "a paralysis of soul." Acedia's omission from the list of the "eight bad thoughts," which eventually became the seven deadly sins, began early in the fifth century, when the influential monk Cassian, even as he recognized acedia's link with sadness, emphasized its physical aspects as laziness. By the next century, the theologian Gregory the Great had dropped acedia from the capital vices, fusing it with sadness; his list of the seven principal sins is still recognizable today. Cassian and Gregory had built on the desert tradition but altered it considerably, and acedia began to disappear from the common lexicon of spiritual life.

For the medieval scholastic theologians, notably Thomas Aquinas, acedia held what Wenzel terms an "intermediate position between body and spirit." It may spring from physical weariness, but ultimately it is the spiritual phenomenon of "aversion of the appetite from its own good," specifically an "aversion against God himself. . . . It is the opposite of the joy in the divine good that [we] should experience." The person afflicted with acedia, even if she knows what is spiritually good for her, is tempted to deny that her inner beauty and spiritual strength are at her disposal, as gifts from God. "Give up long enough on trying to be spiritually lovely," one contemporary philosopher explains, "and you will decide that no one could love anything as ugly as you—and then you have despair." Such a person can seem so trapped within herself that others will say, "Her only enemy is herself." But the true enemy is the acedia that has set into motion the endless cycle of self-defeating thoughts.

Until the early thirteenth century, acedia was seen as exclusively a monastic vice, caused by the rigors of an ascetic life. As the concept was applied to laypeople it lost much of its religious import. It came to mean physical as well as spiritual laziness, and to combat it meant embracing what is now both extolled and disparaged as the Protestant work ethic. If we trace with Wenzel what he calls "the deterioration of acedia" in the late Middle Ages, we find the sin increasingly secularized, until in the Renaissance it is replaced with melancholy—where, to a large extent, it remains today. I suspect that many people now would answer the question "Is acedia depression?" with a reflexive and assured "Yes, of course," depression having become a catchall for not only mental illness but also a wide range of emotions. Pharmaceutical companies advertise in newspapers and popular magazines with lists of symptoms—feeling down, anxious, fatigued, or discouraged—that would seem to cover most everyone at some time, as is no doubt the point. These advertisements can inspire people who need treatment to seek it, but they also serve the purposes of commerce and feed a disturbing tendency to medicalize all human experience.

This is nothing new: in the 1970s, Karl Menninger called "absurd" a statistic purporting that some sixty percent of Americans were afflicted with "chronic states of disorganization, formerly labeled 'schizophrenic.'" Psychiatric counseling and prescription medication were seen as the solution to the problem. This avoids the question of whether despair can be a reasonable or even healthy response to suffering and evil. If we are to address this, it is essential, according to Menninger, that we "[relinquish] the sin of indifference," the "'Great Sin' of acedia." While acedia may appear in many guises, "no amount of sentimentalizing [it] as 'contentedness,' 'minding one's own business,' and 'living and letting live' can cover up its devastating effects." It is easy to feel overwhelmed by the state of our lives and the world, but we still must examine our response. If we shrug and turn inward, are we normal, ill, or somewhere in between?

The very ubiquity of indifference should give us pause. "Inactivity and unresponsiveness in those upon whose cooperative efforts we depend always *feels* to us like sinful negligence," Menninger wrote. "The persistence of this taboo over the centuries . . . testifies to the universality of the temptation to shirk." As a psychiatrist, Menninger knew that "inactivity and idleness may (also) be an expression of fear, self-distrust, or self-misunderstanding. . . . One can never be sure whether indifference is an aspect of sloth (acedia) or a perceptual intellectual deficiency—'a certain blindness in human beings,' as William James called it." Whatever we call it, we might admit that given the condition of our world, "to transcend one's own self-centeredness is not a virtue [but] a saving necessity." We might also apply some common sense.

Discouragement is not necessarily a sign of illness, for people are often discouraged for good reason. Feeling off balance and ill-at-ease may be a sign of sanity, just the goad one needs to face a bad situation. A friend, a professor of philosophy, observes that many depressives accurately perceive that they are living under conditions in which any reasonable person might be despondent. But, she asks with her customary acuity, can the same be said of acedia? Can it ever be considered a rational response to the vagaries of life? From the perspective of Christian theology, the answer would be no, for acedia is understood as the rejection of a divine and entirely good gift. Because we are made in God's image, in fleeing from a relationship with a loving God, we are also running from being our most authentic selves. Even from a secular point of view, we can see that acedia is intrinsically deadly, whereas depression may not be. When we face a grievous loss—of a loved one, a job, a marriage, or health—depression can be an inevitable and appropriate response, providing a time-out to allow for healing. But what if one responded to such a loss with a casual yawn, as if none of it had mattered in the first place? That is the horror of acedia, and its intractable isolation. The journey back from such a deadly solipsism would be extremely arduous, if one could find one's way at all.

Is acedia depression? My answer is, No, not exactly, but I must struggle to articulate the difference with precision. My job is not made easier in the contemporary climate, when not to name acedia as depression can make one suspicious of being in denial, or worse, of judging people who are ill as being morally deficient. This is an area where only a fool would dare to tread, and thus I tread along, trying to keep in mind the useful distinction that Thomas Aquinas makes between acedia and despair. A contemporary scholar summarizes his insight: "For despair, participation in the divine nature through grace is perceived as appealing, but impossible; for acedia, the prospect is possible, but unappealing."

The Vile Temptation

Monastic people have always known acedia to be a particularly vile temptation that can inflict great damage on the pysche. Mary Margaret Funk, a contemporary Benedictine, writes that "dejection and anger afflict the mind; food, things, and sex burden the body; but acedia is lodged in the very soul." In the fourth century, Evagrius marked acedia as one of the spiritual afflictions, far more deadly than the more physical temptations such as gluttony or lust, or the melancholy arising from deprivation or anger. Acedia, he insisted, is something more, a weariness of soul that "instills in the heart of the monk a hatred for the place, a hatred for his very life itself, [and] a hatred for manual labor," which in the early monastic world was always linked with prayer.

We may not think of prayer or manual labor as essential for our well-being, but "hatred for the place" is a thoroughly modern condition. In a consumer culture we are advised to keep our options open, so that we are always free to grab the new, improved model when it appears. It is not easy for us to recognize acedia in ourselves, as it prompts us to see obligations to family, friends, and colleagues as impediments to that freedom. There are situations, as in the case of abusive relationships, when seeking a change is the right course of action. But often it is acedia that urges us, for no good reason, to fantasize and brood over circumstances in which we will be affirmed and admired by more stimulating companions. Whatever the place of our commitment—a monastic cell, a faith community, a job, a marriage—well, we are better off just walking away. If we have come along with the demon this far, Evagrius suggests, acedia will make our self-delusion seem divinely inspired, perhaps sanctioned. The demon of acedia, he writes, "goes on to suggest that, after all, it is not the place that is the basis of pleasing the Lord. God is to be adored everywhere."

How could we ever have imagined that we might find self-fulfillment in this place, among these demanding people? The church choir is incompetent; my colleague talks too much about her children; my wife doesn't understand me. Slamming the door behind us, we head for greener pastures, confident that we are seekers on a holy quest. Certain now that our mission is divinely inspired, we see clearly that commitment is weakness and independence is strength. To "find ourselves," all we need is the open road. But soon we discover that no place will satisfy us, and no one person, no group of friends, can meet our needs. The oppressive boredom we had hoped to escape is lodged firmly within us, and we are in danger of becoming the winnowed chaff of Psalm 1, "driven away by the wind." If we become the straw, we have no hope of gold.

Discernment

The desert monastics came to recognize that they were especially susceptible to acedia when they tried to meditate. The fourth-century Amma Theodora said: "As soon as you intend to live in peace, at once evil comes and weighs down your soul through *accidie*, faintheartedness, and evil thoughts . . . so that one believes one is ill and no longer able to pray." In this situation, the elders emphasized, it is critical to examine the distractions as they arise in the mind, and to determine if one is being tempted by pride, anger, or acedia.

Diagnosing one's true condition requires discernment, and Evagrius excelled at this, so much so that he still offers wise counsel. At the time of prayer, Evagrius observes, we are open to distraction and an enervating disgust with the self, with others, and with God. (Centuries later, Coleridge described this syndrome in "The Rime of the Ancient Mariner": "I looked to heaven, and tried to pray; / But or ever a prayer had gushed, / A wicked whisper came, and made / My heart as dry as dust.") Evagrius also observes that thoughts of anger, and the lust that often follows on its heels, suddenly intrude on the monk seeking inner stillness, increasing his vulnerability to acedia. Memorably, Evagrius writes that acedia "falls . . . upon souls in this state and, dog-like, snatches away the soul as if it were a fawn." As with much of his writing, one senses that he is speaking from experience: his life was marked with an inner turbulence that often translated into drastic changes in his outer circumstance. A student of two of the greatest theologians of his era, Basil the Great and Gregory Nazianzen, and a teacher of the monk John Cassian, Evagrius attained early fame as a preacher and churchman in the rich and stimulating environment of Constantinople. But after a disastrous love affair with a socially prominent married woman, he fled to a monastery in Jerusalem, and later retreated farther into the desert, where he spent the rest of his life among rough-hewn and often illiterate monks who were not impressed with his education and sophistication. On at least one occasion they admonished him to listen before he spoke.

Evagrius listened well enough to realize that these monks had attained a profound understanding of human nature. He termed it *cardiognosis* (knowledge of the heart), which, as one scholar notes, "had been formed in the crucible of [the desert]." In holding firm when acedia struck, and carefully discerning what they were being tempted to do, these monks had learned to practice what we might call reverse psychology. When I know that I should remain in my study, writing if I am able, and if not, being willing to be alone with God, doing nothing, I am easily tempted to leave and seek the company of other people. But if I am honest with myself, I will admit that my inability to be alone is no reason to abandon my solitude: the danger is that I will use others as an excuse to avoid confronting matters that require my full attention. Evagrius defines this temptation as lust, the desire to draw others to ourselves for selfish purposes, and he warns: "Give no confidence to such promptings; on the contrary, follow the opposite course." If I feel a strong urge for solitude, I need to ask: Is it because I wish to foster contemplation, or am I seeking an excuse to avoid other people, for whom I harbor a secret contempt? If it is the latter, then I must not remain in isolation but seek companionship. Only then will I come to better appreciate what Abba Theodore termed "the sweetness of the cell." I may still wish to be alone, he says, but not because I despise my neighbor.

Acedia is a devious temptation, and if the thought of going outside to see whether anyone else is about is not sufficient to distract us from our interior work, we may find ourselves convinced that it is not distraction we seek, but only the opportunity to help people. Perhaps the monk beset by what John Cassian calls "the foul mist" of acedia decides "that he should pay his respects to the brothers and visit the sick." The monk in this condition is in danger of using other people in order to feel good about himself, and may fantasize about performing the "great and pious work" of making more frequent visits to this or that holy man or woman who is more isolated than he, and who has little support from others. The last thing he should do, he decides, is to remain, "barren, and having made no progress, in his cell."

Cassian warns of the real peril that this monk will forget who he is, and "the reason for his profession," which is to practice silence, solitude, and meditation. If he succumbs to one diversion after another, he will lose the capacity to pray, and become more prone to despondency. Theologians have always regarded acedia as an especially serious, or "capital," sin because of its ability to engender and nourish other vices; it is a root out of which both despair and anger can grow. We are to be wary, Evagrius says, when "the irascible part of our soul is stirred up," and anger tempts us to keep others at a distance. Solitude may remove us from the immediate disturbance, he tells us, but it won't help us confront the cause of our irritation and sadness. That will happen only through the mediation of those "others" we are apt to scorn and detest. Then, tending the sick would be appropriate, a humbling act of charity that might free the soul from vainglory and illusions of holiness. Serving others in such a spirit could help us appreciate these words of Anthony the Great: "Our life and death is with our neighbor."

The monastic perspective can assist us specifically with regard to understanding the value of community. Imagine for a moment that the people you encounter at home, work, or school are the very people God has given you to pray with, eat with, and play with for the rest of your life. And you are supposed to thank God for this, every day, several times a day. This is what monastic people take on. And what they've learned from this particular asceticism, in attempting to live in peace with themselves and with others, may constitute their greatest gift to us. How radical to think that we can best know ourselves by embracing commitment, not rejecting it; by relating to others, not callously relegating them to the devilishly convenient category of "other." Monks know that taking on this challenge entails struggling with acedia, and that is one reason they have been so dedicated to discerning its presence within themselves and accurately naming it.

Naming the Demon

The era of the desert fathers and mothers was no less complex than our own—the fourth-century Mediterranean was in great political and social turmoil—but monks such as Evagrius were free of the heavy baggage of Western Christendom's concept of sin. What the Church later defined as sin, desert monks termed "bad thoughts," which to my mind is a much more helpful designation. Given the history of the Church's emphasis on sins of the flesh, contemporary readers may find it odd that the early monks regarded lust as one of the lesser temptations. They identified it as a form of greed, the desire to possess and use another person inappropriately in the pursuit of one's own satisfaction. Anger, pride, and acedia were considered the worst of the "thoughts," with acedia the most harmful of all, for it could inflict a complete loss of hope and capacity for trust in God.

As the "eight bad thoughts" of the desert monks eventually became the Church's "seven deadly sins," acedia was dropped from the list, and the monks' profound understanding of the common temptations that all people suffer lost ground to a concept of sin as an individual's commission of a bad act or omission of a good one. This in turn led to a superficial form of self-justification, for instance: If I don't overeat, then I'm not guilty of gluttony; if I don't commit adultery, I am free of lust. The new emphasis on acts also contributed to the Church's power; it alone could identify the acts that it alone had the power to absolve. The monks' subtle comprehension of temptation as thoughts that the individual may identify and resist before they turn into harmful actions was largely submerged. The insidious thought of acedia was not easily defined as an act, and it was soon subsumed within the sin of sloth.

I regard the early monastic perspective on the basic temptations that all people face as an ur-psychology that is as relevant today as when it was first conceived. In *The Praktikos*, his primary work on these temptations as he experienced them, Evagrius characterizes them as gluttony, lust, greed, sadness, anger, acedia, vainglory, and pride. The idea of sadness as a "bad thought" may strike modern readers as perverse, but Evagrius explains that it often comes upon us when our desires are thwarted, and we call to mind poignant memories of our parents caring for us at a time when we felt more at home in the world. This exercise in nostalgia can be treacherous. As the scholar Lucien Regnault points out, Evagrius came to believe that the demons "cannot act directly on the intellect. They arouse evil thoughts by working on the memory and imagination." Evagrius warns that if we do not resist these seemingly harmless thoughts at the outset, they soon "[pour] out in pleasures that are . . . only mental in nature" and then "[seize us and drench us] in sadness." As we come to prefer living in the past, we grow less able to enjoy the present or invest in the future.

Evagrius is quite astute on the subject of how quickly a person's unresolved anger can turn against him, building an intensity that is inappropriate to its presumed cause. The one who inwardly harbors such an all-encompassing indignation manifests "a general debility of the body, malnutrition with its attendant pallor, and the illusion of being attacked by poisonous wild beasts." John Eudes Bamberger, the Cistercian monk who translated *The Praktikos* into English, and who is a physician, notes that Evagrius's "description of the dynamics of disproportionate anger" is best "appreciated for its accuracy . . . by those who have carefully followed the progression of certain forms of schizophrenia."

I recognize all too well anger as Evagrius describes it: "a boiling and stirring up of wrath against one who has given injury—or is thought to have done so. It constantly irritates the soul and above all at the time of prayer it seizes the mind and flashes the picture of the offensive person before one's eyes." I have endured what Evagrius terms "alarming experiences by night," when indignation overpowers me and disrupts my sleep. I may dwell for a time on the immediate cause of my anger, but if I do not check my rage, I am likely to think of other slights, other people who have been disagreeable, or whom I feel I have good reason to detest. Once when I was furious with my husband, the importance of resisting the "bad thought" of anger was brought home to me. I found myself wide awake in the middle of the night, brimming with resentment. David had acted irresponsibly, and I felt thoroughly justified in my rage. But as my litany of complaint raced on, moving from my husband to others who had recently wronged me, and then to those who had annoyed me in the more distant past, I stopped. Wait a minute, I said to myself, this could go on forever. What's really happening here?

That question had an answer. And only after I had consciously dismissed my anger for the phantom it was could I see past the shadows. My husband had not been able to help himself, and was in fact in a highly fragile state. My anger had masked what I really felt for him, which was fear. Somewhere in my reading of monastic literature I had found a description of anger as the seed of compassion, and I felt this keenly on that night. What my husband needed most was hospitality, and an open ear. I had to reject my feelings of hurt and anger, which were self-indulgent under the circumstances. I needed to clear my vision. But even as I recognize the psychology involved in this change of perspective, I have to admit to its theological import. If anger had imprisoned me within myself, only love could free me, the love that is the gift of a merciful God.

When discussing the psychology of the desert monks, we must remember that for them God was at the center of it all. They disdained discussing theology, and while they often spoke about the importance of loving one's neighbor, they did not specifically mention the love of God.

But God was always their reference point. As John Eudes Bamberger has commented, the monks' concerns were eminently practical, yet they were also directed at more than the psychological and social consequences of bad thoughts and actions. If their hearts and their lives were to mirror God's pure and unconditional love, they needed to concern themselves with anything that clouded that divine image.

To Speak of Sin

A friend who is a monk, a scholar, and, like some contemporary Benedictines, the client of a psychiatrist and a user of psychotropics, once remarked that what we call "issues" the early monks called "demons." It's probably not that simple, but I'm tempted to brandish my poetic license and say that he's right. And what of sin? Shouldn't we dump the sick old theology that makes the depressed person feel not only worthless but evil as well? Of course, but we need to be clear about what we are doing, and recognize that this subject is likely to trigger an intense and also polarized response. Some people bristle at the suggestion that they be held in any way accountable for their mental states, while others regard a concern with underlying causes or motivations as an attempt to excuse bad behavior and evil acts.

The psychiatrist Karl Menninger, struggling with this dilemma in the latter half of the twentieth century, observed that even though one may detect the reasons behind a sin, this "does not correct its offensiveness, its destructiveness, its essential wrongness. If 'ignorance of the law excuses no one,' ignorance of the truth surely cannot absolve one from all sins of omission. Call it sloth, acedia, apathy, indifference, laziness, callousness, or whatever—if refusal to learn permits the continuity of destructive evil, such willful ignorance is surely wrong." It may be, for example, that a person abuses a child because he or she suffered similar cruelty in childhood. This does not diminish the reality of pain for the child now undergoing the abuse, or in Menninger's terms, its "wrongness." And unless that wrong is named and addressed, its harmful effects will be passed on to future generations of innocent children.

By treating acedia as a sin, I am not suggesting that people bear responsibility for being overwhelmed by the medical condition diagnosed as depression, which is not a moral failing but an illness. Yet like any essayist, I am an explorer, and I mean to explore freely what I have experienced for most of my life as "acedia" in the light of literature, theology, psychology, and pharmacology. I need to essay, in all its senses— try out, test, weigh, and probe the distinctions between the disease of depression and the vice of acedia. I suspect that an informed understanding of sin can assist us in sorting them out.

I regard sin as a viable concept, one that helps explain the mess we've made of our battered, embattled world, and the shambles we make of so many personal relationships. It's the abuse of the doctrine that trips us up, as theologians and church leaders have often settled for a facile and narrow view of sin that leaves people either firmly convinced of their own virtue or resigned to believing that they are beyond redemption. I find it instructive that while the early monks tossed around the words "demons" and "bad thoughts" with abandon, they did not speak of sin.

Acedia is best understood not as one of the seven deadly sins, but as the eighth bad thought. Depression may well be one of its names, yet I sense that acedia contains something more than what we generally mean when we say that someone is depressed. I am in good company. Both John Cassian and Thomas Aquinas recognized that acedia operates on the border between the physical and the spiritual life. They considered it both a sin and an ailment—a recurring theme in the history of acedia. As a remedy for the affliction, Thomas Aquinas recommended a hot bath, a glass of wine, and a good night's sleep.

Certainly I am grateful for the great advances that have helped destigmatize mental illness and brought relief to millions, including my husband and me. Still, labeling despair as an illness may be less helpful than it seems. It's a start in the right direction, but only that. We are at a primitive stage in determining the role of genetics and environment in influencing our behavior, and what we believe to be our enlightened and sophisticated understanding of the human character may prove, within a few short years, to be as primitive as Aristotle's notion that four humors are the prime determinants of temperament.

History suggests that we tend to be overconfident about what we know, and that we never know as much as we think we do. Some Victorians believed that they had brought science to an end by discovering all that there was to know, but they were wrong. In fact they were on the verge of a scientific revolution. Whatever age we live in, our perspective is always much more limited than we believe, and even as we progress in our understanding, blind spots remain that astonish and appall those who come after us. Yet it is also true that we have learned enough, over thousands of years, to have developed some idea of what helps us live more fully and compassionately, and to recognize what hinders us. We have not changed so much that the myth of Narcissus has no relevance today; it is a valid representation of a dangerous aspect of the human personality. We still recognize as love the emotion evoked by the poet Sappho, or the author of the Song of Solomon.

When we read the impassioned plea "Set me as a seal upon your heart, / as a seal upon your arm; / for love is strong as death, / passion fierce as the grave" (8:6), these ancient words still have the power to move us, and on a level too deep for words, we comprehend them as truth.

For me, the writings of Evagrius have a similarly evocative freshness and experiential tone. His work remains obscure, in part because his theology was condemned as heretical by a Church council after his death, but he remains an influential figure in the history of Christian thought, in both Eastern and Western traditions. He has been called the "father of our literature of spirituality" and "the creator of 'the first complete system of Christian spirituality.'" I enjoy how he employs the light of humor to penetrate the fog of mystical experience, bringing me down to earth. Of our seemingly limitless capacity for self-aggrandizement, he writes: "I have observed the demon of vainglory being chased by nearly all the other demons, and when his pursuers fell, shamelessly he drew near and unfolded a long list of his virtues." There is no theological ether here, only shrewd insight into the human condition.

As Evagrius and Cassian do not merely predate modern psychology, but also prefigure it, I am willing to grant to their writings the same latitude I give to other ancient literature. Their perspective helps me confront my own bad thoughts, temptations, neuroses, and compulsions, and I also know that I am not alone. A young woman recently told me that reading Cassian on sadness and acedia helped her cope with depression in ways that complemented the medications she'd taken and the therapy she'd received. But if I am to appreciate fully the contribution of these early Christian writers, I need to let go of the comfortable assumption, still pervasive in literary and academic circles, that religion is of no use to us today. Grounded in the nineteenth-century belief in unceasing human advancement and in the writings of such innovators as Freud and Nietzsche, this prejudice takes myriad forms: the smug certainty that religion keeps people at an infantile stage of development that the worldly person must outgrow; that it is a weapon to make people feel guilty for things that are not their fault; that it is the cause of all violent conflict.

Joyce Carol Oates, in a review of Andrew Solomon's masterly study of depression, *The Noonday Demon*, epitomizes a disdain for religion that is common among intellectuals, but she contributes something welcome and rare in acknowledging its profound value, even to unbelievers. She laments the Judeo-Christian origins of Solomon's title, writing that "one might wince at the theological metaphor, with its suggestion of demonic possession—a primitive stage in our comprehension of mental illness we like to believe we've advanced beyond." Yet, she adds, "the poetic figure of speech is a powerful one that no amount of scientific terminology and matter-of-fact discussions of serotonin deficiency, neurotransmitter systems or tricyclics can match. Though we 'know' better, we tend to 'feel' symbolically."

I appreciate how, in a deft phrase, Oates skewers what amounts to religious faith in science, technology, and medicine, which, in confronting the mysteries of our bodies, remains less a science than an art. Maybe we still need to "feel" symbolically because we're human. Let's look at an ancient poem, Psalm 91, from which the early monks coined the term "noonday demon":

You will not fear the terror of the night
nor the arrow that flies by day,

nor the plague that prowls in the darkness
nor the scourge that lays waste at noon.

While we are all too familiar with nighttime terrors, we might well ask: *What* scourge that lays waste at noon? Andrew Solomon explains that he chose *The Noonday Demon* as the title for his book because he found the phrase "describes so exactly what one experiences in depression. . . . Most demons—most forms of anguish—rely on the cover of night; to see them clearly is to defeat them. Depression stands in the full glare of the sun, unchallenged by recognition. You can know all the why and the wherefore and suffer just as much as if you were shrouded by ignorance. There is almost no other mental state of which the same can be said."

Reading fourth- and fifth-century monks such as Evagrius and Cassian, who provide much of the substance of early Christian thought about acedia, we find that, as much as any modern psychiatrist, they knew that awareness of one's underlying problems was key, but by itself could not effect a healing. These monks had learned that it's at noon, when the sun is unbearably hot, and one's energy is drained, that all the knowledge in the world is of little use. Whatever peace and joy one found at prayer in the cool of the morning could all seem false by midday, and the view of "life stretching out for a long period of time" unendurable. "The toil of the ascetic struggle," which had once seemed the very foundation of life, was now exposed as futile. That Evagrius characterizes these thoughts as a "demon" (he does not speak of "possession") matters far less than the exactitude of his description of how despair takes hold of a person. I know that when I am tempted to run from an onerous task in the present, I am likely to picture past times that I now imagine to be better than they were, or to project myself into future events of which I can, in fact, know nothing. I am unable to see the grace that is available to me now, in this place and time. Acedia can flatten any place into a stark desert landscape and make hope a mirage. Time itself becomes unbearable, and I am fifteen years old again, under assault by horrible thoughts that seem mine alone. I have no idea that others have experienced this and lived to tell of it.

A desert monk troubled by "bad thoughts" knew he was not alone. He was expected to seek out an elder and ask for "a word." But the elder consulted was likely to be reluctant, and even suspicious. If he determined that he was being consulted for the wrong reasons, as a diversion from tedium or an excuse to socialize, he would admonish the seeker to stop looking outward for what he needed to look for within. Lengthy confession or conversation was deemed unnecessary, and the elder's good word often consisted of Zen-like instruction: "Go, sit in your cell," said Abba Moses, "and your cell will teach you everything."

This was a common saying in the desert. Fighting acedia with a focused, intentional stability was considered so vital in maintaining a good relationship with God and one's fellow monks that elders sometimes gave their disciples advice that contradicted the monastic norms. One counseled, "Go, eat, drink, sleep, do no work, only do not leave your cell." Astonishingly, given how central prayer was to the monks, another elder advised, "Don't pray at all, just stay in the cell." According to one scholar, this admonition concealed "a fearsome demand," and the elder knew full well "what courage, what heroic endurance was needed to tolerate the demon of *acedia* . . . the most oppressive of all, whose specialty it is to take a dislike to [staying] in one place."

Call It a Day

That sort of perseverance is still required of us in contending with acedia, and it can still be a discouraging endeavor. In a speech titled "In Praise of Boredom," the twentieth-century writer Joseph Brodsky described facing ennui head-on, and allowing yourself to be crushed by boredom, for "the sooner you hit bottom, the faster you surface. The idea . . . is to exact a full look at the worst. The reason boredom deserves such scrutiny is that it represents pure, undiluted time in all its repetitive, redundant, monotonous splendor." Brodsky was addressing American college students, but his words would no doubt resonate with monks, who have long understood "hitting bottom" as recognizing that you are not going anywhere, because you are already there. Can't we just call it a day, and give our overanxious and ironic selves a rest? Might we consider boredom as not only necessary for our life but also as one of its greatest blessings? A gift, pure and simple, a precious chance to be alone with our thoughts and alone with God?

In claiming boredom in this sense, we approach what monks term a "recollection of the self." That sounds pleasant enough, but it is far from a narcissistic endeavor: in a pitched battle with acedia, we will come up against the best and the worst in ourselves. Only after this trial can we enjoy, in the words of Saint Bruno, the founder of the extremely ascetic Carthusian order, a newly dynamic solitude, in "leisure that is occupied and activity that is tranquil." Yet it is always easier for us to busy ourselves than to merely exist. Even important and useful work can distract us from remembering who we are, and what our deeper purpose might be. Monastic wisdom insists that when we are most tempted to feel bored, apathetic, and despondent over the meaningless-

ness of life we are on the verge of discovering our true self in relation
to God. It is worth not giving up, because when we are willing to do
nothing but "be," we meet the God who is the very ground of being,
the great "I Am" whom Moses encountered at the burning bush.

One need not be a monk, or even a religious believer, to confront
this mystery. In a notebook entry F. Scott Fitzgerald speaks of boredom
as not "an end product" but an important and necessary "stage in life
and art," acting like a filter that allows "the clear product [to emerge]."
The philosopher Bertrand Russell describes himself as an unhappy child
who realized at the age of five that "if I should live to be seventy, I had
only endured so far, a fourteenth part of my whole life, and I felt the
long-spread-out boredom ahead of me to be almost unendurable."
What saved him from hating life enough to commit suicide was the
"desire to know more mathematics." Speaking prophetically to future
generations, including our own, he writes that "a generation that cannot endure boredom will be a generation of little men . . . unduly divorced from the slow processes of nature, in whom every vital impulse
withers." If I was saved by poetry, and Russell by mathematics, the challenge we faced was the same, that of daring to become an individual.
Even as I discovered my vocation as a writer, I had to struggle to maintain the boring work habits necessary for nourishing it. The syndrome
that the ancient monks describe is one that I know well. It is just when
the work seems most hopeless, and I am hard pressed to care whether
I ever write another word or not, that the most valuable breakthroughs
are likely to come. When I face trials in my life and work, I have found
that the perspective of another—pastor, physician, counselor, editor—
can bring me to my senses. But it's the work I have learned to do on my
own—the self-editing, if you will—that has proved the most valuable.

Where acedia is concerned, the desert abbas and ammas advocate plentiful self-editing, and they employ harsh imagery to convey acedia's power to distract us from it. John Climacus compares the person led astray by acedia to a dumb beast: "Tedium reminds those at prayer of some job to be done, and . . . searches out any plausible excuse to drag us from prayer, as though with some kind of halter." Most anyone who has endeavored to maintain the habit of prayer, or making art, or regular exercise or athletic training, knows this syndrome well. When I sit down to pray or to write, a host of thoughts arise. I should call to find out how so-and-so is doing. I should dust and organize my desk, because I will get more work done in a neater space. While I'm at it, I might as well load and start the washing machine. I may truly desire to write, but as I am pulled to one task after another I lose the ability to concentrate on the work at hand. Any activity, even scrubbing the toilet, seems more compelling than sitting down to face the blank page. My favorite story about this state of mind concerns a university professor who went on sabbatical to write a book, and resolved to keep to a strict work schedule. A colleague who drove by his house one day was surprised to see him in the yard, wearing coveralls and hauling a hose. "I started to work this morning," the man explained, "and it suddenly occurred to me that I've lived here for over five years and have never washed the house."

It is all a matter of perspective. There is the story of an abba who took a piece of dry wood and told his disciple, "Water this until it bears fruit." How bizarre, perhaps cruel, an instruction that seems; yet in nurturing a marriage over a span of thirty years, and in keeping to the discipline of writing and revising for even longer, I have often found myself watering dead wood with tears, and with very little hope. I have also been astonished by how those tears have allowed life to emerge out of what had seemed dead.

Acedia and Vocation

The concept of acedia has always been closely linked with that of vocation. Acedia was, and remains, the monk's most dangerous temptation, as it makes the life he has vowed to undertake seem foolish, if not completely futile. As one scholar has stated, the monk struggling with acedia is "dealing with more than bad moods, psychic fluctuations, or moral defeats. It is a question of the resolve that arises in the wake of a decisive choice for which the monk has risked his life and to which he must hold . . . to realize [his] full potential in oneness with God. He has bet everything that he has and everything that he is on this." Monastic people live with the tension of having to find meaning in a way of life that the world, for all the reverent lip service paid to "holy orders," considers largely anachronistic and useless. Artists can feel a similar disconnect, and many could no doubt identify with a caustic remark attributed to T. S. Eliot, to the effect that when all is said and done, the writer may realize that he has wasted his youth and wrecked his health for nothing.

Acedia has been observed in other areas in which the labor is long and the rewards are slow to appear, if they come at all. An article published in the 1960s, "Scientific Acedia," elaborates on the vice as "an occupational hazard among men of learning that takes the form of a general withdrawal of motivation for research and an increasing alienation from science." Acedia is a danger to anyone whose work requires great concentration and discipline yet is considered by many to be of little practical value. The world does not care if I write another word, and if I am to care, I have to summon all my interior motivation and strength. But the demon of acedia is adept at striking when those resources are at a low ebb, as John Berryman notes:

> Life, friends, is boring. We must not say so.
> After all, the sky flashes, the great sea yearns,
> we ourselves flash and yearn,
> and moreover my mother told me as a boy
> (repeatedly) 'Ever to confess you're bored
> means you have no
>
> Inner Resources.' I conclude now I have no
> inner resources, because I am heavy bored.
> Peoples bore me,
> literature bores me, especially great literature.

One would expect that literature, especially great literature, would inspire a writer such as Berryman, or at least enhance his faith in the worthiness of his craft. But no, acedia insists, it's just boring. Acedia's genius is to seize us precisely where our hope lies, to tear away at the heart of who we are, and mock that which sustains us.

Liminal Acedia

Acedia's liminal status in the history of Western culture, and in the Christian East, has allowed it to be a slippery operator, persistently eluding our attempts to comprehend it. Trying to talk about acedia is like trying to define a negative or grab a shadow. As the monks' "eight bad thoughts" evolved into the Church's "seven deadly sins," and acedia was hidden within the sin of sloth, it played a terrible trick on us. We came to regard sloth as an insignificant physical laziness, or a pleasant and even healthy lassitude. Evelyn Waugh acknowledges that most of us believe sloth to be "a mildly facetious variant of 'indolence,' and indolence, surely, so far from being a deadly sin, is one of the most amiable of weaknesses."

But I wonder. Specifically, I wonder about our synonyms for *laziness*: *listlessness, languor, lassitude, indolence.* They sound harmless enough, a good, long stretch on plump pillows. *Listlessness* has a seductively soft sound, but at root it means being unable to desire, which is a cause, and a symptom, of serious mental distress. *Languor* derives from a Latin word meaning "to feel faint," and *lassitude* from a word meaning "to fall forward because of weariness." It is related to *alas,* connoting misfortune and unhappiness. The harder sound of *indolence* clues us in to even more serious trouble. It is defined as "habitual laziness," and in its root we find a very bad habit indeed. *Dolor* is an ancient word for "pain," and indolence is the inability to feel it. We've now come close to the worst that acedia can do to us: not only does it make us unable to care, it takes away our ability to feel bad about that. If we can no longer weep, or desire, or feel pain and grief, well, that's all right; we'll settle for that, we'll get by.

Whether there is a wily devil lurking out there or we have merely bedeviled ourselves with delusions concerning the true nature of sloth, I am intrigued that over the course of the last sixteen hundred years we managed to lose the word *acedia*. Maybe that's one reason why, as we languish from spiritual drought, we are often unaware of what ails us. We spend greater sums on leisure but are more tense than ever, and hire lifestyle coaches to ease the stress. We turn away from the daily news, complaining of "compassion fatigue," and enroll in classes to learn how to breathe and relax. Increasingly, we need drugs in order to sleep. We are tempted to regard with reverence those dedicated souls who make themselves available "twenty-four/seven" and regard silence as unproductive, solitude as irresponsible. But when distraction becomes the norm, we are in danger of becoming immunized from feeling itself. We are more likely to indulge in public spectacles of undemanding pseudo-care than address humanity's immediate needs. Is it possible that in twenty-first-century America, acedia has come into its own? How can that be, when so few know its name?

If only it were as easy as shouting "Rumpelstiltskin" and watching the fiend dissolve in a rage around his fire. But acedia has been called by many names. To the ancient Greeks it was the black gall; to the fourth-century monks it was a vicious and tenacious temptation to despair. Petrarch called it the nameless woe, and Dante named it a sin. It became known to Robert Burton and others in the Renaissance as melancholy. In Shakespeare, it is the boredom of Richard III, arguably as responsible as ambition in triggering his monstrous violence. Jonathan Swift and Alexander Pope called it spleen; to Baudelaire, and to many writers in the years to follow, it was ennui. To Kierkegaard it was the soul turned into a Dead Sea, over which no bird can soar without falling to its death. To the nineteenth-century French, it was the *mal du siècle,* or the illness of the age. To twentieth-century playwrights—Chekhov, Ionesco, and Albee among them—it fuels the acrimony that underlies domestic relationships, making us suspect that relationship itself is absurd and unworkable. Acedia is the place where we wait for

Godot, and it is the state of waiting. It is the fashionably negative pose of ironic detachment, of valuing life as "less than zero."

I can hear scholars howling, with some justification, that I am mixing it all up, failing to make the necessary and proper distinctions. That is their job, not mine. I am deeply indebted to the work of Reinhard Kuhn, who in *The Demon of Noontide: Ennui in Western Literature* examines acedia's baleful effects on the human spirit over many centuries. He finds that already in the literature of antiquity, "the seeds of the modern plague were present," noting echoes of Aristotle's "black bile" in Joyce's Stephen Dedalus, the *horror loci* (fear of place) of Lucretius and Horace in Baudelaire's "The Voyage" and Beckett's tramps, and the squeamishness of Seneca's Serenus in the nausea of Sartre's Roquentin.

As for me, I need to tell a story. More than twenty years ago, not long after I had been surprised to find myself in the description of acedia made by a fourth-century monk, I conceived this book. I had no idea how long and painful the labor would be, or I might have rejected it from the start. But in conversations with my husband, David, who was also a poet, I began to work with the connections I was making between my experience of acedia and my experience as a writer. David suggested that I look at Aldous Huxley's essay "Accidie." I tried interlibrary loan, but despite its author's renown, this work, like much that has been written about acedia, was not easy to locate. It took some time to track it down, and when I did I found something that changed my life.

IV. *Psyche, Soul, and Muse*

A Poet's Education

Aldous Huxley's "Accidie" begins with a look at the desert monks and their depiction of the *daemon meridianus*, or noonday demon, as a "fiend of deadly subtlety, who was not afraid to walk by day." The monks learned, Huxley notes, that this demon could seize upon any weakness, however small, in order to take a monk "through disgust and lassitude into the black depths of despair and hopeless unbelief. When that happened the demon smiled and took his departure, conscious that he had done a good day's work."

Huxley then traces, in a brisk tour de force, "the progress of acedia" through the Middle Ages to the twentieth century. Considered a demon or a vice by early Christian monks, acedia in the Renaissance was thought of as a physical ailment, called the vapors, or spleen. By the early eighteenth century, "accidie was still, if not a sin, at least a disease." But, Huxley adds, "a change was at hand." What the poet Matthew Green termed "the sin of worldly sorrow" in 1837 was becoming "a literary virtue, a spiritual mode. . . . Then came the nineteenth-century and romanticism; and with them the triumph of the meridian demon.

Accidie in its most complicated and deadly form, a mixture of bore-dom, sorrow, and despair, was now an inspiration to the greatest poets and novelists, and it has remained so to this day."

When I read this, I felt that Huxley was describing my education as a poet. For many years, ever since I entered the resolutely secular atmosphere of Bennington College, I had assumed that religion was no longer a part of my life. This was not a conscious rebellion on my part. I had gladly attended church with my family all through high school, had sung in a choir, read books such as *Man's Search for Meaning* for a Sunday class, and discovered the writings of Evelyn Underhill on my own. I also had staggered through a dense little paperback containing Søren Kierkegaard's *Fear and Trembling* and *The Sickness unto Death*, not even half comprehending what was there but persisting nonetheless.

At Bennington, I decided that religion did not interest me any-more. Literature made a viable substitute, and my English professor during freshman year, the poet Ben Belitt, immersed his students in a contemplative, line-by-line reading of Joyce's *A Portrait of the Artist as a Young Man*, and also led us through exquisitely detailed and probing exegeses of such poets as Hopkins, Pound, and Eliot. For the first time in my life I was elated by poetry, astonished to find that so much mean-ing could be packed into so few words. I could read this way forever, I thought, and make teaching literature my life's work. But Belitt had other ideas. He was the first person who suggested to me that I was a poet, and that I had not only to read, but to write as well.

Hesitantly, humbly, awed to discover how much poems could sig-nify, I made a first attempt, mustering some fifteen words. Soon I was writing in earnest, and reading all the poetry I could find. As a junior

I indulged myself in a yearlong seminar on seventeenth-century verse that made me wonder whether that was the last era in which religion and poetry could coexist so amicably. Faith seemed to be something I had lost, but I was heartened that John Donne and George Herbert, both Anglican priests, had produced some of the greatest poetry in English. Over the next year, as I steeped myself in the Romantics— Wordsworth, Shelley, Keats—and the French Symbolists, I came to believe that outgrowing a religious faith was something I needed to do in order to become a writer.

A child of the 1960s, I was attracted by the rebel stance of Shelley, Byron, and Baudelaire. To challenge authority, convention, and traditional religion: that was the poet's calling. To disorder the senses and embark on Rimbaud's drunken boat, that was the sacrifice the writer made in order to reveal the full potency of human experience. As an impressionable adolescent, seeking in poetry a refuge from shyness and social incapacity, I found it attractive to cultivate a disdain for the day-to-day, and for less enlightened people who were content with their mundane existence. The Romantics had been fighting a legitimate battle, what the poet Louise Bogan termed "a difficult and unpopular [one] against the 18th century's cold logic and mechanical point of view." She found it unfortunate that "so much of that early boldness and originality" was, however, "dissipated in excesses of various kinds," so much so that by the mid–twentieth century, poets had become associated in the popular imagination with drug and alcohol abuse, mental illness, and suicide. It was discouraging for an aspiring young writer to follow a postwar generation of poets whose madness and self-destruction had been so public: Dylan Thomas, Sylvia Plath, Anne Sexton, Delmore Schwartz, John Berryman.

I fell into a trap that ensnares many novice poets, writing only when I was depressed and allowing the writing to lead me into an excitable, hyperactive state. This method can foster literary productivity for a while, but in the long run it is self-defeating. The poet Donald Hall has said that while "no one can induce bipolarity in order to make poems," the question remains: "Does the practice of the art exacerbate a tendency? Surely for the artist the disorder is creative in its manic form—excitement, confidence, the rush of energy and invention." Yet once that energy is expended, exhaustion sets in, and the time that flowed so quickly seems unbearably slow. A restless anxiety stirs within, and acedia can take hold.

Huxley's "Accidie" made me reconsider two fallacies I had appropriated as truth: that despair is the state most conducive to writing, and that place and time are enemies of the creative spirit. My literary education in this type of desperation is neatly summarized in Franz Kafka's short story "The Departure": "'Where is the master going?' 'I don't know,' I said, 'just out of here, just out of here. Out of here, nothing else, it's the only way I can reach my goal.' 'So you know your goal?' he asked. 'Yes,' I replied, 'I've just told you. Out of here—that's my goal.'" I had never considered acedia's role in making what Huxley terms "the sense of universal futility, the feelings of boredom and despair, with the complementary desire to be 'anywhere, anywhere out of the world,' or at least out of the place in which one happens at the moment to be," seem indispensable for creating poetry. Huxley's cool assessment opened a door into my self-imposed prison, and let in a blast of fresh air.

"The Gift of Faith Has Been Denied Me"

I encountered Huxley's essay at a critical time in my life. The cerebral young woman I had been was becoming someone much more grounded. I had entered my first long-term, committed, and stable relationship, and my husband and I had moved from New York City to my grandparents' home in western South Dakota. Using recipes I found in my grandmother's kitchen, I learned to bake bread. I worked in her garden and struggled to keep her perennials alive. I planted my own herbs and vegetables. The people I encountered every day were not other writers but farmers and ranchers, and something of their deep respect for God, the land, and the weather began to rub off on me.

In my thirties, though, unease nagged at me, as I attempted to reconcile what I had long felt to be, and in fact had been educated to see as, irreconcilable: my vocation as a writer, and a life of faith. I occasionally attended the Presbyterian church up the street, where my grandmother had been a member for more than sixty years and where I had gone to Sunday school during childhood summers. But I still considered it my grandmother's church and not my own. My friendship with the pastors there led me to a Benedictine abbey some ninety miles north, and the monks' liturgy of the hours deeply attracted me, although I could not have said why. After my first visit, I dreamed about the place every night for more than a week. One dream was set in a chemistry lab, where a monk I had met was conducting a class. He was no chemist, but a scholar of monasticism; my dream may have signified that he had something to teach me about human chemistry. At the time I found it curious that a monk might teach me anything.

The monastic men and women of the fourth century went into the desert for the specific purpose of combatting their demons. When I moved to South Dakota with my husband, I had no such design. I wanted a quiet place to write and to nurture our relationship. But by planting myself firmly in a marriage, in my grandparents' house in a part of the world considered by most to be a desert, I had done something untoward, and more radical than I knew. In a place with few distractions, where it is possible to go to monasteries for excitement, I had taken on the burden of time. When so many of my generation were "finding themselves" by renouncing commitments, I was attempting to make one work, staking my claim on the conviction that this new-found stability would not destroy my writing but allow it to flourish. Faith was another matter: I was burdened by religious doubts and felt keenly Anne Sexton's lament "I love faith, but have none." I thought that what was true of another poet I greatly admired, Louise Bogan, was also true of me. She had a deep-seated appreciation for liturgy but admitted that "the gift of faith has been denied me." Like Bogan, I readily acknowledged religion as a human need having a great symbolic resonance, and even beauty. As she once commented, "The Elysian fields are underground and the Christian heaven is overhead for two deep psychological reasons." Still, I was bewildered by my desire to attend church and reclaim the faith of my ancestors as my own.

After that initial visit to the abbey, which I made not out of a burning spiritual desire but to hear a talk by the writer Carol Bly, I wrote to a monk I had met, unloading on him a host of questions about religion that were troubling me. He responded with a thoughtful letter, and with a book from the monastery library, *On Being a Christian*, by Hans Küng. My heart sank when I opened it and tried to read. It was a massive, abstract work of theology. Sighing, I put it back into the mailer, and noticed that the monk had written on the envelope, in a neat calligraphic hand, something to the effect of: "If this doesn't work, try Flannery O'Connor's letters." It was an inspired suggestion: O'Connor was exactly what I needed, a woman whose vocation was to both Christian faith and writing. I was heartened by her assertion that "most people come to the Church by means the Church does not allow, else there would be no need their getting to her at all. . . . The operation of the Church is entirely set up for the sinner, which creates much misunderstanding among the smug."

A devout Catholic, O'Connor could be stern about theological matters but charitable about the peccadilloes of others. In a letter written at Yaddo, a literary retreat, she says of an alcohol-sodden party: "I left before they began to break things." She also noted, that "at such a place you have to expect them to sleep around. . . . This is not sin, but Experience." I'd had more than enough "Experience" at Bennington and in New York City, and if I had moved on, improbably, by settling in one place, with one man, it remained to be seen whether our South Dakota home would be good for me, for us, and for our writing. It was unclear to me exactly where the Christian religion fit into all of this, and some friends cautioned me about the dangers of mixing religious faith with the poetic muse. One who had known both Anne Sexton and John Berryman was particularly concerned. As I studied these writers, reading poems, letters, journals, and interviews, I sensed that while their religious quest had produced brilliant work, the peace that faith can bring had eluded them. I noted with fear and foreboding that their desire for faith had itself become destructive, fueling the delusional high of the manic-depressive cycle. The poet Maxine Kumin, a friend of Sexton's, writes that "an elderly, sympathetic priest, one of many priests [Sexton] encountered—accosted might be a better word—said a saving thing." Sexton herself wrote of the encounter, recalling that after the priest had read her poems he told her, "'Your typewriter is your altar.' I said, 'I can't go to church. I can't pray.' He said, 'Your poems are your prayers.' . . . As he left me he said . . . 'Come on back to the typewriter.'"

The priest's good counsel, Kumin notes, did keep Sexton "alive at least a year beyond her time." But the writing that sustained Sexton was also feeding her mania. In the poem that concludes her last book, *The Awful Rowing Toward God*, Sexton writes of playing poker with God in a crooked game. She finds the situation comical, and as God laughs, the poet joins in, saying, "I . . . love you so for your wild card, / that untamable, eternal, gut-driven *ha-ha* / and lucky love." In the end, the God whom Sexton found in her verse was not one who could save, and she killed herself soon after reading galleys for the book.

Much of John Berryman's work also was written in a kind of fury. One friend of his told me of going to a Manhattan hotel to check on the poet, after he had phoned to say he was in town and wanted to see her, but had then not contacted her again. Finding him exhausted and raving from drink and lack of sleep, she called an ambulance. She also carefully gathered up manuscript pages for what would become his masterpiece, *The Dream Songs*, which Berryman had scattered about the room. Like Anne Sexton, he was drawn to both Judaism and Christianity. His last book of poems, *Delusions, etc.*, was inspired by the psalms and the prayers of the canonical hours. The poems that conclude the book, most of them prayers, fluctuate wildly between ecstasy and despair. "The Facts and Issues" opens by saying of Christ, "I really

believe / He's here all over this room / in a motor hotel in Wallace
Stevens' town." Counting his blessings, Berryman describes himself as
"happy to be here / and to have been here, with such lovely ones / so
infinitely better, but to me / even in their suffering infinitely kind."
The poem reaffirms the confident opening lines, concluding with an
expression of faith in Christ as redeemer, who suffered and died "to
make this filthy fact of particular, long-after, / far-away, five-foot-ten
& moribund / human being happy. Well, he has! / I am so happy I
could scream! / *It's enough!* I can't BEAR ANY MORE. / *Let this be it.*
I've *had* it. I can't wait." In another late autobiographical work, the
novel *Recovery*, Berryman's protagonist Severance tries to say the Lord's
Prayer, only to be overcome by anguish: "'Kingdom'; not the hid
treasure or the pearl of great price but the lucky find! the risking
all! to have *one* thing—Christ to Martha, his gentle and inexorable re-
proof defending Mary. Wise Mary, the better part. It: sobriety, and a
decent end."

Sadly, John Berryman could not find that "decent end" for himself; he committed suicide after an alcoholic relapse. In a foreword to
Delusions, etc., his friend Saul Bellow wrote that "at last it must have
seemed that he had used up all his resources. Faith against despair,
love versus nihilism had been the themes of his struggles and his
poems. What he needed for his art had been supplied by his own person, by his mind, his wit. He drew it out of his vital organs, out of his
very skin. At last there was no more. Reinforcements failed to arrive.
Forces were not joined." The deck was stacked against Berryman,
Sexton, and Plath, and not only because of tragic personal circumstances: the suicide, in Berryman's childhood, of his father; Sexton's
manic depression; the deep-seated psychosis of Plath. Cultural factors

also worked against them, notably the idea, as explored by Huxley in his essay, that boredom, hopelessness, and despair are essential for artistic inspiration. They were also contending with what the critic C. M. Bowra termed the "belief that the imagination was nothing less than God as it operates in the human soul," a dangerous proposition indeed. In his survey of art history from the Byzantine era to the twentieth century, the theologian John Cobb observes that what had previously been considered holy, part of a transcendent world with the power to "transform, redeem, unify and order" had "moved in a continuous process" from communal expressions of faith "into the inner being of artists themselves." Many had come to assume that what the Church called the Holy Spirit was no more, and no less, than artistic inspiration. This is a far more insidious proposition than what the Romantic poets had in mind, and for many artists, it has proved an insurmountable burden.

Poets are both revered and ignored in American culture. For many people poetry is that vaguely subversive stuff that you enjoy as a small child but detest by the time you're in high school, having labored in vain to find its "hidden meanings." Yet cultural expectations of the poet remain high, as exemplified in a passage from the biologist Lewis Thomas: "We have a wilderness of mystery to make our way through in the centuries to come, and we shall need . . . not science alone. For perceiving significance where significance is at hand, we shall need minds at work from all sorts of brains . . . *mostly the brains of poets of course. The poets, on whose shoulders the future rests,* might, late nights . . . begin to see some meanings that elude the rest of us" (emphasis mine). In an increasingly secular age, many people do trust writers rather than priests with their confessions. But the ancient and communal roles of shaman, seer, and storyteller are not an easy fit for writers in the contemporary world. Even if they are praised for what they offer through their work, they can feel isolated and lacking recourse to help.

If writers are often stymied by depression or addiction, many are also wary of psychoanalysis, psychotropics, and twelve-step programs as potentially detrimental to their art. Therapists find that some writers use treatment as an excuse to procrastinate, while others fear that the sessions will drain them of material they should be using in their work. Medications such as Prozac have been rejected outright by some writers, because, as one counselor puts it, the drugs tend to "eliminate their desire to write together with their regret over not doing so."

Storytelling itself can be a redemptive act for the writer. In a sequence in *Love & Fame*, in poems with such titles as "The Hell Poem" and "Purgatory," John Berryman writes of seeking salvation in a psychiatric ward, and finding it as he listens to other patients, many of whom are in even greater distress than he is. He applied his poetic genius in witnessing to their stories, and in "Death Ballad" addresses two alcoholic teenagers who have attempted suicide. The poem concludes: "Only, Jo & Tyson, Tyson & Jo, / take up, outside your blocked selves, some small thing / that is moving / & wants to keep on moving / & needs, therefore, Tyson, Jo, your loving." As 1 Corinthians 13 puts it, faith may fail, but love does not. Berryman's extravagant love—for literature, for wit, for his students—was extolled and admired by his many friends. But he was haunted by the struggle to love life itself. He made a poignant request of his wife, Eileen Simpson, after they had separated. One brief, chilling phrase captured not only his persistent fear that he, like his father, would be a suicide, but also his hope that

God would receive him anyway. He reminded Simpson, "I would like if possible to be buried in consecrated ground."

Night and Day

I used to tell friends in New York, "If I ever marry a poet, please shoot me." Now that I had done it, those friends were thousands of miles away. The enforced intimacy my husband and I enjoyed in our small town meant that we had to be each other's reader and critic, as well as best friend and confidant. It became clear to me that the ultimate question that Huxley's "Accidie" had raised for me was not "Can a poet have faith?" but "Can a poet be well?" Let alone two poets, together? The evidence suggested that poets had not been well for some time. Gérard de Nerval may have brightened his Paris neighborhood by walking a lobster on a leash, but not when he hanged himself from a railing in the Rue de la Vieille Lanterne. His literary contemporaries were haunted by the thought that the poet had killed himself because his muse had failed him. Six years later Charles Baudelaire wrote in a letter: "I have fallen into an alarming debility and despair. I have felt myself attacked by a kind of illness *à la Gérard*, namely the fear of being unable to think any more, or to write a line." Writing too much can also prove dangerous to a poet. Two poets idolized by many young women of my generation, Anne Sexton and Sylvia Plath, had, shortly before their suicides, churned out four to six poems a day. In the posthumously published *Winter Trees*, Plath described her brain as "a gray wall . . . clawed and bloody," and asked, "Is there no way out of the mind?" Sexton wrote her last book in less than three weeks, with, she noted, only "three days out. One for exhaustion and two for a mental hospital . . . Writing in seizure, practically not stopping."

What Plath and Sexton demonstrate is not that writers must nobly endure self-destructive compulsions, but that no artist can maintain such a high level of creative intensity. When one has been writing in the heights of what Sexton termed "a fugitive frenzy," one needs a way to come down safely. Taking a walk may work, but other means can be more tempting: tranquilizers, marijuana, and above all, booze. Drunkenness may be, in Bertrand Russell's memorable phrase, a "temporary suicide," but alcohol can also be, William Styron reminds us, a "magical conduit to fantasy . . . and to the enhancement of the imagination." Going up, coming down, and paying a steep price. A clergywoman who knew Sexton in her last days once said to me that "it wasn't poetry that killed her, but alcohol." This is probably true of John Berryman as well.

By the time my husband and I met, in 1973, we were practicing poets: that is, we had arranged our lives so that we had time to write. David had quit a job as an advertising executive after an epiphany in an Atlanta hotel: Either kill yourself, or go back to writing poems. He had moved in with his widowed father in Hartsdale, New York, taken a job in a Bronx printing factory, and was putting together a manuscript of verse in his free time. I was more sheltered, still in my first postcollege job in arts administration. Two years before, I had won a young writers' competition for a book of poems, but after the euphoria of publication wore off, I was at a loss. Although I still spent weekends writing, no matter how much I worked on them, my poems were dead on the page. I felt as if the creative spirit had abandoned me. More experienced writers assured me that this was a common occurrence, and not just with first books. Completing a manuscript and sending it to a publisher can engender great anxiety: The book is finished, and there may not be another. The book is finished, am I finished as well? The dour Romanian philosopher E. M. Cioran hit the mark when he described a book as "a postponed suicide."

David and I quickly discovered that our writing styles and habits were like night and day. He was far more conversant with the English literary tradition than I; at eleven, he had become enamored of Tennyson and the Brownings. An education in Greek and Latin had disciplined his memory, and he knew an alarming number of poems by heart. He once stunned a college audience by reciting Gerard Manley Hopkins's lengthy "The Wreck of the *Deutschland*" from memory, and he often delighted student writers with enthusiastic renderings of "Jabberwocky" in English, French, and German. David preferred to write in blank verse, unrhymed but metered lines. I, by comparison, was a free-verse bum and sensation junkie; I loved reading and writing poetry for the way it made me feel. I sometimes wrote in syllabic verse, but this was due more to musical training than to deliberate effort. David said that I had "an ear for English," and added, only half joking, that he never could have married anyone who did not.

Friends often asked us how two poets could live and work together without getting in each other's way. David worked best late at night; I flourished in the early-morning hours. Our best conversations often took place at four a.m., when he was on his way to bed and I was waking up. He had always been a night person, and if I had to rouse him for a morning appointment he required at least two hours before he was fit to leave the house. He said that he'd never found an alarm clock loud enough to wake him. I seldom needed an alarm, and would rise full of energy and ready for the day. David's grandparents had been born in Ireland; mine were of English descent, born in the United States. He had rum runners and freedom fighters in his background; my ancestors are more likely to have been chaplains and pastors. David would say that for all our cultural differences, we had a common origin. "Dwyer" derived from the Danish for "pirate," he said, and "Norris" from "Norse," those raiders and pillagers from the north. We did feel a bit like pirates after our move to South Dakota, as if we had gotten away with something. We had an inexpensive place to live in and my grandfather's enormous V8 Oldsmobile to drive. Above all, by living off savings, part-time jobs, and the occasional grant, we were free to focus on writing.

David completed the poetry manuscript he'd been working on when we met, and in 1976 it won the Juniper Prize of the University of Massachusetts Press and was published as *Ariana Olisvos: Her Last Works and Days*. Ariana was an old woman David had been inventing for years, based on his grandmothers and a beloved great-aunt, who had been a stockbroker. He cherished the way she had taken him under her wing, teaching him such useful and worldly things as how to open a bottle of Champagne; he treasured the gold cuff links he had inherited from her. David had fun with Ariana, giving her his childhood experience of being taught classical Greek by his father. David had meant to make Greek scholarship, along with writing poetry, his life's work. Although a nervous breakdown at age nineteen had forced him to drop out of college, a few years later he was accepted into the graduate program in classical Greek at the University of Chicago. His thesis (which he never completed, as he became ill with a painful intestinal disease that was misdiagnosed for well over a year) was on Lesbian Aeolic, the language of Sappho.

David poured much of himself into Ariana. He gave her a Victorian childhood, in which some of his literary heroes—the Brownings, Swinburne, and Andrew Lang, editor of *The Blue Fairy Book*—made cameo appearances. And by having Ariana die of cancer, David could write about his own mother's lingering death from metastasized breast cancer when he was in his twenties. He made Ariana tough-minded and brave—a side of himself that was sometimes eclipsed by his accommodating nature and conversational flights of fancy. David learned to change his mother's mastectomy dressings and give her morphine injections so that he could accompany her on one last visit to her beloved Adirondacks.

In his author biography for the book, David said of himself that he "lives in Lemmon, South Dakota, where he works as a farmhand and a bartender." He found both jobs inspiring. He wrote a poem in which the French poet Stéphane Mallarmé pays a visit to the Ranger Bar and tosses dice with the locals, and another based on the sounds an old tractor and baler made struggling up a hill. In the poem "Love and Poetry at Ground Zero," he envisioned nuclear missiles in silos on the Great Plains (the nearest such silo was some sixty miles from us) as sleepless fairy-tale monsters who speak in deceptively inviting tones to passersby. After I wrote a poem about the plains at night, "The Middle of the World," he wrote one called "The Middle of Nowhere," about peeing by the side of a gravel road in the presence of the Northern Lights, "these swells of stripped / hydrogen atoms and disaffected / quarks that splash our electromagnetic / outer reefs, above Sioux County, / North Dakota." Typically, David employed his poetry as a vehicle to bring together his interests in mathematics, science, and natural beauty: "I shiver and pee in the black / ditch, wave functions /

collapsing around me like waves. / I know where I am: not far from home; / not far from our glamourous, ex- / travagant star; lost in uncountable, / unaccountable light."

David and I had moved into a house that my grandparents had occupied for more than sixty years. Nearly everything we used was theirs: furniture, bedding, kitchen utensils, even the SweetHeart soap I remembered from childhood summers. We felt like temporary occupants, entrusted with the house and belongings until the true owners should appear. After wearing an old canvas jacket of my grandfather's, David addressed the subject of the ghosts in the house in the poem "To Kathleen, with a Rabbit": "I cannot say that I know / all their land is talking about, less / still what their talky old house has in mind. I'd just / as soon live with those voices, though, till / I can hear them." The "talky old house" was also the inspiration for the new poems I was writing. It was full of family presence; my grandfather's buffalo robe and my father's Navy greatcoat in the closet, my mother's small wooden playhouse in the basement, along with a doll in a wicker carriage. In the prehistoric seabed of western South Dakota, I was no longer at sea.

v. *Up and Down*

Crisis

David and I supported each other through the minor ups and downs of the writing cycle. When one of us was working on new poems, the other would be revising older work, or not writing at all. We adopted a farming term, "downtime," which refers to the period spent waiting for repairs or replacement parts. David tended to get through his downtime by taking up higher mathematics or computer science, playing with prime numbers or random access codes. In a more literary mood he might consult his Oxford texts of Hesiod or Homer. Once you've troubled to learn classical Greek, he'd explain, you don't want to let it go. I would go for a walk or a swim, start a novel I'd been meaning to read, or try a bread recipe from an old library book. I might turn to a piddling but necessary job, bookkeeping for my family's farm corporation, or to our own monthly bill-paying.

If we were both "up" and fully engaged in writing, we tried to make room for each other. If we were both "down" and mildly depressed, we would gather our forces. As David cooked, we'd visit in the kitchen. I'd mumble, "I used to be a writer," and he would say, "Yeah, me, too," and then we'd laugh at ourselves. For us, this was a workable way to live. I loved his poetry, and he loved mine, and while we did not collaborate, we each trusted the other as our first and most invaluable reader. When there was no new work to read, we could encourage each other not to give up.

David seldom spoke of his earlier mental breakdown, except to characterize it as a classic reaction to a first, failed romance, and to say that Freudian psychiatry had saved him. I harbored doubts about the usefulness of traditional psychiatric methods for me. I felt that doctors expected young women to be neurotic; thus, we could not fail to be so. In one infamous study from the 1960s, psychiatrists were asked to describe the qualities of a mentally healthy adult and those of a mentally healthy woman. The results demonstrated that if a woman was a sane adult—that is, independent and assertive—she could not be a mentally healthy woman. Also, I was from a middle-class family, and in the 1960s psychotherapy was mostly for the wealthy. Before I went to college I had never known anyone who was the client of a psychiatrist, and at Bennington I was unnerved to find that among many of my peers, having "a shrink" was the norm, if not an outright status symbol. Some had begun analysis in childhood and now identified so closely with their neuroses that they seemed incapable of change. But I also learned that psychiatry could work wonders, as I saw friends who had left college return, no longer psychotic and suicidal, after spending months in mental institutions.

Before I met David, when I was feeling low, I sought quiet time alone or with friends. An off-season weekend in Montauk with my typewriter and chilly walks on the beach, or physical labor in my friend and mentor Betty Kray's Rhode Island garden. At Betty's behest, after the tumultuous end of a love affair, I saw a Jungian analyst for a while, and found her helpful. But that ended with the move to South Dakota, where the nearest Jungian was more than five hundred miles away. As psychotropic drugs became more advanced and also more commonly prescribed, David and I opted not to use them. We believed that our ups and downs were part of the creative process, and we didn't want to risk being flattened emotionally, which could stunt our work. If we weren't exactly well by the world's standards, we were coping, having made our adjustments to the demands of both the poetic muse and our marriage.

Problems surfaced as we approached forty. David's habitual use of alcohol as a means of inspiration caught up with him. I tended to avoid mixing alcohol and writing, for even one or two drinks made me sleepy. But for years, David had been able to drink everyone else under the table without suffering noticeable effects. He would then stay up half the night working, writing either lyric poetry or computer programs. When he began to suffer from drunkenness, he found it unpleasant, but he panicked at the thought of having to give up drinking—he felt he would then lose his creativity. He said that William Styron's experience of alcohol, so vividly rendered in *Darkness Visible*, mirrored his own. Styron speaks of relying on alcohol "as a means to let my mind conceive visions that the unaltered, sober brain has no access to." He regarded alcohol as "an invaluable senior partner of my intellect" and "a friend whose ministrations I sought daily—sought also, I now see, as a means to calm the anxiety and incipient dread that I had hidden away."

David had not hidden from me the formative details of his life: his college education interrupted first by a mental breakdown, then by grave illness; his mother's early death. But there was much that he had kept from me, and from himself—a depth of dread and anguish he'd held bottled up for years. It was all about to come rushing out. There were many triggers: The approach of middle age. The sudden death of his beloved mentor, William Forrest, a professor at Le Moyne College in Syracuse, New York. This was also the year that my friend Betty Kray was dying of ovarian cancer. She worried that I was spending too much time with her, in Rhode Island and New York City, and warned me that David might be feeling abandoned. As usual, she was right. I had thought that my husband appreciated having the extra time alone to write. With a grant from the National Endowment for the Arts, he had been working on a second book of poems, which had recently been accepted for publication. I had no idea how bad all this good news would turn out to be.

I was well aware that my rekindled need for religion had been unsettling to David. We talked about it openly, and frequently. When I began attending the Presbyterian church near my grandparents' house, David had been bemused yet accepting. He believed strongly, he said, in religious freedom. But, said the former Roman Catholic altar boy who hadn't been to Mass in years, only partly teasing, "Of course, that's not a *real* church." David enjoyed serving fine meals to the ministers in town, and several became our friends. One pastor's wife, a full-time mother to young children, had a degree in mathematics from Cambridge, where she had met her husband. She and David enjoyed conversing about higher mathematics, an interest her husband also shared. It was amusing to watch him with David, engrossed in an arcane bit of computer science in a grocery store aisle. If one of his parishioners approached, the reverend would shift suddenly into pastoral mode, and plain English.

The Protestant Kathleen was fine with David. When I began to make regular visits to the Benedictine abbey nearest our home, however, he grew anxious and fearful. I did all I could to convince him that I did not intend to convert to Catholicism, let alone put pressure on him to go back to the Church. Over dinner in the refectory one night, a monk told him, plainly, "You've got to get that Catholic monkey off your back." But I failed to recognize the depths of David's despair. His mother had been in many ways a conventional pre–Vatican II Catholic, who took her children to have their throats blessed every year on the feast of Saint Blaise and made regular pilgrimages to Mother Cabrini's tomb in the Bronx. Yet at a time when young Catholic women were expected to attend Catholic educational institutions and enter teaching or nursing, David's mother went to Barnard and earned a Ph.D. in chemistry.

David and his mother had been exceptionally close, and she delighted in her son's intellect. He used to say that from the time he was very small, when he asked her a question—how ammonia cleaned the window, or why the sky was blue—she would explain in great detail. But when he was an adolescent, Mother Church came between them: he wondered how a scientist could believe in Christian dogma, and his mother grieved over his loss of faith. For years he attended Mass only to please her, building up a store of resentment that he couldn't express, and she died before the rift could be healed. David carried a hidden wound, one that he thought had mended over time. But in truth, he had not begun to deal with it. And I was Pollyanna Protestant, unwittingly blundering into what for David was hostile territory.

You put it together: turning forty, the death of a mentor, a modest literary success that David could not fully enjoy, as he was crippled by a guilt that convinced him he didn't deserve any good thing. And now his wife, like his mother, was being drawn to a Catholicism he could not fathom or accept, going to a place where he could not follow. While I did not understand all of the forces that were tearing David apart, I knew that something was terribly wrong. I was used to his staying up all night to write; now he exhibited new and disturbing behavior. He would stay up for thirty-six or forty-eight hours, becoming incoherent, if not from alcohol, from a lack of sleep. Once when I was out of town, a policeman, a neighbor, stopped David for erratic driving, expecting to find that he was drunk. But he wasn't, and being exhausted was not in itself a crime. The officer told David he could drive home, but he would be trailing him and, if necessary, would put him to bed himself. A small blessing in a small town.

When David could talk about his condition, he spoke of an overwhelming sorrow that was all the worse because he could not weep. I asked him whether he'd consider getting treatment, as therapy had helped him twenty years before. The nearest psychiatrists were in Bismarck, North Dakota—just four of them, I believe—and David picked one from the yellow pages and called for an appointment. Sometimes I would accompany him to Bismarck and shop or visit friends; other times he went alone, returning late at night. I thought I saw some improvement, but his condition still worried me. On the day he mailed his completed manuscript to his publisher, he seemed deeply troubled. When I asked if he could talk about what was wrong, he said no. He told me he had an appointment with clients at a nearby grain elevator; he had to help install a computerized payroll program that he'd written. We could talk when he came home.

When David didn't return that night, I phoned local taverns and friends, to ask whether anyone had seen him. The next morning I called the secretary at the grain elevator, who told me that the new program was up and running, and they hadn't seen David for weeks. On rare occasions David had gone off by himself for a day or two, but he always kept in touch. The lie he had told frightened me, and I stayed by the phone all that day. The next day I went to our post office box, expecting to find word from him. I was encouraged to see his handwriting on an envelope postmarked Bismarck. Good, I thought, his doctor is there. Yet what was inside was clearly a suicide note. I walked in a daze to the mailroom window and told the clerk that I needed to call the police. Hope—what Emily Dickinson termed that "thing with feathers"—was battered but still alive in me. I reasoned that if David had mailed the letter from Bismarck the day before, he must be alive there today.

On that bleak winter morning, I was showered with kindness. The postmaster came out from his office to wait with me until the police chief arrived. He asked if he could photocopy the note. I felt a qualm but of course assented. He then asked whether he could offer me a ride. We drove to my pastor's house, and there, for the first time, as the minister and his wife prayed for David and me, I cried. But I soon laughed to hear our small-town police chief phone the head of the Bismarck Police Department and say, "Now, Dave may look like a bum, but he's very intelligent. And he's a good guy. He won't give you no trouble." I gave all the information I could about where David might be, and the names of hotels where we had stayed, of bars he might frequent, and of his psychiatrist.

My pastor offered to drive me to the monastery, and from there one of the monks would take me the rest of the way to Bismarck, another seventy-five miles. We left town not knowing whether David was dead or alive. It was bitingly cold, well below zero, and I found it hard not to think about him dying from exposure. The pastor listened as I described David's condition over the past few months. He then said, "I hope you realize that if he has killed himself, it's not your fault." He seemed surprised when I replied that I did know that. I felt I had done everything I could do to get David to open up about what was troubling him. Normally, we could talk things through. But if he had decided to commit suicide, that was the kind of insanity that shuts everyone else out.

During that drive I recalled the ceremony in which I had become a Benedictine oblate (an associate of a particular monastery). David had brought me flowers and wished me well, but had arrived late and seated himself apart in the darkened church, out of the circle of light around the altar and the choir stalls, where I sat with the monks. During the Mass he looked stricken and alone; later he told me that he'd been startled to see how much the oblation, an abbreviated form of monastic profession, resembled a wedding. But since then David had become close friends with several of the monks. He loved it when I came home from being with the Benedictines, because I was always in a good mood. I didn't understand why the crisis had come now.

When we arrived at the abbey, one of the brothers came from behind his desk in the reception area and hugged me. "He's alive," he said. The police had found David and had taken him to St. Alexius, a Benedictine hospital.

Other monks entered, some in their habits, some in blue jeans. I was comforted by their presence and quiet concern. Our great friend Father Robert West, the director of oblates and master of the wine cellar, came around with a car. He had called ahead to arrange for me to stay with the Benedictine sisters in Bismarck. When we arrived at the hospital emergency room, the police were still there. They'd had invaluable help from a motel housekeeper, who had found David's Browning automatic pistol and drafts of the suicide notes he'd been writing. The police had adjusted the door lock so that he could not shut himself in the room, and then canvassed the neighborhood. They found him in a seedy bar, drinking gin and reading the newspaper. One of his friends later remarked that David could never have killed himself without first checking out the day's comics and "Dear Abby." I believe that he was trying to put off the inevitable, was hoping to be found. A policeman told me, in a tone of mournful wonder, "Ma'am, he was so depressed." There had been a murder-suicide the week before, a rare occurrence in Bismarck, and the police were glad to have prevented another death. One of them asked to buy the pistol from me. The David I knew would have found this highly amusing, but I was not sure who this new David was.

The doctor on duty explained that he was running a number of tests to help him determine whether to admit David to the psychiatric ward or to the hospital proper. He had been drinking heavily and not eating well, and he was dangerously dehydrated. The doctor pointed to a door: "He's in there." I entered the room, looked around, and almost left. There was only one patient in the room, hunched in a wheelchair, and it wasn't David. I looked again, disbelieving. It was as if David had turned inside out, his familiar features so distorted by anguish that I could not recognize him. Noticing the crucifix on one wall, I sighed; the man before me looked far more crucified than that. David could barely speak, and when he did, he shook his head and said only, "No. No." He would not look me in the eye. I stayed with him, saying little, until an aide came to wheel him to the psychiatric unit. I held David's hand, and before he got into bed I gave him a gentle hug, but he didn't respond.

That night, I looked out of my guest room onto the snowy bluffs of the Missouri River and was overcome by a sense of gratitude. I was grateful that David was alive, and in a safe, warm place. With the help of a drug, he would be able to sleep. As the stillness of the monastery began to seep into my bones, allowing me to acknowledge how exhausted I was, I immersed myself in the poetry of the Song of Solomon, and felt myself connected in unexpected ways to its story. I, too, had searched for my lost love. I had taken him away from his mother's house halfway across the country to the house where my own mother had been raised. And yes, love is stronger, fiercer even, than death. If I had been emotionally drained by the events of the past few days, I was no longer frightened. The word *crisis* derives from the Greek for "a sifting," and even in my distress I sensed that there might be a purpose to our present upheaval: to jostle, sift, and sort things until only what was most vital would remain. When I found the man I loved in that emergency room, I had seen him as if for the first time. Although I knew him well, I had never witnessed the true extent of his pain.

Against all reason, my hope was certain: Now that he had truly broken, he would be able to heal.

Do You Want to Be Made Well?

When Jesus saw him lying there and knew that he had been there
a long time, he said to him, "Do you want to be made well?"

—JOHN 5:6

The next days were full of shocks. The good news was that David's hospital psychiatrist would be the same doctor who had been seeing him for the past six months; the bad news was that it had all been a lie. The doctor had never met David, and seemed mildly amused by the deception. After David had been in the hospital for a few days I received a call from the business office informing me that we had no medical insurance. I called Blue Cross and learned that David had stopped paying the premiums months before. He later admitted that in his downward spiral he had been trying to mess things up so badly that they couldn't be fixed and I would reject him. Suicide would then be his only option.

As disconcerted as I was, I was convinced that now that David's lies had been exposed, we could better confront the serious issues behind them. Losing our medical insurance, which once would have seemed a disaster, proved to be the least of my worries. I grieved that David had been carrying so much guilt, all alone. The psychiatrist diagnosed him with "psychotic melancholia," and said something about him that David later repeated to me, with a hint of pride: "You have exceptionally well-defended neuroses." Friends warned us that this doctor had a reputation for overmedicating his patients. However, for David he prescribed only a sleeping pill to be taken as needed, and that was the sole medication he received during his stay in the hospital, and for many months after.

I am aware that this flies in the face of current therapeutic orthodoxy. One physician I recently told this story to responded indignantly; she called David's treatment "an absolute waste of time." But it was, for David, exactly right. His healing would come largely through interactions with others. His hospital roommate was an adolescent with an eating disorder, low self-esteem, and homework, and David, a born teacher, could not resist offering to help him. I knew that the worst was over when I entered their room and found the two of them sorting out a math problem. David smiled at me for the first time in a week. He disliked the jargon that was tossed around in group therapy; he thrived on more informal exchanges with other patients. The women, especially, took to him, as women had all his life. They told him stories of cruel and neglectful fathers and husbands, stories he never forgot. There was a small glassed-in lounge—the only place in the hospital where smoking was permitted—and David asked me to keep him supplied with cigarettes, not only for him but also to share. He started to look more like himself. He asked for writing supplies and his copy of John Donne's sermons.

Depression has many causes: genetic disposition and chemical imbalance in the brain, as well as unwelcome change, notably loss in all its forms. Can we agree that there are many treatments as well? My husband thought himself incapable of prayer; at the crisis points of his life, Freudian psychiatry brought healing. One might say he had faith in it.

For me, a measure of healing has come less from psychology than from religion, specifically the ancient practices of prayer and psalmody. Once, when I was all but paralyzed by despair, a wise physician prescribed physical exercise and spiritual direction. It worked.

Picture me at the Bismarck police station, waiting to pick up the few possessions David had left in that motel room: a canvas briefcase, a notepad, pens and pencils, and a copy of *Tristram Shandy*. After completing the paperwork, I sat in the vestibule, waiting for a ride to the monastery, and read my psalter. Throughout this crisis, the psalms had been my constant companions, calming me and helping me endure. When a friend from New York phoned to offer emotional support, she asked, "How about you? Are you seeing a doctor? Do you have something to take for this?"

"I have the psalms," I answered. "And they're *enough*?" she asked, incredulous. "Yes," I replied, not knowing how to explain myself. I had been so fully embraced by the healing hospitality of the Benedictine women of Bismarck, and by the psalms that I read with them in daily prayer, that it had not occurred to me to ask for tranquilizers. I felt that I needed my wits about me, and needed to feel whatever I was to feel. Yes, the psalms were enough, at least until I went back home to find that our phone wasn't working. Then, as I attempted to write a letter to Blue Cross, in what would be a futile attempt to reinstate our medical insurance, the computer monitor quit. Everything was breaking down: first my husband, then the phone, and now the damn computer. The terrible comedy enraged me, but it also permitted me to weep, copiously, for the first time in days. If someone had handed me a psalter at that moment, I would likely have thrown it across the room. Yet I went back to the psalms at bedtime that night, and in the morning. I owed so much to them, and to the monastic communities that pray them faithfully, day in, day out.

I commuted between Bismarck and Lemmon for several weeks, and the sisters offered to keep a room in their guest quarters for me. The sisters and I celebrated Mardi Gras together and entered Lent. David was slowly recovering. He could look me in the eye again, and talk with me, and even laugh. After a week he was allowed to accompany me on walks outside the hospital. He told me he had started composing a poem, titled "Provident Life," inspired by an insurance company sign that he could see from his room, and he began to talk about going home. One day the monk who'd been subbing as a chaplain in the hospital, a good friend of ours, asked if I would like to go to dinner. A night out sounded grand. I splurged on a bottle of Champagne, and we talked until the staff kicked us out of the restaurant. Clutching the unfinished bottle—I planned to use the stale Champagne as a hair rinse in the morning—I entered the monastery as the clock struck midnight, a misguided and tipsy Cinderella. But in the wintry desert of western North Dakota, something good was stirring to life. I could feel the blossoming of hope.

Home

After David had spent three weeks on the psychiatric ward, the doctor sent him home. He scheduled a number of follow-up office visits and group therapy sessions, and made it clear that David could request a prescription for an antidepressant at any time. David and I began the process of picking up where we had abruptly left off. Much had changed, of course, but the marriage itself was reassuringly familiar. I was on high alert and had to learn to let David be alone again. He admitted that he was not yet certain that he wanted to live, but at least he was talking about his self-destructive urges rather than acting on them in secret. Our only source of income, apart from a small stipend from the family farm corporation, was the work I was doing for the North Dakota Council on the Arts in public schools, and David now accompanied me when I went to a small town for a week or two, sharing the funky motel rooms with paper bath-mats and uncertain TV reception, eating the same café food. David the philosopher was intrigued, in one town, to find that the only thing you could order that didn't come with toast was toast. In another town we had free meals courtesy of a school principal who owned a roadside hot-dog-and-ice-cream stand. It was spring, and David enjoyed afternoon walks in the countryside. I was always relieved to find him waiting for me when I returned after a day of teaching.

Our good friend Annie Wright, widow of the poet James Wright, offered us invaluable advice during this time. We knew that Jim had once been hospitalized after a breakdown and had come home to heal. One evening, years before, when we were having dinner at the Wrights', he had demonstrated his contribution to a therapy session in which patients were asked to imitate an ordinary household object. Solemnly, with hands raised over his head, slicing air, and his feet crisscrossing in little steps, he "became" a pair of scissors. David had mentioned his own breakdown at college, and said that shortly before he was hospitalized, he had gone on retreat at a Trappist abbey in Genesee, New York. He found that the manual labor—shoveling manure from a barn—had helped for a while. When I phoned Annie about our current situation, she told us that we would see progress, but it would be maddening, a matter of six steps forward, two back, then three steps forward, one back. "You won't believe how long it will take," she said, giving me a useful mantra for the next three years.

Regular sessions with the psychiatrist were helping David, but he was less certain of the value of group therapy. I wanted some help for myself; advocating for David in the hospital and coping with the insurance mess and the medical bills had worn me out. I needed to learn how to relax again and regain my sense of self. Years later, when I saw the film *A Beautiful Mind*, I recognized myself in the woman who, when asked by a friend how she is doing, responds by talking about her husband's condition. When pressed to speak for herself, she admits that she doesn't know whether she is a wife, a nurse, or something in between. I felt that David and I would benefit from marriage counseling, but he was too "talked out" and asked me to wait. Once his group therapy ended, some six months after his discharge from the hospital, we were ready for intentional work on the basics of listening to each other. What David feared most was a relapse, and he was encouraged when, after several months, the counselor said she thought we had become much more attuned to each other, so that if either of us started to go off track, the other would notice immediately. We sensed that our marriage was more stable than ever before.

David eventually asked his psychiatrist for an antidepressant and was put on a low dose of Prozac. While he did not have the intense uplift that some users report, he felt that it took the edge off his despair. It made him less afraid, and that was good enough. We were able to resume our more or less normal life, and if progress was slow, at least it was progress. Routine events took on a renewed beauty. David enjoyed a passage I had found in Louise Bogan's memoirs, in which she writes of seeing, out the window of a psychiatric ward, a woman hanging clothes and of "wishing that I, too, could . . . hang out clothes in a happy, normal way." When she walked with other patients at "the hour when children begin to scent supper," she observed an air of despondency come over the group. The women "knew the hour in their bones. It was no hour to be out, taking an aimless walk." David could see himself in Bogan as she discovered to her surprise, shortly after her release from the hospital, that her unaccustomed sense of peace did not depend on "the whim of any fallible creature, or . . . economic security, or the weather. I don't know where it comes from. Jung states that such serenity is always a miracle. . . . I am so glad that the therapists of my maturity and the saints of my childhood agree on one thing."

After fourteen years together, David and I were at last speaking more openly. He had been raised in a family in which people held things back, and I in one in which few topics were taboo. He buried his anger within, while I let mine out in quick, short blasts. I was fully capable of breaking dishes in frustration, but I never threw them at him and I tried not to say hurtful things. An argument we had, witnessed by one of my sisters, became a family legend. Slamming a kitchen cupboard shut and sputtering with rage, I wanted to tell David that I hated him, though I knew that wasn't true. So I shouted, "*I don't like you very much!*" This broke us up, a laugh-until-you-cry gut-buster, and defused the tension. My sister was not reassured, and a few days later startled my mother by reporting over the phone, "I think they're getting divorced."

When David could tell me to my face that he was hurt or angered by something I had done, I rejoiced, even as I fought back, or recognized my need to apologize. When things were going well, I urged him to resist the temptation to turn success into failure. "You don't need to create trouble," I'd say. "Troubles come of their own accord." If I was, as he sometimes said, "Little Miss Protestant" to his "recovering Catholic," he now found something worthwhile in my faith. Eileen Simpson, in her memoir of her marriage to John Berryman, *Poets in Their Youth*, wrote that while many of their friends were "openly antagonistic to religion, John was not. Although he was unable to believe, it was very important to him that I should." If I missed church for two Sundays or more, David would gently chide me: "It's good for you. You ought to go."

I considered it a miracle that I had attained some measure of religious faith just in time to face the crisis in David's health, and in our marriage. If I had ever thought that I was seeking salvation for myself, I realized now that David and I had become, in the Gospel phrase, "one flesh," and that salvation for me was salvation for him as well. And I was helpless to save either one of us. We needed help, and plenty of it. From God, from Benedictine men and women, from pastors, physicians, postmasters, and psychiatric nurses, from police officers and a motel housekeeper. From the suffering Jesus on the cross, and the risen one who embodies hope.

When Jesus asks the man, "Do you want to be made well?" he does not answer directly, yes or no. He explains that he has no one to help him go down to the pool when the water is stirring. This is the healing pool of Bethesda, whose waters are stirred by an angel. Although unnamed in Scripture, the angel is traditionally understood to be Raphael, whose name means "God's medicine." The man is too frail to reach the pool on his own, and when he attempts it, others always get ahead of him and block his way. Jesus listens, then says, "Stand up, take your mat and walk" (John 5:8).

Faith

"Stand up, take your mat and walk"? What kind of answer is that? To a sick person, a depressed person, that is precisely what is not possible. And don't try to say, as Jesus does, that it's my faith that makes me well. That's just plain discouraging if I take it to mean, as far too many people have, that my lack of faith keeps me ill. Surely we can drop that particular bludgeon from our theological arsenal. Note that in this healing story, Jesus does not impose any conditions. He does not ask the man whether he is a believer, only whether he wants to be made well. This gives me hope that there is a faith for those of us who, like Miss Dickinson, may "believe, and disbelieve a hundred times an Hour, which keeps Believing nimble." My Christianity understands that while pain and distress have many causes, lack of faith is not one of them. At times, as when my husband and I were sent home from the psychiatric ward, faith can be a matter of taking up one's mat and walking.

Like faith, marriage is a mystery. The person you're committed to spending your life with is known and yet unknown, at the same time remarkably intimate and necessarily other. The classic "seven-year itch" may not be a case of familiarity breeding ennui and contempt, but the shock of having someone you thought you knew all too well suddenly seem a stranger. When that happens, you are compelled to either recommit to the relationship or get the hell out. There are many such times in a marriage. When the other person does something unforgivable, can you forgive? When you do something unforgivable, can you accept forgiveness? At home, after David's three weeks in the hospital, we were like strangers, unsure of each other and unsure of our future together. Every step was wobbly, like a baby's step, and suicide was the bogeyman. If anyone had asked, "Do you have faith enough for this?" it would have seemed the wrong question, one we were ill equipped to answer.

We shortchange ourselves by regarding religious faith as a matter of intellectual assent. This is a modern aberration; the traditional Christian view is far more holistic, regarding faith as a whole-body experience. Sometimes it is, as W. H. Auden described it, a matter of "[choosing] what is difficult all one's days as if it were easy." David did not "choose" his mother's lengthy illness and death, his recurring intestinal problems, or his disposition toward melancholy. But he was Catholic enough to regard these troubles as no more, and no less, than his share of human suffering. To his everlasting credit, this made him more, and not less, compassionate. Many years into our marriage, what he did choose, and what I chose as well, was to stay together. We took our two steps forward, three steps back, then one forward and five back. But we kept on walking. For us, it was the only way.

No Prescriptions Here

This may not have worked for you. But I am telling stories, not writing prescriptions. Our desire for the latter is so strong in this country that we overuse antibiotics to our detriment, rendering once helpful medications ineffective. We cause another kind of harm, I think, when we assume that literature, particularly literature about depression, is necessarily prescriptive. I once wrote an article about dragging myself to church out of a sense of family obligation, only to find myself confronted with the hymn "There Is Sunshine in My Soul Today." Hardly what I was feeling, and normally I would have scorned its verses as pietistic, insufficiently concerned with anything except "Jesus & me." But acedia had lately made my world obscenely small, and the hymn allowed me to feel alive for the first time in days. Singing it was a glad response to grace. "I have the strength to take it all up again," I wrote. "This is a day to begin." After the piece was published, I received a letter chastising me for trivializing the serious illness of depression, and for suggesting that people can snap out of it. I had done no such thing. I had described one of those common but precious awakenings of the heart that point to something greater than the self and give us hope. I stand by it.

A coalescence of music, Scripture, and other people in a worshipping congregation had brought me to my senses. I had been dwelling in a drought-stricken land, like the famished prodigal, who, envying the pigs their husks and slop, suddenly remembers that he is a beloved child who has a home. I know that, in the words of a great hymn, "Come, Thou Fount of Every Blessing," my temperament makes me "prone to wander from the God I love." But if I have forgotten who I am, getting back on the road may help me remember. I am both humbled and exalted by the reception I receive when I make my move: the world itself seems to open up and accept me.

Losing one's way and then finding it may mimic the cyclical nature of depression, but it is also part of the natural rhythm of day and night, of the waxing and waning moon, and of seeding and harvesting. However true and even beautiful this turning of times and seasons may be, I tend to resist it as a necessary aspect of the spiritual life. Monastic writers have always emphasized that maintaining a life of prayer means being willing to start over, after one has acted in a sinful or destructive way. Both pride and acedia will assert themselves, and it may appear that we are so far gone we may as well give up and not embarrass ourselves further by pretending to be anything but failures. It seems foolish to believe that the door is still open, that there is always another chance. I may accept this intellectually, but I have come to appreciate its depths only through experience. Just when I seem to have my life in balance and imagine I can remain in this happy state forever, I lose sight of the value of contemplation and prayer, and try to live without it. Soon enough, once again, I am picking myself up out of the ashes.

The early Christian monks staked their survival on their willingness to be as God had made them, creatures of the day-to-day. They regarded repetition as essential to their salvation, and valued perseverance in prayer and manual labor as the core of their spiritual discipline. When acedia tempted them from these tasks, they were admonished to make their way back as quickly as possible. It is all a matter of falling down and standing up again, no matter how many times. Typically, the desert fathers provide a gnomic commentary on this aspect of their lives: "Abba Moses asked Abba Sylvanus, 'Can a man lay a new foundation every day?' The old man said, 'If he works hard, he can lay a new foundation at every moment.'"

VI. *Give Me a Word*

To the Desert

By the fourth century, both pagan and Christian ascetics were less interested in schools of thought than in ways of living. They pursued detachment from the world as a means of freeing themselves for contemplation, and developed lists of the characteristic temptations and obsessions that disrupted their spiritual practice. While the pagan philosophers tended to remain in cities, the monks went to the desert in an attempt to grow closer to Christ. Some monks lived together and followed a common rule of life, and even hermits often had neighbors with whom they celebrated a weekly eucharist. Elders attracted disciples who lived with or near them. Most of these monks had no written rule; they tended their souls with the discipline of prayer, the memorizing and reciting of Scripture, manual labor, and what we now term spiritual direction.

A novice monk who doubted his vocation was encouraged to seek out an elder and ask for a word. The response given was often both practical and profound. When Abba Pambo asked, "What ought I to do?" Abba Anthony replied, "Have no confidence in your own virtuousness. Do not worry about a thing once it has been done. Control your tongue and your belly." Addressed to individuals in specific situations, the remarks were passed down orally among the monks. Eventually they were compiled in written form. Many psychological insights found in these sayings are found also in pre-Christian philosophers. The Roman Stoic Seneca, for example, wrote that to escape *taedium vitae* (weariness with life) "it is your soul you need to change, not the climate." This was a recurring theme for monks as well, particularly because acedia mocked their good intentions by reminding them of the comforts they had forsaken and urging them to abandon their hard way of life. One abba said, "If some temptation arises in the place where you dwell in the desert, do not leave that place. . . . For if you leave it then, no matter where you go, you will find the same temptation waiting for you." Amma Syncletica employed a typically homey metaphor: "Just as the bird who abandons the eggs she was sitting on prevents them from hatching, so the monk [and] the nun [grow] cold and their faith dies, when they go from one place to another."

In going to the Egyptian desert the first Christian monks were rejecting a church that was newly respectable, wealthy, and top-heavy with clerics and bishops residing in urban palaces. The desert was then considered a fearful place, where only demons dared live. Attempting to confront these demons on their own turf, the monks learned that as external distractions were diminished, interior distractions increased, and they began to study their thoughts as they arose, noting which were life-giving and which destructive. Evagrius speaks of the vital importance of recognizing and distinguishing between the different types of bad thoughts, and warns that we must "take note of the circumstances of their coming . . . which are the more vexatious, which yield . . . more readily and which [are] the more resistant?" The reason for this careful self-observation, Evagrius says, is that we need "effective words against them, that is to say, those words which correctly characterize the [demon] present. And we must do this before they drive us out of our own state of mind."

The monks believed that their most effective weapons in this struggle were the words of the Bible, and they committed to memory as much Scripture as possible. This was a practical measure, as books were rare, but it served also to equalize the educated monks and the illiterate majority. With powers of concentration that are nearly unfathomable today, novice monks set about to learn the psalms and the Gospels by heart. And that was just for starters. To help monks struggle against the "bad thoughts," Evagrius compiled an extensive *Antirrheticus*, a list of Scripture passages appropriate to resist each temptation. Against the thought "that sets before our eyes the long duration and the harshness of the years of our life," for example, he suggested this line from Psalm 103: "As for us, our days are like grass; we flourish like the flower of the field." In the Dakotas, where pasture grasses often turn brown by late summer, this is a hearty dose of realism. To acknowledge our mortality need not be depressing, if it encourages us to enjoy the beauty of life while it is still fresh and new.

For contemporary people with easy access to books, the Internet, and television, the power of words as experienced by the monks is almost beyond comprehension. But even now, repeated exposure to Scripture can be a revelation. One day when the air was so frigid that it hurt to breathe, I was on my way to visit David in the psychiatric

ward. As I cursed the cold and the icy pavement under my feet, these
words of a canticle from the Sunday divine office came to mind:

> Bless the Lord, winter cold and summer heat . . .
> Bless the Lord, dews and falling snow . . .
> Bless the Lord, nights and days . . .
> Bless the Lord, light and darkness . . .
> Bless the Lord, ice and cold . . .
> Bless the Lord, frosts and snows;
> sing praise to him and highly exalt him forever.
> (Daniel 3:45–50)

Unaccountably consoled, I was grateful that without my willing it, or
being aware of how it had happened, the liturgy of the hours I had
prayed was having its desired effect. The words were now a part of me,
and when I most needed them, the rhythms of my walking had stirred
them up, to erode my anxiety and self-pity, and remind me that blessings may be found in all things.

Thoughts and Words

I can readily find myself in the descriptions of the bad thoughts—
avarice, anger, vainglory, pride, and all the rest—provided in the desert
stories. And I am grateful to the Benedictine Mary Margaret Funk for
her book *Thoughts Matter*, in which she looks at the tradition in light
of contemporary monastic life, and translates some of the earlier language for us. If we resist the daunting term *gluttony*, we still know what
it is to have "bad thoughts" about food in a society in which eating dis-

orders are a major health concern. Similarly, if the words *avarice* and *greed* seem a bit much, we can admit that in a culture addicted to consumption, where credit card debt seems epidemic, our "thoughts" about things cause real trouble.

Funk employs the traditional monastic terminology to some extent. "We are not our thoughts," she writes. "Thoughts come and thoughts go. Unaccompanied thoughts pass quickly. Thoughts that are thought about become desires. Desires that are thought about become passions." While good thoughts have the potential to become virtues, bad thoughts are likely to become "bad passions or habits of action." The ancient monks would agree with Funk that taking measure of our thoughts and attempting to redirect them is of primary importance. It is also a discipline available to anyone.

What I find most liberating about this practice of discerning thoughts is that it's not a proficiency test. In confronting my many failings, I don't have to feel guilty or helpless when I fall short and have to try again. I can rely on old Abba Ammanos to remind me that he "spent fourteen years . . . asking God night and day to grant . . . victory over anger." And I can be assured that my struggle to derail my own bad thoughts before they become sinful acts does not come about because I am evil by nature. We often use the phrase "It's human nature" when looking at the mess people have made of the world. But I stand with the early monks in believing that humanity, as created by God, is good. When our bad thoughts lead us to act selfishly and without compassion, we distort that original goodness. The monastic endeavor has always been to keep alive the image of God within, and now as in the fourth century this means contending with acedia.

Monks on Prozac

Monasticism is both an ancient and a contemporary phenomenon. The Benedictine Jeremy Driscoll has commented that while he takes part in an ancient tradition, he is not living in the past. "This is my century too," he writes. "I travel in planes, see the movies, use a computer. It makes me think about how I think." In today's world, monks must consider the spiritual significance of what many people take for granted: faxes, cell phones, e-mail, "personal" computers. Benedictines tend to be practical in working through this central conundrum of their lives, being at the same time fifteen hundred years old and thirty-five or sixty. A sister working outside the monastery may be issued a cell phone, but not a sister whose ministry is at home. Monks or nuns who are traveling may sign out a communal phone, in the same way that they reserve one of the monastery's automobiles. A monk who is teaching in a college or working on a doctoral dissertation will be granted a laptop for individual use, while others must rely on an old desktop in the community room.

People who cling to a romantic image of monasticism are often at a loss when confronted by the reality of the monastic life as it is lived today. They may disapprove when a monastery establishes a website so that people can e-mail prayer requests, or take offense when Benedictines offer nontraditional retreat programs with contemporary therapeutic methods. I have noted with interest the hostile reactions of some people when they learn that monasteries customarily require psychological assessments (such as the Minnesota Multiphasic Personality Inventory, or MMPI) of those who wish to join, or that some Benedictines see psychiatrists and take drugs such as Prozac, Wellbutrin, or Zoloft. Both conservative Catholics and, oddly enough, secular cynics tend to regard this phenomenon with an aggrieved air. The Catholics find yet another sign of the collapse of their traditional religion, as if a monk who needs Prozac were one who lacks faith. The cynics see only hypocrisy: Why, these "holy people" are not so holy after all, they're like the rest of us. To which the monastic choir responds with a glad and resounding "Amen!"

While a monastery cannot help reflecting to some extent the society of which it is a part, it is also a place apart. What may be the distinguishing feature of these communities in a polarized America is the extent to which, to paraphrase Walt Whitman, they contain multitudes. Look beneath the surface uniformity of monastic habits, and you will find people struggling, and mostly succeeding, to live together in peace despite a wide range of opinions on religion, spirituality, politics, sexual identity, diet, and health. Here is a monk who has been involved in interfaith dialogue with Buddhists or Jews for forty years, peeling potatoes with one who believes that anything other than Roman Catholicism is of the devil. Here is a nun convinced that to vote for a Democrat is a sin, praying alongside another who can't understand how any Christian can vote Republican.

Where mental illness is concerned, as recently as the mid-1960s a depressed monk or nun might be told by a superior, as a psychiatrist reported of one of his patients, "You are not a good [nun], because a good [nun] can never be depressed." It would not surprise me to find a Benedictine who still views mental illness as some sort of moral or spiritual failure, but that attitude is not the norm. The monastic communities with which I am most familiar do not hesitate to encourage a troubled member to seek help. One of the women David met in the Bismarck psychiatric ward was an elderly Benedictine, who told him that she checked herself in whenever her depression became too much to bear. When the prioress came to visit, she found David and the sister happily engaged in needlepoint to pass the time.

Once, at a conference of Benedictines, I witnessed an impassioned response to a presentation a sister had given on using the ancient practice of discernment to treat mental illness in the present day. She defined discernment clearly enough, as fostering "our ability to do the right deed with the right intention or motivation." But her suggestion that monastics had gone too far in jettisoning this valuable part of their heritage in favor of modern therapies brought a heated reply. The conversation after her talk was riveting and revealing: while people felt strongly on the subject, as Benedictines they were also careful to listen to one another. This meant that the anger some people may have felt—how could she consider rejecting the advances made in psychology?—became good energy, allowing for an open and frank discussion. The group was free to explore questions that in another setting would have triggered predictable and hardened responses: Are there essential differences between therapy and healing? What place do religious faith and the discipline of prayer have in helping people maintain their mental health?

Belief in the efficacy of therapeutic methods is such a part of American culture that for many psychology has replaced traditional religion. Some are tempted to regard religion itself as just another form of therapy, and an inadequate one at that. In *The Noonday Demon,* Andrew Solomon discusses people whose religious faith and practice have helped them cope with depression; but in an interview he expressed regret that "only half of Americans with severe, incapacitating depression have ever tried to get aid of any kind, *even* from a clergyman" (emphasis mine). One of the saddest Christians I have ever met is an ordained minister, a college chaplain, who was told that his school had no need of a chaplain anymore, because it had a fully staffed counseling service. The school, like many founded by Protestant denominations in the nineteenth century, had for years been loosening its religious ties, and the stance of the college administrators did not surprise me. I was dismayed that the minister, whose seminary training had included courses and internships in psychology and pastoral care, could think of nothing to say in rebuttal. I wanted him to shout from the rooftops that there might be an important difference between a pastor and a psychotherapist, and that some students would benefit more from one than the other.

The Devil I Know

It was at Bennington College, which has never considered hiring chaplains, that I allowed literature to take the place of religion in my life. And when I felt the stirrings of a religious conversion in my thirties, it was the literature of the psalms that drew me in. I also came to love the sayings of the desert fathers and mothers, and regretted that I had not found them sooner, for they help me live with myself as I am. I need their stubborn realism, their reassurance that my struggle with bad thoughts does not mean I am a bad person. I am glad to apply to my own life the words of Abba Poemen, who when asked about who might benefit from the words of Matthew 6:34, "Do not worry about tomorrow," responded: "It is said for the man who is tempted and has not much strength, so that he should not be worried, saying to himself, 'How long must I suffer this temptation?' He should rather say every day to himself, 'Today.'"

This literature also provides me with the most useful definition of prayer I have found. It is, Abba Agathon said, "warfare to the last breath." This had great relevance for me when, the first time I went to a monastery for Holy Week, I began having nightmares. When I complained to a monk that I had come for peace, not disturbing dreams about evil, he advised me to accept what was happening as a good sign. "What better place than a monastery," he said, "to face the devil's assault?" He sent me to the desert tradition, to the life of Anthony the Great and his observation that "without temptations, no-one can be saved," and to this teaching of Abba Pastor: "The virtue of a monk is made manifest by temptations." This insight frees me from guilt, from thinking that I've brought my troubles on myself because I lack faith. It also gives me hope. There is, of course, a vast difference between my life and that of a fourth-century ascetic. But there is also something recognizably similar. Were I to approach an abba or amma asking for a "word" to help me cope with the assaults of acedia on my soul, I would likely be reminded that if I am especially susceptible to acedia, it is because I harbor within myself the virtue of zeal.

That comes as a relief. It helps explain the extremism that lies beneath my more or less sane façade. I am both an extrovert and an introvert, energized by other people, even crowds of people, but also content to keep to myself for days on end. The diverse places in which I feel at home—Manhattan, the western Dakotas, the island of Oahu, and most any monastery—reflect the poles of my personality. My energy levels are set on high or low: I can happily juggle any number of activities or do very little. At my most sluggish, I experience a mild agoraphobia, which makes it hard for me to meet outside obligations, even to shop for bread or a quart of milk. Over the years, physicians have verified that my ups and downs are garden-variety, not clinical manic depression, or to use the more current phrase, bipolar disease. Over the years, I have learned to live with the flow. And that is part of the problem.

During periods of high energy, I enjoy a sense of balance and can easily find the time for prayer, work, exercise, socializing, and rest. And often, when I am low—whether in spirit, energy, or both—I seek out activities that will steady me: baking, reading, walking, and writing if I can, but not fretting if I cannot. In both my spiritual life and my work, I can often ride out the periods of drought that follow a drenching rain of creativity and purpose. But as I grow older this process becomes more exhausting. One of my mantras is a plea from Psalm 51: "Put a steadfast spirit within me." I pray it, but I must admit that I don't always mean it. Would a more steadfast spirit deaden me somehow, or dampen the writer in me? This up-and-down, unsteadfast person is who I am; this is the devil I know.

When I was a child, I loved the Exodus stories that told of the people of Israel being led through the desert by a pillar of cloud by day, a pillar of fire by night. I felt that such miracles were certain to engender nothing but faith. But when I read those stories as an adult I found something else, the power of that old, familiar "devil I know" to drive the people to doubt that they will find enough food and water. All the miracles are in the past; the people see only danger ahead. Fear sets in, along with a desire for the food they once had in Egypt. Their exhilaration at being liberated evaporates in the dry desert air, and they accuse God of bringing them there to let them die. Nostalgia glosses over the cruel conditions under which they had formerly lived, until they actually begin to prefer slavery to freedom. When God rains food down on them, all they can say is, "What is it?"—they are unable to recognize sustenance when it is right before them. As the nineteenth-century

Hasidic rabbi Hanokh said, "The real exile of Israel in Egypt was that they had learned to endure it."

Let's call it sickness, a desert malady. Anyone could lose perspective in that heat, weakened by hunger, thirst, and uncertainty. Yet a curious fact about illness, including depression, is that it can bring us to clarity. We value the quality of attention that comes to us when we are not well. In "I'm Not OK, You're Not OK," her review of *The Noonday Demon*, Joyce Carol Oates observes that "those afflicted with depression are often ambivalent about it, as no one is ambivalent about physical illness." Her latter assumption belies the fact that people of many faiths have experienced ailments and incapacities as a gateway to spiritual insight. But her observation about depression reflects the fact that many people are conflicted about a state in which the ploys they've used to color things in their favor are stripped away, and they sense that they are witnessing the world as it is. The light may be harsher than we would like, but at least it forces us to see.

From his extensive research, Andrew Solomon reports evidence that depressed people have a more realistic view of the world than others. He writes of one study that showed "depressed and nondepressed people are equally good at answering abstract questions. When asked, however, about their control over an event, nondepressed people invariably believe themselves to have more control than they really have, and depressed people give an accurate assessment." In a test involving a video game, "depressed people . . . knew just how many little monsters they had killed," while the nondepressed people consistently overestimated their kills by four to six times the actual amount. For all of that, Solomon reminds us that "major depression is far too stern a teacher: you needn't go to the Sahara to avoid frostbite."

Still, we find ways to love that old devil we know. And "love" is not too strong a word. "Curiously enough," Solomon admits, "I love my depression. I do not love experiencing my depression, but I love the depression itself. I love who I am in the wake of it." He cannot help respecting that which gave him knowledge of "my own acreage, the full extent of my soul." Solomon's perception is an ancient one; in the first century the Stoic Seneca observed that people "love their vices with a sort of despair, and hate them at the same time." Solomon is also in agreement with the desert fathers and mothers who made their stand in the desert in order to combat their demons and assess themselves more honestly. When he asserts that "the opposite of depression is not happiness but vitality," he is echoing the existential monastic view that the opposite of acedia is an energetic devotion. When I am at my worst, mired in torpor and despair, simply recalling this can give me hope.

"Hope" is the title of Solomon's last chapter, and in it he writes, poignantly, of valuing his depression because it unearthed "what I would have to call a soul, a part of myself I could never have imagined until one day . . . when hell came to pay me a surprise visit. It's a precious discovery." It is also a costly one, and the price is exacted again and again. All too often we are like the man in the Gospel story who is cleansed of evil spirits only to find that the demons who have been displaced keep wandering, looking for a place to land. When they see that the house of his soul has once more been made neat and clean, they descend on him and make his condition even worse than before.

How is it possible to maintain our sanity, let alone to foster hope? Acedia is a particularly savage enemy, because it is not content with just a part of us. Evagrius writes that "the other demons are like the rising or setting sun in that they are found in only a part of the soul. The noonday demon, however, is accustomed to embrace the entire soul and oppress the spirit." Evagrius, Cassian, and Andrew Solomon might agree that hope is nurtured when we can recall the peace of mind we once attained, and regard it as real, at least as real as our most troubled and anxious state. But we must start small. Often my first act of recovery is doing something as menial as dusting a bookshelf or balancing my checkbook. If I am tempted to devalue such humble activities, I remember that acedia descended on Anthony as soon as he went to the desert, but when he prayed to be delivered from it, he was shown that any physical task, done in the right spirit, could free him. Likewise, Evagrius gives sound advice to anyone who has begun to recover from an assault of the demon: "What heals acedia is staunch persistence.... Decide upon a set amount for yourself in every work and do not turn aside from it before you complete it."

If my pride recoils from endeavors that seem futile in the face of my world-weary despair, I have to remember that disdaining ordinary, mundane chores that come to nothing can lead to my discounting personal relationships as well. Why honor my mother and my father, when they will grow old and infirm and then abandon me by dying? My own "antirrheticus" for that thought comes from Psalm 27: "Though father and mother forsake me, / the Lord will receive me." Under acedia's siege I might ask: Why vow myself to a spouse, if it is "until death do us part"? We all die anyway, and even our sun will one day burn itself out, destroying life as we know it on earth. Does this mean that I don't need to bother about loving, or living, here and now? I am better off asking: Why is it that acedia brings such thoughts to the table just as I would feast on life's bounty? Only then can I fight back, embracing love and commitment as a source of strength and peace instead of despondency. Only then will I have defeated acedia. At least for now.

Both ancient and modern writers speak of the profound serenity that can come after a period of torment and trial. As Solomon puts it, "Depression at its worst is the most horrifying loneliness, and from it I learned the value of intimacy." The pain is real, but remedy may yet be found. For Evagrius, the struggle with acedia is worthy because it leads not only to peace but also to joy. If, as the scholar Christoph Joest has written, acedia for Evagrius was the culmination of all the temptations, then its absence is the fulfillment of all virtues, which find their ultimate expression in love. That is why the struggle is worth our while.

Eden

I once told an Anglican nun that I was planning to write a book about acedia, and she was intrigued, because, as she said, not much had been done with it since the sixth century. Then she cautioned, "When you take on acedia, you've taken on the devil himself." I laughed uneasily, but was too full of literary ambitions to dwell on what she meant. My improbable encounter with the monastic tradition had moved me in deep ways, and I wanted to find out more about how it was that this ancient and foreign way of life was helping me understand who I was. Correspondences have always interested me far more than distinctions, and I felt ready to plunge ahead.

When I moved to Lemmon, South Dakota, in 1974, I did not see myself as fleeing New York City, as the early monks had fled Alexandria or Constantinople. But like the monks, I learned that my nostalgia for urban life could adversely affect my ability to appreciate my new home.

I was dismayed to find that in a tiny town that offered very little in the way of distraction, I nevertheless managed to be distracted much of the time. I had imagined a quiet place to write, but not that I would first need to foster more quiet within. If I had willingly left behind the comforting anonymity that a city can provide, I had not escaped the urge I often felt to run from the demands of daily life.

As I was newly in love, I could easily envision the dry prairie land as a garden in which my husband and I would make our own Eden. The closeness we were forced by our isolation to develop might not have come so readily in an urban setting, and I am grateful for the opportunities for personal and literary intimacy that small-town life provided. I did not yet comprehend marriage itself as a form of asceticism, and was slow to grasp what it would require of me. I remained prone to acedia, to what the early monk John Climacus termed "a slackness of the mind . . . [and] a hostility to vows taken." But I did not see this: In facing the demands of my own vowed life and my husband's frequent medical crises, both mental and physical, I shoved acedia aside without much thought. Time and time again, I had to be in shape for battle. Constantly drawing on my capacity for zeal meant that I could ignore the tendency to acedia that remained dormant within me. I could put off giving the devil his due.

When I would tell physicians that my husband had enough medical history for five or six people, they would look over the list of his prescriptions and agree. David had been robust when I first met him, carrying two hundred twenty pounds on a six-foot frame. But some years into our marriage, an old pattern repeated itself. He had been nineteen when an acute psychological crisis presaged a life-threatening physical one, and at twenty he required a six-hour operation to remove his badly inflamed gallbladder. He was forty when he was admitted for the three-week stay in the Bismarck psychiatric ward, and within a year he developed frightening symptoms—projectile vomiting, malaria-like night shivering—that thrust us into in a lengthy search for a diagnosis. Eventually he required emergency surgery, which revealed that stones had formed in his common duct. The surgeon took a slew of biopsies—"I could have sworn you had cancer," he told us later, sounding puzzled—and rearranged David's intestines. His recovery entailed spending more than thirty days in the hospital, unable to eat anything by mouth. I took care of the home front, my job made easier because David was typically graceful in accepting his lot. He charmed the nurses, orderlies, plant-waterers, and janitors. "They're trying to save my life," he commented, "why would I not appreciate that?" As soon as he was able to walk, he measured the hallways so that he would know the distance he was covering. Soon he was doing six miles a day. I brought him all the books and magazines he could handle, and tracked his recovery by the number of medical equipment stands he had to push down the hall—three, then two, then one—and the number of grim appliances hanging from each.

David and I laughed together over the surgeon's remarking, "I hope no one ever has to cut you open again, because nothing is where it's supposed to be." That was less funny when, four years later, David landed in the emergency room of a hospital in Vermont, where I was teaching a summer writing workshop at Bennington College. After the initial consultation, the doctor recommended exploratory surgery. It was my birthday, and as David was being wheeled off he regretted not having a present for me. "Just survive this," I said, as I kissed him. The doctor had explained to us that he had little idea of what he would find—"cancer" was the unspoken word between us—or how long the operation would take. I said that I understood, and would be in the surgery waiting room. By then it was evening and no one else was there. I turned off the television and sat for a while in blessed silence.

Later I phoned David's brother and sister, and my parents. I also called several Benedictine friends to ask for prayers. An acquaintance from the writing workshop came from a dinner party to see if I wanted to go out for a drink. I decided that ice cream would be safer, so we went to a nearby diner, where a chocolate cone was a welcome birthday treat. I decided to finish it in the waiting room. Several hours passed before the doctor appeared, saying, "That went much better than I had any reason to expect." What he had found was not cancer but adhesions from the previous surgery. He said that we'd been just in time, as David was an hour or so from requiring a complete colostomy, and perhaps six hours from dying. True to form, he rebounded from this latest adventure much sooner than his doctors expected. I began to tease him about having not nine lives but eighteen.

After this we enjoyed several years in which David was reasonably healthy. In the fall of 1997, however, he developed a severe case of pneumonia. We later heard that the radiologist had asked, on seeing David's X-rays, "Is this guy going to make it?" But after being admitted to the hospital, he responded well to treatment. When I left him settled for the night, he was reading a novel and had given me a list of books he wanted me to bring the next day. When I returned in the morning, I found that he'd been moved to a room directly across from the nurses' station. The nurse who sat at his bedside told me that David had anxiously awaited my coming, claiming to hear my footsteps every time someone passed his room. He was hallucinating and he was terribly restless, picking at his IV tubes as if he didn't know why they were there. I was shocked at his condition, but the staff told me that this probably would not last more than twenty-four hours. Good as that was for me to know, David's fear was palpable, and in his confusion he needed constant reassurance: *No, that is not a sniper out the window, aiming a shotgun at us, it is a tree in the wind. I'm here, sweetie, I'm fine. No one is trying to hurt us.*

David was on a talking jag, and once his paranoia eased a bit I was touched that much of what he said concerned better times in our life together. There was our elopement to Sundance, Wyoming, where after our wedding at the county courthouse we were toasted by strangers at the Dime Horseshoe Bar. There was the fall we had spent in his family's tiny cabin in the Adirondacks, hiking or canoeing into the town of Long Lake by day and reading by lantern at night. There were his childhood memories of sleeping rough in the mountains, making hammocks out of rope, and drinking campfire coffee from chipped blue-enameled cups. He spoke fondly of the flight he had taken several years before to the South Pacific; he had asked the flight attendants so many technical questions about what happened to the navigational instruments when the plane crossed the equator that the pilot had invited him into the cockpit to see for himself. As David rambled on, I felt as if we were inhabiting a Surrealist poem. That was strangely comforting, because I was the only person in the world who could have put together all the disjointed things he was saying. The marriage itself had become a healing force, not only for David but for me as well.

I arranged to spend the night in David's hospital room. I woke suddenly when he stood up to go to the bathroom and immediately crashed to the floor. (Later we found out that he did not have enough potassium in his system to support his bones.) The nurses rushed in and found no injuries. It took two nurses and me to get him to the toilet and back. A male nurse was then stationed in the room, and since I couldn't get back to sleep, I talked with him for the rest of the night. He was a native of North Dakota, and a Vietnam veteran. Seeing lives lost in the war had convinced him that he should go into nursing, where he might help save people.

By morning David was himself again and had little memory of the previous day. The doctor, who had been our physician for many years, told us that most people in a hallucinatory state take out their fear and frustration on the nursing staff. "But you," he told David, "were a perfect gentleman." This was no surprise to me. David's preternatural sweetness had surfaced in difficult conditions before.

Our life together went on. Because of that bout with pneumonia, his physician ordered regular checkups, and in early December 1998, an X-ray showed a spot on one of David's lungs. It proved to be malignant, and the diagnosis changed everything. Time itself seemed suspended, and even as I busied myself with practicalities—getting us to Honolulu a week earlier than we had planned, setting up an appointment with an oncologist there—I could not escape a stark sense of terror. One of David's cousins had died from the same form of lung cancer, which is not caused by smoking. His malignancy had been discovered too late for medical intervention, and he had died within a few months. Was treatment still possible for us? I use the plural form, because that is how it felt. The uncertainty of David's condition was a dreadful burden, but it was one we could share.

After a series of tests and medical consultations that seemed to drag on forever, a plan emerged: surgery followed by radiation, and perhaps chemotherapy. David came through the surgery and radiation in Honolulu in good shape, and we went home to South Dakota in late spring. While the loss of one lung had slowed him down, he was again walking for miles every day around our prairie town, up to the cemetery, down Main Street, and home. But two rounds of chemotherapy over the summer devastated him, and in late November he suffered severe weakness and shortness of breath. At first his doctors thought it was a recurrence of pneumonia; it turned out to be far more serious. In yet another emergency room we were told that David had come within hours of death. He had developed a large blood clot in his one remaining lung.

We had been preparing to visit my family in Hawai'i for Christmas; that was now out of the question. We were down to basics: Was David going to live, or would he succumb to the flu that was plaguing North Dakota's hospitals? If he survived, would he continue to require assistance for the basic tasks of living? Would he need to be in a nursing home? He was more frail than I had ever seen him, but as always, he cooperated with the therapists who came to his bedside: respiratory therapists, physical therapists, occupational therapists. After he had been in bed for a week, the nursing staff wanted him on his feet. It took four people to help him walk a short distance. A woman whose mother was being moved to a hospice played Christmas carols on a piano in the oncology ward lobby, and I watched through tears as David struggled down the hall. I wondered if he would ever walk on his own again.

By the time he was released from the hospital I had found us a handicapped-accessible room, equipped with a mini-kitchen, in a Bismarck motel. We had no idea how long we would be there. David would need daily therapy for at least a month; his oncologist thought he was still too weak to visit the rehab site as an outpatient. But we decided to try: if it didn't work, we could arrange for a therapist to come to us. David now required supplemental oxygen, so I had to overcome my mechanical klutziness to be able to set up and change his tanks. To judge from my husband's expression, he initially feared my ministrations more than death itself. But talking, eating, walking, and bathing exhausted David. He needed help with all of it.

It was disconcerting not to know whether he would recover enough to return to our home in South Dakota, or whether we would ever get to Honolulu. The Christmas season was awful, yet not without small joys. My family sent Hawaiian flowers, which we placed in the motel lobby, and also a pine wreath that scented our room. The temperature was below zero for much of the time, but there was a grocery nearby, and also a McDonald's, where I got David an occasional cheeseburger, fries, and chocolate shake to help him gain weight. In the middle of a blizzard, while he was asleep, I bundled myself up and walked to a nearby mall to see the movie *Dogma*, reveling in the suspension of disbelief it drew from me. How could I care so much if two angels banished from heaven made it to a church in New Jersey in time to exploit a theological loophole, redeem themselves, and incidentally destroy the universe? Alan Rickman alone, as a put-upon angel, sneering at people whose biblical knowledge is based on Charlton Heston movies, was worth the trudge through the wind and snow.

The comforts of routine eased our sense of dislocation. Every weekday we took the motel van to a pulmonary rehab clinic for David's therapy. After dropping him off I took the walkway to the hospital's gym and dispelled my tension on the treadmill. After the first week the therapists gave David homework, and soon the motel housekeepers were cheering him on as he walked down the hall, trying to go a little farther each day. I followed with a chair in which he could rest before walking back to our room. Friends helped with errands. Monks who were in town visited. The receptionist at our computer store came by with homemade soup. Having lived without television for several years, we took a guilty pleasure in watching *The Sopranos*.

Our friend the hospital chaplain frequently gave us rides back to the motel. As Christmas Eve approached, he asked me if I wanted to attend services at a church south of town where he would be presiding at Mass. I readily agreed, feeling sad that I had neglected church during much of Advent. Acedia often descends on me at this time of year, and while I love the richness of the Advent readings, which incorporate the Bible in its entirety, from Genesis to Revelation, I inevitably fail at consulting them faithfully in preparation for the Christmas season. This year in particular, I felt dead inside.

On the afternoon of Christmas Eve, I noticed that David was in poor spirits, and asked whether he would like me to stay with him that night. He replied, quietly, "That would be nice." His tone signaled to me that inwardly he was shouting, "Don't leave me alone!" I canceled my plans for church and made popcorn in the microwave as David consulted the television schedule. The only thing of interest was hardly Christmas fare: Franco Zeffirelli's *Hamlet*, with Mel Gibson and Glenn Close. The flow of Shakespearean language was a balm for our souls. "Blank verse," David said, contentedly. It did seem curious that as the birth of the Prince of Peace was being celebrated all around us we were stuck with a rash of stabbings and poisonings in Denmark.

After more than a month of daily therapy, David's doctors determined that he was strong enough to fly to Hawai'i with the aid of a wheelchair and supplemental oxygen. The trip went well enough; the first thing David said upon exiting the plane in Honolulu was, "I can tell I'm at sea level." For the first time in months, he could breathe on his own. But I am getting ahead of my story. For I did celebrate Advent that year, despite myself, despite the laxity of my spiritual reading, and my utter indifference to worshipping with other Christians. The monks had given me their schedule of Scripture readings, which I had studiously ignored. One morning, though, as I was waking in the motel room, I thought, "Oh, hell, it's getting close to Christmas—I might as well see what's up." After consulting the liturgical calendar, I opened the Gideon Bible to Isaiah 43 and found this:

> But now thus says the LORD, who created you; O Jacob,
> And He who formed you, O Israel:
> Fear not, for I have redeemed you;
> I have called you by your name;
> You are Mine.
> When you pass through the waters, I will be with you;
> And through the rivers, they shall not overflow you.
> When you walk through the fire you shall not be burned,
> Nor shall the flame scorch you.
> For I am the LORD your God, the Holy One of Israel,
> your Savior.
> —Isaiah 43: 1–3 (NKJV)

Taking in these words as I listened to the steady sound of my husband's breathing, I was profoundly glad for everything. This is a blessed time, I thought to myself. We wait and want for nothing. We are free to love, which is the ultimate freedom. Our situation might appear hopeless to others. But we are Adam and Eve, before the Fall, and all we know is heaven.

A Little Riff on Heaven and Hell

I suspect that any married person, or any monk for that matter, has at one time or another felt the loss and diminishment expressed by the fourth-century Abba Megethius when he said to his fellow monks, "Originally, when we met together we spoke of edifying things, encouraging one another. We were 'like the angels'; we ascended up to the heavens. But now when we come together, we only drag one another down by gossiping, and so we go down to hell."

For the early Christian abbas and ammas, both heaven and hell were to be found in present reality. While both were envisioned as an inheritance—one to be hoped for, the other avoided—neither existed apart from everyday experience. No doubt these monastics would have greeted Sartre's famous existentialist credo "Hell—is other people" by saying, "Yes, of course, and heaven as well."

Eugène Ionesco wrote that "there is no religion in which everyday life is not considered a prison; there is no philosophy or ideology that does not think we live in alienation: in one way or another . . . humanity has always had a nostalgia for the freedom that is only beauty, that is only real life, plenitude, light." Heaven or hell? Either place is within our reach, for we carry it within us. Today is the first day, and the last. Heaven or hell: this is the moment, here, now. Make of it what you will.

VII. *Acedia's Progress*

Good Times and Bad

During that December, David seemed more like an octogenarian than a man in his early fifties. Shopping for his prescriptions and warmer socks in a crowded mall on the hectic days before Christmas made me weary, and I feared for both of us. We would rather have been spending the holidays in Hawai'i than North Dakota, and my family was disappointed that David would not be preparing his customary snack for Santa on Christmas Eve—antipasto and fettuccine Alfredo—and a traditional Christmas Day feast, with roast turkey, garlic mashed potatoes, and a chocolate mousse in classic French style. Our young nieces had dubbed David "Uncle Mousse." I was "Auntie Omelet."

Exiled from that familial and subtropical warmth, we at least had each other. But our life had been stripped so bare as to be oddly ascetic. Our cell was a motel room, with a loud though effective heating unit. Our food was that of the contemporary nomad, deli sandwiches, and microwavable meals that managed to be both oversalted and bland. In this gaudily carpeted desert, one thing that was familiar was my acedia. It was the same as it had been the year before, and the year before that. Acedia, it seems, is my companion in good times and bad. No matter what happens in my life, or how I am feeling, it is my primary temptation. The desert monks would recognize in my annual Advent blahs a textbook case of the struggle with acedia, when prayer seems not only a useless activity but also an impediment to freedom. This is truth as the devil tells it, using the lure of being free to be myself to enslave me in a sterile narcissism. For acedia is not merely a personal vice. Left unchecked, it can unravel the great commandment: as I cease to practice my love of God, I am also less likely to observe a proper love of my neighbor or myself.

If the Church has made too much of the sin of pride, which seduces us into thinking too highly of ourselves, it has not made enough of the sin of sloth, which allows us to settle for being less than we can be, both as individuals and as a society. The Presbyterian pastor John Buchanan believes that passivity and indifference that make us less able to engage in vital occupations and concerns are as problematic today as intentional evil. But they are also an ancient curse. The Judeo-Christian story places it in Eden, where the primal sin involves refusing to take responsibility. Put on the spot, Adam tries to excuse himself by blaming Eve, and Eve then blames the serpent. Neither cares where the buck stops, as long as it rests with someone else. God responds to this display of sloth by sending the first people, who had been intended for the holy leisure of paradise, into a land where they must labor for their sustenance.

Religious vocabulary is demanding, and words such as *sin* and *repentance* carry so much baggage that even many Christians are reluctant to employ them. In a culture marked by theological illiteracy it is tempting to censor terms that are so often misconstrued and misused.

Many people who would not dream of relying on the understanding of literature or the sciences they acquired as children are content to leave their juvenile theological convictions largely unexamined. If they resented religion when they were young, as adults they are perplexed and dismayed by its stubborn persistence in the human race. But religions endure because they concern themselves with our deepest questions about good and evil, about the suffering that life brings to each of us, and about what it means to be fully human in the face of death.

We are right to distrust the idea of sin as it is often presented, but are foolish indeed if we throw out the living baby with the old church bathwater. The concept of sin does not exist so that people who may need therapy more than theology can be convinced that they are evil and beyond hope. It is meant to encourage people to believe that they are made in the image of God and to act accordingly. Hope is the heart of it, and the ever-present possibility of transformation. The doctrine would not have remained a living tradition for such a long time if it had not been, as the theologian Linda Mercadante describes it in her book *Victims and Sinners,* "a rich, holistic way of conceptualizing the human dilemma—one that functioned to steady and inform thousands of generations." Were I to deny this, and discount the wisdom of my ancestors, I would grow not wise but overconfident in my estimation of myself and in what passes for progress.

Were I to listen with an open ear, I might come away from a Lenten sermon on fasting better able to spurn the tempting feast of malicious gossip and the satisfying art of maligning others in order to feel good about myself. When the church speaks in this way we do well to pay attention. Or when a master preacher such as Fred Craddock defines the sin of sloth so clearly that it stings like a slap in the face. What we casually dismiss as mere laziness, he says, is "the ability to look at a starving child . . . with a swollen stomach and say, 'Well, it's not my kid.' . . . Or to see an old man sitting alone among the pigeons in the park and say, 'Well . . . that's not my dad.' It is that capacity of the human spirit to look out upon the world and everything God made and say, *I don't care.*"

The sin of sloth in this sense is all too recognizable in the United States, where the term "granny dumping" is used to define the practice of anonymously depositing our elderly on the doorsteps of nursing homes and where urban hospitals have been known to abandon indigent patients on skid row, some still in their hospital gowns and with IVs in their arms. But even as such outrages are exposed, we are beset by a curious silence: the more that society's ills surface in such evil ways, the less able we are, it seems, to detect any evil within ourselves, let alone work effectively together to fix what is wrong. The philosopher Alasdair MacIntyre finds that while our "present age is perhaps no more evil than a number of preceding periods . . . it is evil in one special way at least, namely the extent to which we have obliterated . . . [our] consciousness of evil. This . . . becomes strikingly apparent in the contemporary modes of instant indignation and denunciation. It is marvelous," he adds, to observe "how often the self-proclaimed defenders of the right and the good do not seem to have noticed [in themselves] the vices of pomposity . . . exaggeration, and self-righteousness." Such behavior is not new to human history, MacIntyre concludes; but "it was left to our time for what had been an eccentric vice . . . to become a dominant social mode." Acedia, which is known to foster excessive self-justification, as well as a casual yet implacable judgmentalism toward others, readily lends itself to this process.

Though we may think ourselves far too liberated to be considered prigs, the writer Marilynne Robinson insists that this is exactly what we have become. She points out that the polarized tenor of our social discourse epitomizes the dictionary definition of *priggishness,* as "marked by overvaluing oneself or one's ideas, habits, notions, by precise ... adherence to them, and by small disparagement of others." It may be easy to profess not to believe in sin, but it is hard not to believe in sinners, so we embrace the comfortable notion that at least they are other people. "I'm a good person, but God hates homosexuals." "I'm a good person, but God condemns homophobes." "I'm a good person, but the homeless are irresponsible bums." "I'm a good person, but those who denigrate the homeless are evil." "Good people like me support our president." "Good people like me oppose the president." The loud litany of self-aggrandizement that reverberates through our culture convinces me that, for all of our presumed psychological sophistication, we remain at a primitive stage in our capacity to understand the reality of sin. It's as if we believe that if we just don't talk about it, it will go away, and we'll all be nicer to one another. As a Christian, I beg to differ. Our bad thoughts are real, and they lead to bad acts. Check any newspaper.

In the fourteenth century, Chaucer warned that "a great heart is needed against acedia, lest it swallow up the soul." But in a priggish culture such as ours, this magnanimity of spirit is precisely what we lack, and if we persist in denying any truth but our own, the danger to society is that our perspective will remain so narrow and self-serving that we lose the ability to effect meaningful change. Robinson wonders, in fact, whether we have made such a fetish of social concern and criticism that we have eroded our belief that genuine reform is possible. Anger over injustice may inflame us, but that's a double-edged sword.

If our indignation feels too good, it will attach to our arrogance and pride and leave us ranting in a void. And if we develop full-blown acedia, we won't even care about that.

At bottom, to dismiss sin as negative is to demonstrate a failure of imagination. As the writer Garret Keizer asserts in *Help: The Original Human Dilemma*: "Everyone believes in sin, the people who charge their peers with political incorrectness and the people who regard political correctness as the bogey of a little mind." He adds, "What everyone does not believe in, as nearly as I can tell, is forgiveness." It requires creativity to recognize our faults, and to discern virtues in those we would rather disdain. Forgiveness demands close attention, flexibility, and stringent self-assessment, faculties that are hard to come by as we career blindly into the twenty-first century, and are increasingly asked to choose information over knowledge, theory over experience, and certainty over ambiguity. This mentality may be of some use in business, but in a family, including the family of faith, it is a disaster. It permits us to treat our churches as if they were political parties instead of the body of Christ, making them vulnerable to crass manipulation by ideologues. It allows Christian seminarians to give the psalms short shrift, and to assume an attitude of superiority toward these ancient poems, as relics of a more primitive time, when people still had enemies, and still wished them ill. "I can't pray that," I have heard pastors say of the cursing psalms, or the confessional ones, which admit to loving lies more than truth, to resenting others or desiring revenge. We're not like that. We're good people, or good enough, having willed away the prejudice, tribalism, and violence in our hearts. We are at a loss to explain their presence in the world around us.

Yet if we pay attention to what is going on, we may come to the uneasy realization that the root meaning of *acedia,* as 'lack of care,' could serve to define our present state. We grow inured to the horrendous violence engendered by suicide bombings and genocidal "little wars" around the world, and sigh when we hear of road-rage fatalities at home, or of the murder of a teenager for the trendy jacket or athletic shoes he is wearing. A refusal to care about the needs of others marks the unapologetic incompetence of a government worker or call-center operator, and also the disregard of corporate executives for the pain caused by a move to a place where cheaper labor might be exploited and more dangerous working conditions accepted. In the elderly, acedia expresses itself as a resigned withdrawal in a society indifferent to the ravages of aging, while in the young, it is a studied boredom with all that the world has to offer.

In April 1999, two teenage boys in a Denver suburb slaughtered thirteen people at their high school before killing themselves. The numerous homemade bombs they placed in the building convinced police that their intent was to destroy the school and kill everyone in it, well over a thousand people. Whatever disaffection these young men had felt among their peers, they were in the throes of a lack of caring so severe as to be pathological. A student who had considered himself a friend of the pair said in an interview that as awful as their action was, he couldn't help feeling that "they finally did something." An astute observation, in a time of acedia, when murder on a large scale may be counted as something to break up the everyday routine and grant notoriety to teenage outcasts. In a culture crazy for celebrity and careless of basic needs, it should come as no surprise that a pair of teenage "losers" might come to value "doing something," even something unspeakably violent, over life itself. The actions of the Columbine duo confirm what the criminologist S. Giora Shoham says of acedia, that it is more than a "breakdown in meaningful interaction among human beings," it is a thorough disengagement. "The accidic," he writes, "is an 'outsider' who is completely detached from both the 'positive' and 'negative' sides of the value continuum."

They "finally did something." In some ways the two teens at Columbine were only taking their culture's excessive attachment to irony to its logical and deadly extreme. The essayist Benjamin Barber reminds us that, "like sentiment, which has been called unearned emotion, the new irony is a form of unearned skepticism." The theologian Henri de Lubac puts it another way: "Cynicism is the reverse side of hypocrisy. It does not give us the truth about [ourselves]." But the jaded adolescent, confusing cynicism with maturity, may ask, "What is truth, anyway? And why should I care, if no one cares about me?"

Respectable Acedia

As a viable sense of sin has eroded in modern times, acedia has become more acceptable. In his pithy essay on the subject, Aldous Huxley explores why, although boredom, hopelessness, and despair have always existed, in his own time "something has happened to make these emotions respectable and avowable; they are no longer sinful, no longer regarded as the mere symptoms of disease." It may be that after two world wars people could not presume that the great technological advances of the industrial age would lead to cultural and moral advancement as well. Chemical weapons, forced-labor camps, gas chambers, death marches, the firebombing of civilian populations in Spain, England, Japan, and Germany, and nuclear attacks on two Japanese cities revealed that while human beings had become more efficient at genocidal violence, it was not easy for us to consider ourselves civilized, let alone "good." Leszek Kolakowski, once Poland's top Marxist philosopher, and now, according to the theologian Martin Marty, "a friend to faith," notes that "the absence of God became the ever more open wound of the European spirit," when it became clear that "the new shining order of anthropomorphism"—which, it was hoped, would take the place of "the fallen God"—never arrived.

The German Jesuit Karl Rahner, writing in a devastated Munich shortly after the end of World War II, reflected that "it has gone strangely with [us] in the recent decades of European intellectual history." While many felt that, having "struggled passionately against the tutelage of Church, state, society, convention, morals," they could now claim true autonomy, they often found it an empty freedom. What had originated as "a great, honest struggle" devolved for many into "a foolish protest that mistook licentiousness and unrestraint, the freedom of error and ruin, for true freedom." Far from finding release, Rahner concluded, modern people fell into "a very odd slavery . . . slavery *from within*."

Slavery from within, in all of its manifestations, was exactly what the early Christian monks were contending with, and Rahner mines a vein well-known to these ancients. His contemporaries, he writes, seem more helpless than ever in struggling with "the powers of desire, the powers of egotism, the hunger for power, the powers of sexuality and pleasure and simultaneously the impotence caused by worry which undermines . . . from within, by insecurity, by loss of life's meaning, by anxiety and futile disappointment." Not exactly the eight bad thoughts, but close enough. Having lost the sense of a useful religious tradition, and with the insights of the early monks obscured over time, Rahner's self-proclaimed "free" person was ill equipped to take note of what Aldous Huxley, who was decidedly not a Christian, warned was the noonday demon emerging as the primary sin of the age. "It is a very curious phenomenon," Huxley observed, "this progress of accidie from the position of being a deadly sin . . . to the position first of a disease and finally of an essentially lyrical emotion, fruitful in the inspiration of much of the most characteristic modern literature." In the nine-teenth century, Baudelaire could write, coolly, of a young, urban man as monarch of his own small kingdom: "Bored to nausea with his dogs and other creatures. / Nothing amuses him: not chase, nor falconry, / Nor people dying opposite his balcony." More than a century later Andrei Voznesensky speaks of the heart itself as an Achilles, and com-ments, "In these days of unheard-of suffering / One is lucky indeed to have no heart."

Industrial Acedia

In determining the cause of acedia's progress during the modern era, Huxley looks to the aftermath of the French Revolution, Napoleon's spectacular rise and fall, and the triumph of mechanized production. "The discovery that political enfranchisement, so long and stubbornly fought for, was the merest futility . . . so long as industrial servitude re-mained," he contends, was the most bitter disillusionment of all. The early decades of the twentieth century saw the first major conflict of the industrial age; naively designated the "Great War," it shocked European sensibilities beyond repair as it destroyed an entire genera-tion of young men. But the aftermath of World War II proved paradoxical, for even as it spawned an era of unparalleled prosperity in the United States, Europe, and eventually Japan, it left a residue of unease. The agents of this prosperity, a new breed of multinational corporations, may have invented the "free world" as we know it, but they also fostered servitude on a global scale. The only lasting freedom, it turned out, was that of corporations to do as they please, for entities such as I. G. Farben and ITT, for example, to profit from doing business with both the Allies and the Axis powers. In the future we will no doubt discover that powerful firms such as Bechtel, Halliburton, Raytheon, and SAIC have been involved in similar practices in our own time. In the early 1960s, President Eisenhower warned in vain about the threat to democratic principles that he saw emerging in a powerful and largely unaccountable "military-industrial complex."

The words *accidie* and *acedia* may have been restored to the *Oxford English Dictionary* by this time, but at least one dictionary of the era had no room for them. The 1951 edition of *Webster's New World Dictionary of the American Language* goes from "accident insurance" to "accipiter," and from "aceae" to "ace in the hole." I observe acedia flourishing, however, undetected and unnamed, in the postwar triumph of both weapons-making and consumer manufacturing. An unprecedented array of automobiles, dishwashers, frost-free refrigerators, and gas-powered lawn mowers were brought forth, lavishly promoted and soon regarded as necessities. The pharmaceutical industry grew exponentially to meet a need for medications that could help people cope with undercurrents of anxiety, the fear that this recent prosperity was hollow at the core. Modern conveniences might save people from tedious labor, but they could do nothing to assuage the sense of being in a precarious position in a rapidly changing world. Instead of feeling carefree, many people felt burdened with more and more "necessities," until they were less able to distinguish between needs and wants, between self-indulgence and self-respect. They became, in short, perfect consumers.

Our politicians are fond of telling us we live in a "free country." But they less often invite us to consider what our freedom consists of and what it is for. In asking those questions we touch on a great dissonance in American culture. In her essay "Keeping the Sabbath," Dorothy Bass observes that "in Deuteronomy the commandment to 'observe the Sabbath day' is tied to the experience of a people newly released from bondage. Slaves cannot take a day off; free people can." In that light, how many in the world are free? The poor can't risk losing a day of fishing or farming or factory work. The sweatshop manager doesn't provide time off for illness or leisure. And the rich are reluctant to put the brakes on in a society that offers such great rewards for greed, ambition, and workaholic habits that erode the spirit.

The effects of "eroding the spirit" can't be quantified and are therefore not significant. Neither are individuals. Our diminishing value can be traced through corporate jargon; businesses that once referred to employees as "personnel" rechristened them "human resources" and have now adopted an even chillier term, "human capital." People who are "capital" are readily disposable, and in recent years corporations have been emboldened to regard full-time employees as liabilities, and thus limit or altogether eliminate health care, pensions, and other once common benefits. But these same corporations do need consumers, and they spend prodigious amounts on advertising campaigns (the military terminology is no accident) intended to seduce us into thinking that freedom is the ability to purchase what

Sears once promised as "The good life. At a good price. Guaranteed."
As the concepts of good and freedom, for centuries the province of
theology, become small arms in the ever-expanding arsenal of marketing tools, the purpose of life itself can change. One Internet multi-
billionaire recently stated that his goal is to die with more toys than
the next guy. He may do just that. Thomas Merton said it starkly and
prophetically in the 1960s: that in a society focused and "organized for
profit and for marketing . . . there's no real freedom. You're free to
choose gimmicks, your brand of TV, your make of new car. But you're
not free not to have a car."

Once considered suitable only for marking animals and slaves as
property, branding is now a social norm, and for a price, some
Americans have agreed to have brand names tattooed on their fore-
heads, necks, and pregnant bellies. One man was looking to replace the
family car; a woman wanted the $10,000 for private school tuition for
her son, another was paying medical bills. And how readily we have
relinquished the sanctity of our own names, in order to walk down
the street as Calvin, Tommy, or DKNY, willing to be free advertisements, if only our choice of clothing and shoes might impress others
as to our superior character and worth. The sixth-century theologian
Gregory the Great would recognize our condition as an outgrowth of
acedia, which can foster deep resentment that leads to avarice. If the
psychological connections that were obvious to Gregory remain obscure to us, we might recognize ourselves in the observation of the
contemporary Benedictine Hugh Feiss that "the confused heart, having lost joy within itself, seeks . . . consolation outside . . . itself. The
more it seeks exterior goods, the more it lacks interior joy to which it
can return."

It is indeed acedia's world when we have so many choices that we grow indifferent to them even as we hunger for still more novelty. As luxury goods and pornographic images permeate the culture, no longer the province of a select few, we discard real relationships in favor of virtual ones and scarcely notice that being overly concerned with the thread count of cotton sheets and the exotic ingredients of gourmet meals can render us less able to care about those who scrounge for food and have no bed but the streets. Now more than ever we need contrarians like Thomas Merton, who once told a Louisville store clerk who had asked what brand of toothpaste he preferred, "I don't care." Merton was intrigued by the man's response. "He almost dropped dead," he wrote. "I was supposed to feel strongly about Colgate or Pepsodent or Crest or something with five colors. And they all have a secret ingredient. But I didn't care about the secret ingredient." Merton concluded that "the worst thing you can do now is not care about these things."

We should care that as the public sphere becomes increasingly chaotic and threatening, what we think of as freedom consists of retreat and insularity. Marketers welcome this development, but a consumerist mentality allows us to turn spiritual practices, which traditionally have been aimed at making us more responsive to the legitimate needs of the wider world, into self-indulgence. We can pay good money to seek advice, which is plentiful, about finding the prayer method that best suits us and deciding where best to position our meditation space: in a custom-made gazebo, or over the three-car garage? One glossy advertisement I have seen shows a woman facing the ocean in a yoga position; off to the side is a beachfront high-rise with condominium apartments costing from $1 to $5 million, and a sales pitch: "The outer world is frenzied. The inner world needn't be." When people pray over finding the color scheme, carpet, candles, images, and incense that will best enhance their spiritual life, they would do well to recall the literal meaning of the third commandment, against blasphemy. In Hebrew, it is an admonition against offering nothingness to God. As Graham Greene observes in the novel *A Burnt-Out Case*, "[People] have prayed in prisons . . . in slums and concentration camps. It's only the middle-classes who demand to pray in suitable surroundings."

In England, the television show *Spirituality Shopper* offers a variety of religious experiences in a sense that William James could not have imagined. One woman, when asked to select something from the spiritual superstore—among the choices were an introduction to Buddhist meditation, a Jewish Sabbath-eve meal, and a Christian Lenten charity—chose Sufi whirling. Missing, of course, was any sense that religious traditions build up meaning only over time and in a communal context. They can't be purchased like a burger or a pair of shoes.

As we grow more reluctant to care about anything past our perceived needs, acedia asserts itself as a primary characteristic of our time. "Given the state of our world," Alasdair MacIntyre writes (and, I would add, not just the state of our inner "wellness"), we might ask whether it is time to "restore the concept of evil that it once had in Western culture. It is clear that we lack an adequate concept of evil . . . because we lack any adequate concept of good." The danger for us and our society, he points out, is that "inadequate thought and speech always translate into inadequate action." If sloth means, as the pastor John Buchanan contends, "not living up to the full potential of our humanity, playing it safe, investing nothing, being cautious, prudent, digging a hole and burying [our treasure]," it is critical that we take into account what this means for society at large.

Historians, Buchanan writes, "observe that whenever totalitarianism of any kind rears its ugly head, it's because ordinary people have stopped caring about the life of the community and the nation." He cites Simone Weil, who declared that Hitler's rise to power would be inconceivable without "the existence of millions of uprooted [people]" who could not be roused to care about anything except their immediate circumstances. It is all the more appalling that these were often people who believed that human progress had made them more advanced and free than any who had come before. This common fallacy allows us to complacently measure the world by the scope of our own limited outlook; but as the Carmelite Constance Fitzgerald reminds us, our failure to acknowledge our inner blockages can make us incapable of recognizing the blockages we have created in the culture. "We see cold reason, devoid of imagination," she writes, "heading with deadly logic toward violence, hardness in the face of misery, a sense of inevitability, war, and death." Even worse, we come to assume that these conditions—injustice, poverty, perpetual conflict—are inevitable, the only possible reality, and lose our ability to imagine that there are other ways of being, other courses of action.

One such blockage—I'll call it acedia—seems to me to be at the heart of the question of what we will tolerate as a society. The problem of homelessness in this country now seems intractable, but it scarcely existed, apart from skid row alcoholics, only decades ago. For many people, the problems of homeless families whose children go to bed hungry every night, or the at least 40 million Americans who do not have medical insurance and adequate health care, are just "the way things are," beneath the radar of their concern. The writer Wendell Berry laments the extent to which economics has been elevated to a position that God once held, as "ultimate justifier." We have come to "treat economic laws of supply and demand" as though they were "the laws of the universe." If there is a religion that encompasses all the world, it is the pursuit of wealth. But Christians must recognize that in slothfully acquiescing to its petty gods, we deny Christ a place on earth even more effectively than do the loud atheists and antitheists of our time.

To Say "God Is Love" Is Like Saying "Eat Wheaties"

In a series of talks in the 1960s, Thomas Merton foresaw our contemporary world as one-dimensional, a world in which "all words have become alike . . . To say 'God is love,'" he commented, "is like saying, 'Eat Wheaties.' . . . There's no difference, except . . . that people know they are supposed to look pious when God is mentioned, but not when cereal is." Now that expensive handbags and jackets are displayed in store windows as reverentially as icons, and swimsuits alleged to have a slimming effect are advertised with the tagline "Why pray for a miracle when you can wear one?" even that distinction has been compromised. And it matters. When magazines such as *Time* and *Newsweek* pretend that the news consists of page after page of unpaid advertisements for the latest gadgets, we may, as Merton predicted, fall into the trap of "[thinking we] are informed," when in fact we are "living in an imaginary world."

In this hyped-up world, broadcast and Internet news media have emerged as acedia's perfect vehicles, demanding that we care, all at once, about a suicide bombing, a celebrity divorce, and the latest ad-

vance in nanotechnology. Advertisements direct our attention to automobiles; medications to combat high blood pressure, hemorrhoids,
and insomnia; the Red Cross; a new household cleanser. When the
"news" returns, there are appalling segues, such as one I witnessed recently, the screen going from "Child Sex Offender Search" to "Gas Prices
Rise." It all comes at us on the same level, and an innocent from another world might assume that we consider these matters to be of equal
value and importance. We may want to believe that we are still concerned, as our eyes drift from a news anchor announcing the latest
atrocity to the NBA scores and stock market quotes streaming across
the bottom of the screen. But the ceaseless bombardment of image
and verbiage makes us impervious to caring.

As Thomas Merton predicted, our world has been flattened, and
we've been had. Our concern with being up-to-date on the latest
product—be it a lotion promising to make our skin more youthful or
a trend in politics, medicine, or spirituality—is both "hypnotic [and]
narcissistic, which is what a closed circle always is." Presented with a se-
ductive product or idea, "you allow yourself to be seduced by it, and
then . . . you're happy." The problem, as Merton notes, is that "this is
the way the abuse of language functions." Inundated with "self-
validating, hypnotic formulas [that] are immune to contradictions"—
he uses as an example a maxim employed by military officers during
the Vietnam War: We are destroying a village in order to save it—we
lose the ability to reflect on either world events or our own lives.

It is hard work to look beneath the surfaces presented to us and examine the cultural and historical forces underlying current conditions.
Why should we care enough to make the effort? In positing this question, we are well advised to name and confront our acedia. For it is an

unseen enemy; like a windstorm, it is witnessed only in its damaging effects. Acedia is not a relic of the fourth century or a hang-up of some weird Christian monks, but a force we ignore at our peril. Whenever we focus on the foibles of celebrities to the detriment of learning more about the real world—the emergence of fundamentalist religious and nationalist movements, the economic factors endangering our reefs and rain forests, the social and ecological damage caused by factory farming—acedia is at work. Wherever we run to escape it, acedia is there, propelling us to "the next best thing," another paradise to revel in and wantonly destroy. It also sends us backward, prettying the past with the gloss of nostalgia. Acedia has come so far with us that it easily attaches to our hectic and overburdened schedules. We appear to be anything but slothful, yet that is exactly what we are, as we do more and care less, and feel pressured to do still more.

We may well ask: If we are always in motion, constantly engaged in self-improvement, and even trying to do good for others, how can we be considered uncaring or slothful? In *Sloth*, the late playwright Wendy Wasserstein concluded a brilliant parody of a self-help book, titled *Sloth and How to Get It*, with a cogent observation of the "über-motivated" people of our time. "When you achieve true slothdom," she writes, "you have no desire for the world to change. True sloths are not revolutionaries, [but] the lazy guardians at the gate of the status quo." The culture may glorify people who do Pilates at dawn, work their BlackBerrys obsessively on the morning commute, multitask all day at the office, and put a gourmet meal on the table at night after the kids come home from French and fencing lessons, but, Wasserstein asks, "are these hyperscheduled, overactive individuals really creating anything new? Are they guilty of passion in any way? Do they have a new vision for their government? For their community? Or for themselves?" She suspects that "their purpose is to keep themselves so busy, so entrenched in their active lives, that their spirit reaches a permanent state of lethargiosis."

Just look at us, with more money and less sleep than we know how to handle, except to go into debt, and take pills that get us up in the morning and others that let us rest at night. If we are to believe Bertrand Russell, who remarked that "one of the symptoms of approaching nervous breakdown is the belief that one's work is terribly important," then a good many of us are on the edge. Despite the abundance of available therapies, we are still bewildered in the face of our neuroses and spiritual poverty and may be less well equipped than a fourth-century monk to deal with them. In our desperate seeking after more precise terms to define our condition, we have become like the hapless citizens of Jean-Luc Godard's savagely comic film *Alphaville*, who, in a dystopian future, receive new government-issued "Bibles" every day, dictionaries from which words are continually vanishing, because, as one character says, "they are no longer allowed." She adds, mournfully, that "some words have disappeared that I liked very much," among them *weep, tenderness,* and *conscience.* Recalling a man she knew who wrote intriguing but "incomprehensible things," she says, "they used to call it poetry."

I wonder whether that future is now, and why, if we have effectively banished the word *demon,* we are still so demon-haunted. It may be acceptable to speak again of demons. *The New Yorker* recently published a cartoon depicting an unshaven, bleary-looking businessman leaving for work, holding a liquor bottle along with his briefcase, and saying to his wife, "It's Take Your Inner Demons to Work Day." To me this haggard man, even in his slothful appearance, epitomizes our latest, purely acedic mantra, "I don't have time to think," which presumes that we also don't have time to care. Our busyness can't disguise the suspicion that we are being steadily diminished, not so much living as passing time in a desert of our own devising. We might look for guidance to those earlier desert-dwellers, who had no word for depression, but whose vocabulary did include words for accidie, discernment, faith, grace, hope, and mercy.

They gave one another good counsel: Perform the humblest of tasks with full attention and no fussing over the whys and wherefores; remember that you are susceptible, at the beginning of any new venture, to being distracted from your purpose by such things as a headache, an intense ill will toward another, a neurotic and potent self-doubt. To dwell in this desert and make it bloom requires that we indulge in neither guilt nor vainglorious fantasizing, but struggle to know ourselves as we are. In this process we will not escape sadness and pain; it can help to employ Amma Syncletica's distinction between two forms of grief, one that liberates, another that destroys. "The first sort," she writes, "consists in weeping over one's own faults" and over "the weakness of one's neighbors, in order not to destroy one's purpose, and attach oneself to the perfect good." Yet "there is also a grief that comes from the enemy, full of mockery, which some call accidie. This spirit must be cast out, mainly by prayer and psalmody." If we recognize the bad thought of acedia for what it is, we can indeed cast it out using the very means it has employed to torment us. Amma Syncletica called on prayer and psalmody for a reason. As the slogan has it, life's a bitch, and then you die: so you might as well find a psalm and sing anyway.

VIII. *Acedia's Decline*

The Freedom of Self-knowledge,
the Burden of Self-consciousness

Knowing that I was writing about acedia, a friend gave me a book titled *The 7 Lively Sins: How to Enjoy Your Life, Dammit.* Designated as "Self-Help/Humor," the book at first seems regressive, a relentlessly cheerful "sin for dummies" manual. The sparse text, set off in brightly colored cartoon bubbles, tends toward peppy slogans and photos: bright red lollipops, for instance, tell us that "guilt sucks." As the author, Karen Salmansohn, veers into the realm of theology, ranting against what she understands to be the Christian doctrine of sin, she poses a question that has intrigued countless people, Saint Augustine not least among them: "What if a life reveling in the seven sins would bring you overwhelming happiness, [and] never-ending fulfillment?" Her answer is that sins are good for us, and anyone who says otherwise is way too uptight. Just imagine how envy might enliven us: "Follow your drool" is her take on Joseph Campbell's "Follow your bliss." She sees sloth as "all about the path to rejuvenation . . . self-responsiveness . . . self-compassion, [and] the pursuit of peace and relaxation." To more fully savor our pride, she advises us to shun self-criticism and learn to say, "Damn I'm good."

Even if Salmansohn's book is meant as a total put-on—and I don't believe that it is—it is not so funny, after all, because more than a thousand years of bad theology have made it possible. For far too long, the concept of sin has been applied oppressively, legitimating needless suffering. This silly book is exactly what the Christian church deserves, and Salmansohn dutifully assesses the damage done by what she terms the "spirit killers" of masochism, guilt, fear, and apathy. Her suggested cure for apathy, enthusiasm, is an ancient and effective one, even if she promotes it with a tarted-up citation of Emerson: "Nothing great was ever achieved without enthusiasm . . . and lots of double [F]rappuccinos." Now Salmansohn is not far—only a million or two Frappuccinos away—from the early Christian monks, who named zeal the best weapon in the psyche's toolbox for contending with acedia. When I found Salmansohn's admonition to not desire "mildly" but to "wildly want what you want," I registered a gleeful astonishment, echoing Louise Bogan, that my ancient desert monks and a contemporary lifestyle coach could agree on at least one thing. Abba Lot said to the wise old Joseph, "Abba, as far as I can, I say my little office, I fast a little, I pray and meditate, I live in peace, and as far as I can, I purify my thoughts. What else can I do?" Abba Joseph rose and stretched his hands toward heaven. His fingers were like ten lamps of fire as he responded: "If you will, you can become all flame."

One great difference between these monks and today's pop psychologists is that the monks' process of discernment was likely to result in more self-knowledge, less self-consciousness. In our day, this is often reversed. People whose speech remains stuck in therapeutic jargon, for all the "work" they are doing on themselves, often remain stubbornly unreflective. Even if they can catalogue their neuroses with great facility, they seem stuck within them. Theirs is an ancient and noble tradition. Petrarch is credited with giving additional meaning to acedia in the fourteenth century; he admitted to taking, as one scholar notes, "an almost voluptuous pleasure in [his] own emotional sufferings." Petrarch describes his condition with this cautionary observation: "I feed upon my tears and sufferings with dismal pleasure so that I am loath to leave them."

Today, to suggest that a change might be in order, starting with a healthy drop in self-absorption, is anathema: it's a free country, and don't lay your values on my self-respect. If the early monks paid close attention to themselves, it was only because they knew that rigorous self-analysis was an indispensable spiritual practice. Change was the point of the discipline, and they nailed narcissistic self-definition, correctly, as vainglory. To people schooled in a religion that has often seemed to define sin as a grocery list of dos and don'ts, these monks can seem, as the Dominican Simon Tugwell explains in *Ways of Imperfection*, "rather casual about morality." They were not at all concerned, he writes, "that people should behave correctly according to the rules, but rather that people should be able to see their situation clearly for what it is, and so become free from the distorting perspective which underlies all our sins."

The pursuit of such freedom is a spiritual concern, and the field of secular psychology has roots in this basic religious quest. Andrew Solomon sees "talking therapies," for example, as coming "out of psychoanalysis, which in turn comes out of the ritual disclosure of dangerous thoughts first formalized in the Church confessional." But long before that rite was established, another sort of charged encounter, "the manifestation of thoughts," was being practiced by Christian monks. In the fourth-century desert the disciple's relationship to an elder was of paramount importance. Since the novice monk was to admit not only bad thoughts or actions but also whatever was occupying his mind, conversations with his mentor were, as one scholar writes, far "more inclusive than simply confession of sins . . . or even manifestation of conscience in the modern sense."

It was believed that in revealing his thoughts the novice would be able to penetrate and defuse harmful illusions concerning the self. As the elder, by virtue of long experience in the practice of discernment, was considered more able than the disciple to determine what was beneficial and what was harmful to his soul, holding back any thought was regarded as a grave error. The demon of acedia, as it easily hid behind other thoughts, particularly pride and anger, was felt to be a severe temptation, encouraging the young monk to shield himself from scrutiny. But the price of acquiescing was steep: through slothful inattention a callousness of spirit would arise, creating in the monk a mean heart in the full sense of the word, both petty and cruel.

The Benedictine monk Columba Stewart comments that "the whole life was about opening up: of self to another and of the self to God, with no obsessive concentration on the self or on the relationship with one's abba. . . . Perhaps another way to understand this is to remember that it was the commitment to truth, to seeing things as they are, which disposed the monk for contemplation of God," and that this required stripping away "the mask of fantasies and projections about [oneself]." The relationship of elder and disciple was of necessity founded on a profound trust, not just in one's monastic confreres but also in God, and its purpose was less therapeutic than pastoral. Stewart notes that "the elder, far from being a center of power and a 'director,' served in his or her transparence to divine light as a lens which focuses the light of truth on the dark places in the disciple's heart." The hope was that as the novice learned to spurn his selfish and egotistical self in favor of his true self, he would also come to know a selflessly loving God.

One purpose of any religion is to deflect our egocentricity and put it to good use. As Karl Menninger puts it, "[The] Buddha, Confucius, Lao-tze, Socrates, Zeno, and all the Hebrew prophets from Amos to Jesus taught that sin, hate, alienation, aggression—call it what you will—could be conquered by love." In the Christian spiritual tradition, as in many other faiths, two requisite qualities of that other-directed love are generosity and humility. "What God does in us always produces humility," writes the Carmelite Ruth Burrows. "All that comes from self, be it delight or suffering, tends to boost the ego." She regards any authentic religious experience as entailing "a slow, demanding generosity," one that does not short-circuit within us but flows outward naturally, until what we believe becomes what we do. The thrust of many self-help authors, however, seems to be to assure people that the ultimate goal of their spiritual practice is to reveal what good and deserving people they are.

The Cistercian Gail Fitzpatrick gives a stern warning to anyone who sets out on a spiritual pilgrimage seeking only affirmation. "It is the very nature of the desert," she writes, "to introduce the monk to its element of the wild. Those who seek its peace find instead a raw encounter with all that is untamed and unregenerate in their hearts." This revelation, understood both as a difficult training in how to love and as the gift of our merciful God, results, Fitzpatrick says, in our learning that we engender compassion not through our strengths, but through our common weakness.

This is not a popular point of view, but it is one of the many ways that monastic wisdom contradicts the cherished yet largely solipsistic dogmas of the contemporary age. The desert monk Isidore the Priest, for example, said that "of all evil suggestions, the most terrible is the prompting to follow your own heart." What a refreshing reminder that honest self-reflection is not as easy as we would like it to be, and that pursuing what we most desire might not be good for us or those around us. In the monastic frame of reference, being suspicious of our motives need not mean indulging in self-loathing or unnecessary guilt, for God has provided us with everything we need to cope with our bad thoughts and temptations. The corresponding virtues, or good thoughts, are always at our disposal. When Evagrius asserts that "virtues do not prevent the demons from assaulting us, but they do preserve us guiltless," he is elucidating an all-but-forgotten aspect of the doctrine of sin. The bad thoughts come to everyone at one time or another. No one is exempt from anger, jealousy, greed, gluttony, lust, pride, acedia. Our job is not to deny them or run from them, but to make our way through to the virtue on the other side. The virtue of greed is a fearlessness concerning one's future needs that translates into sharing what one has at present. Lust's virtue is a self-giving love that can endure all things. Acedia's virtue is a caring expressed in thoughtful and timely acts that enhance our relationship with others.

Evagrius notes that the demon of acedia manipulates both our presumption and our despair, puffing us up with thoughts of the great accomplishments we will make and then crushing us when our efforts fall short of expectations. We may be left feeling that we have gained nothing and that we were idiots to have attempted anything in the first place. Our only remedy then, he writes, is, "as far as we are able, [to] exalt the mercies of Christ." The *Catechism of the Catholic Church* also links acedia with arrogance, providing a key to understanding the psychological dynamics of the vice. "Painful as discouragement is," it states, "it is the reverse of presumption. The humble are not surprised by their distress; it leads them to trust more, to hold fast in constancy." Humility has always been a staple of monastic life, together with a stability of spirit. But modern life is increasingly unstable, marked by a lack of constancy and trust. In defense we adopt a disproportionate self-regard that does not allow us to perceive as sanity the early monks' refusal to see themselves as good or in the right. We are likely to recoil from Abba Poemen's response to the question "What is integrity?" He replied, "Always to accuse [oneself]." It is important to recognize that he and other monks were suggesting that people become not doormats wallowing in self-abnegation, but individuals with a realistic perception of their place in the world. These monks were also well aware that in order to give up the instinctive impulse toward self-justification, a person needed a healthy self-regard in the first place. This is a subtle point, yet a critical one.

The advice to blame oneself assumes, a scholar has written, that a person is already "anchored in [an] essential disposition which puts [one] at peace with God." Thus "there is no guilt-complex, since the *me* being blamed and accused is in no way the authentic me, the deep me, but the apparent me." This superficial me may show a confident face to the world but inwardly is plagued by fears and compulsions, and remains blind to its true condition. All too often, it harbors an acedia that arises from unacknowledged anger and manifests as passive-aggressive behavior. Evagrius believed that acedia in its most dangerous form derived from a lack of self-knowledge, "[coming] into being when someone . . . does not perceive the meaning of his temptation and as a result fights against it without understanding." I am often "without understanding" in my attempt to navigate the dense thickets of my good thoughts and bad. When I am mired in acedia, enthusiasm seems foolish and false. And it is no easy matter to spurn the comforts of pride even though I know that only a proper and balanced self-respect can free me to love myself as I am, and also better respect and love others. I am slow to respond to my heart's wisdom, although I know that anything less is deadly. So, I struggle.

I have to watch for passive-aggressive tendencies in myself, remembering that interior freedom is one thing, but to disdain to act—out of pride, indifference, or contempt—quite another. I have to resist the temptation to remain a spectator when I need to become involved. What I most hate about my own neuroses, and the foul mood of acedia that too frequently afflicts my soul, is how selfish they make me. By "selfish" I do not mean observing the basic care of the self, knowing when to retreat, to hunker down in waiting out a storm. In the current vernacular, I may need "time out," I may need to "cocoon." But a cocoon is effective only as a means of change. If I withdraw too completely, I die inside. If I get so close to the pool of Narcissus that my reflection appears, I must break the spell and trust in other people, and also in my need for them. When self-consciousness traps me in a barren self-absorption, I must try another way of seeing, and try to forget myself so that I am more, not less, fulfilled.

From the fourth century on, monks have recognized that people have both physical and spiritual ailments for which there are both physical and spiritual remedies. But the modern mind-set has been slow to value that earlier insight. At its root, *therapy* derives from a word meaning "to hold up, to support." Therapy gives us the satisfaction of being useful. Like the philosopher Diogenes, who is said to have rolled up and down the streets of Corinth in a cask so he would not be seen doing nothing when the army of Philip of Macedon stormed the city gates, when trouble strikes we roll out the support groups and counseling sessions. And often therapy does some good. Yet it can also feed our sense of self-importance, and inadvertently fuel our fear of futility. Therapy is not the same as healing.

The word *healing* comes from a word meaning "entire" or "complete," and signifies a restoration to wholeness. For that reason it is a more "holistic" word than *therapy*. While many people are helped by psychotherapy, I suspect that there are also many like me who have benefited from occasional counseling but have received more help from spiritual practices such as prayer and *lectio divina*, or holy reading. Perhaps the most radical aspect of the psychology of the desert monastics is the extent to which they believed that Scripture itself had the power to heal. In *The Word in the Desert*, his study of how thoroughly the early monks integrated Scripture into their lives, Douglas Burton-Christie notes that they regarded these "sacred texts [as] inherently powerful, a source of holiness, with a capacity to transform their lives."

Appreciating this monastic perspective on the Bible means abandoning the modern tendency to regard it as primarily an object of intellectual study, or as a handy adjunct to our ideology, be it conservative or liberal. The desert father who expounds on the inherent value of meditating on Scripture by observing, "Even if we do not understand the meaning of the words we are saying, when the demons hear them, they take fright and go away," insults our intelligence. What is left to us, if we relinquish our intellectual comprehension? Isn't it necessary to retain more control than that? Maybe not, if we want to experience the Word of God as these monks did, as "a living force within them."

I need the words of Scripture because of the challenges they bring, and because what I find in them I can find nowhere else. I also need the monastic version of self-knowledge that finds expression in the Benedictine vow of *conversatio morum*. Literally this is a conversion of morals, but in spirit it signifies a willingness to keep "living together with," which is one meaning of *conversatio*. The vow asks me to perceive my essential human task as living with myself as I am, even as I continue to confront myself and my behavior so that I might more fully conform my ways of thought, talk, and action to what is good. That I fail far more often than I succeed does not discourage me; it is to be expected. A prayer employed in the Episcopal Church before people come forward to receive communion is a pointed reminder that religious faith is intended not only to confirm us as we are, but also to affirm our desire to become something more: "Deliver us from the presumption of coming to this Table for solace only, and not for strength; for pardon only, and not for renewal."

I can imagine a life without psychotherapy, but not without *conversatio*, for it promises to help me distinguish between fruitful self-knowledge and sterile self-consciousness. I might also become more adept at spotting the difference between truth and sincerity. Self-consciousness feeds on sincerity, and both have attained cult status in America. In the current political climate, as if giving credence to Oscar Wilde's contention that sincerity is the worst vice of the fanatic, the sincere religious beliefs of a few have trumped even some basic tenets of science. But as Henri de Lubac reminds us, "It is not sincerity, it is Truth which frees us, because it transforms us. It tears us away from our inmost slavery. To seek sincerity above all things is perhaps, at bottom, not to want to be transformed."

Acedia, Depression, and Vocation, Revisited

I find it revealing that acedia is still a given of monastic life, whereas depression is not. As one Benedictine sister puts it, acedia is to monastics what acne is to adolescents: unfair, inopportune, and inevitable. Also, as one monk comments, it can leave permanent scars. Monastic people compare the onset of acedia to a marathoner's "hitting the wall." Like a runner, the monk can rely on endurance to some extent, but it will not take him all the way. An abbot has commented that it's an awful change to witness in a person, once the initial enthusiasm of a monastic vocation wears off, or more accurately, drops off. "People really go off a cliff, and their despair is expressed as, 'I'm a fraud, you're all frauds, and I have to get out of here.'"

Monks may joke about the monastery as a refuge for the passive-aggressive, but the effects of acedia on community life can be devastating. The Cistercian Michael Casey characterizes acedia as "an inability to identify with the group and a strong inclination to stand apart from it. It is not open rebellion," he says, "since it is characterized by a lack of energy." Monastic communities have considerable expertise in recognizing acedia, and any director of novices knows that the vice is expressed in both physical and psychological symptoms, and can lead to extreme behavior at either end of the spectrum. A monk might demonstrate a sullen and resentful laziness toward his assigned work as well as the daily chore of meditative reading. Contrarily, he might push himself too hard in these areas to demonstrate that he is more committed than his brothers. A nun may willfully ignore her sisters, or she might obsess in her efforts to care for them, almost preying on those in need. Acedia, because it can tempt people to flee the monastic life altogether or to pursue an impossibly ascetic regimen, presents a challenge to Benedict's concern with maintaining a healthy balance. Perhaps this was on his mind when he placed a warning in his instructions for the observance of Lent. While he states that "the life of a monk ought to be a continuous Lent" (Rule 49:1), he insists that each monk obtain the approval of the abbot for his extra Lenten practice. This helps the monk avoid a secret laziness or "presumption and vainglory" (49:9) in taking on extreme feats of piety. Benedict also asks for basic courtesy, that monks take care that "no brother is so apathetic as to waste time or engage in idle talk in neglect of his reading and so not only harm himself but also distract others" (48:18).

I recognize myself in one aspect of acedia that Evagrius detected in the monk who is "quick to undertake a service, but considers his own satisfaction to be a precept." All too often when I volunteer for a job at church, it is because I feel like it: I have the time, and I know it will make me feel good in every sense of the word, fulfilled and virtuous. Yet often the tasks I don't particularly want turn out to be the ones I most need to perform. One test to determine whether I am receiving a call from God or from my ego is to ask whether this is something I would rather not do, or feel incapable of doing well. If either is the case, my best course may be to set my feelings aside and try to do the job.

As acedia can tempt people to do good things in a wrong spirit, and all the wrong things in trying to do good, discernment is of prime importance. In one monastery I know of, a novice became disillusioned within a few weeks of his entrance. His romantic notion of the monastic life had been shattered when he found his fellow monks discussing the World Series during recreation. He had thought that they would— and should—be speaking only of holy things. The young man stayed on for about a year, but finally grew so angry that he decided to leave. His parting shot was to tell his fellows that they were a bunch of reprobates. The director of novices commented that he was probably right about that. "But," he said, "he is right for the wrong reasons, so he had to go."

For contemporary monks suffering from acedia, the cure is much the same as in the fourth-century desert. When a monk says, "I can't bear to live this way for the next forty years of my life," the answer is still that he need be concerned only with today. "I recommend physical labor," one abbot has said, "woodworking, gardening, even mopping the halls, anything to get them out of that closed circle of the self. Sometimes it helps them to know that we've all been through this." When he has suspected serious depression, discernment is a concern: "Doctors have some twenty indicators to use in diagnosing depression, and I don't hesitate to refer a monk to them if it seems likely to help."

But as an increasing number of school districts, health clinics, and corporations employ such psychological checklists, they become more subject to misuse. One psychiatrist, the lead author of a recently published study suggesting that estimates of the numbers of Americans suffering from depression are about twenty-five percent too high, concedes that as "larger and larger numbers of people are reporting symptoms [on these lists]," researchers have "no way to know whether we're finding normal sadness response or real depression." It is a tough dilemma: another researcher comments that while "we do need to be very careful not to overdiagnose a normal response to loss and call it a disorder," these checklists have identified and helped many people in need of treatment.

Sometimes the distinction between a situational depression and serious illness is obvious. A neurosurgeon quoted in the *New York Times Magazine* article "A Depression Switch?" described one patient's condition as clearly due to "a neural circuit run amok." The woman had a job she loved, and enjoyed a good relationship with her husband and children, but had experienced the sudden onset of a severe emotional numbness. She lost all sense of connection, and ordinary acts that had once given her pleasure, such as deciding what to wear and preparing meals, became exhausting, requiring great effort and will. Her condition proved stubbornly resistant to antidepressant medication and counseling, and her physicians considered but rejected electroconvulsive therapy. One doctor explained that "these therapies usually ease rather than cure depression while sometimes bringing side effects like insomnia or memory loss, and their potency often proves fleeting." The neurosurgeon was called in to employ a technique called deep brain stimulation, or DBS, that is used also in the treatment of Parkinson's. It involves implanting electrodes in a particular section of the brain and "sending in a steady stream of low voltage from a pacemaker in the chest." This treatment worked, and the woman was again able to enjoy her life.

In contrast, consider the middle-aged man described by his psychiatrist as having no "major depression that required medication" but only a "chronic dissatisfaction." Having been in therapy for many years, he had received substantial understanding and empathy, but, as the doctor noted, "they often aren't enough to get patients to change, let alone grow."

He suspected that the therapy's main effect had been to allow the man to "maintain his status as a victim of a troubled history. And this was something" that "he was loath to surrender." In the course of his adult life the man had refused to apply his talents and advanced education in making a living, and remained dependent on parents whom he deeply resented. The doctor proposed a course of treatment lasting no more than six months, a move out of the parental home, and the obtaining of a job commensurate with his abilities. At their final session, the patient told the doctor, "You weren't nice, but I think you helped me."

I find that depression generally has an identifiable and external cause that acedia lacks. I can look at my life and see where the trouble is coming from. But acedia arises out of nowhere, as it were, emerging from my inner depths without warning, and without any reason that I can determine. Also, I have found that depression is amenable to treatment in ways that acedia is not. Depression will disrupt my life so that I cannot fail to notice and take action, consulting a counselor or physician. Acedia is more subtle, and when it wells up in me, only the venerable practice of spiritual discernment is of much use. From the fourth century on, this process has meant attempting to determine how one bad thought begets another, and how they interconnect. The ancient monks saw acedia as the worst of the thoughts because it so effectively hid itself behind other vices and mocked any attempt to sort out the root causes of distress. A contemporary psychologist, Solomon Schimmel, comments that "we may not at first recognize the connection between a deadly vice and its indirect effects, but a deeper probing will often reveal it. Anomie, for example, the despair of finding meaning and purpose in life, is traceable in part to the materialism of greed, the spiritual apathy of sloth, and the narcissism of pride."

If my depression often has a more discernible cause than acedia, it can also be more vague. Questions of accountability that do not arise when I am depressed are essential to dealing with acedia, for it is usually linked to a specific duty or obligation that I am tempted to refuse. For this reason it also has a broader social implication that depression lacks. Both tend to isolate me, but I will seek to relieve my isolation in different ways. When I am depressed I can often still function as if I were not, and sometimes just being out among other people will alleviate my symptoms. With acedia I am more conscious of willfully rejecting not only what other people may have to offer me but also what I can offer them. *The Libertine*, a film about the seventeenth-century poet John Wilmot, Earl of Rochester, brilliantly illustrates this aspect of acedia. Johnny Depp plays Wilmot as a man who is well aware that he has gifts that he might apply in the artistic, social, and political spheres. He responds by engaging in a thoroughly dissolute life, drinking and whoring until he succumbs to syphilis at the age of thirty-three. The only passions he exhibits are, appropriately, a fierce anger and an equally cruel if colder ennui. When I saw the film I was reminded of the helpful distinction that Thomas Merton makes regarding Cassian's differentiation between acedia and sadness. Merton comments that the "sadness caused by adversity and trial in social life" generally comes from "a lack of peace *with others.*" But acedia is far more insidious: it is "the sadness, the disgust with life, which comes from a much deeper source—our inability to get along *with ourselves,* our disunion *with God.*"

Disgust with life often has to do with the life one has chosen, and when the bad thought of acedia attacks one's very identity, it causes great pain. The Benedictine monk Gabriel Bunge has noted that doubts about the validity of one's vocation may start small, and only slowly creep into the consciousness. But "with the passage of time [they] erode one's inner certainty, like constant dripping on a stone." This may correspond to what psychiatry observes as the cumulative effect of episodes of severe depression, and its effects—the numbing of the soul, and an increased inability to conceive of ever being happy again, let alone stable—are no doubt similar.

Writers often doubt their vocation and find themselves in droughts that, unlike the normal rhythm of arid seasons and more productive ones, can cause unnatural silences. Joan Acocella observes that "writer's block" is a modern phenomenon, the result of a change in perceptions of artistic inspiration. "Before," she states, "writers regarded what they did as a rational, purposeful activity which *they* controlled. By contrast, the early Romantics came to see poetry as something externally, and magically, conferred," and were convinced that they would produce their best work in their early years. Wordsworth spoke of poets in their youth, who "begin in gladness," but "thereof come in the end despondency and madness." Later, Acocella points out, the French Symbolists became known for not writing at all.

Another poet, Coleridge, sounds as if he may have been suffering from both acedia and despair when he lamented in a notebook entry from 1804: "Yesterday was my Birth Day. . . . So completely has a whole year passed, with scarcely the fruits of a *month*. O Sorrow and Shame . . . I have done nothing!" For young writers the pressure of having to make a living can diminish their ability to concentrate on the work that matters most to them, while older writers sometimes fear that they have used up their material and have little left to offer. Writers are also blocked by alcoholism, but Acocella reports that therapists who work with them are finding that many are drinking less and exercising more. It is good to know that I am not alone in this regard. If exercise will keep both my blood cholesterol and my serotonin at medically acceptable levels, so much the better.

Acocella finds that some practitioners are baffled by their writer patients' attitudes toward therapy. One expressed disappointment that his patients so rarely wanted to discuss their art. They had sought practical help with a range of mundane issues, including "noisy children [and] obtuse reviewers. And, once [the doctor] helped them deal with these matters, they quit treatment." The therapist was surprised by what I suspect many artists would take for granted, that they "didn't care what underlay their creative function. They just wanted to get back to it, as long as it lasted." This seems reasonable to me, and thoroughly sane. To Edmund Bergler, the twentieth-century analyst who coined the term "writer's block," and once remarked that he had "never seen a 'normal' writer," I can honestly reply: That's all right. I am not certain I have ever seen a "normal" psychoanalyst.

A crucial distinction between depression and acedia is that the former implies a certain level of anguish over one's condition, while in the latter it remains a matter of indifference. But it is an unearned indifference to the vagaries of experience and emotion, because one hasn't really endured them. Acedia will always take the path of least resistance and attempt to go around, rather than through, the demands that life makes of us. To combat acedia Evagrius recommends a close and dispassionate observation of our thoughts as they arise: What are they? How do they appear, and in what order? What do they suggest to us? Which are the most troublesome or resistant? Monks have always insisted that we can in fact think about our thoughts and feelings, and consider how we are to act on them.

This traditional practice of observing one's thoughts as they arise, and, as one Benedictine describes it, "laying them out, rather than resisting them," bears a striking resemblance to a new technique in cognitive therapy, a "behavioral activation" treatment in which patients "acknowledge their thoughts and feelings as they arise, without judgment, and then let them go." Here we are not so far from what Evagrius, in the latter part of *The Praktikos*, describes as driving a nail out with a nail. As the demons assault us by means of our thoughts, he asserts, it is by the same means that we can fight back, turning their own weapons against them. You might, for example, drive out thoughts of vainglory with thoughts of humility, thoughts of greed or lust with thoughts of temperance. Where the monk would attempt to place "a psalm or a prayer alongside the thought" and thus seek to redirect his focus toward God, a therapist might ask us to determine how our negative thoughts promote negative actions. The desire to shun a social event that might expose us to pain, for example, can put us in a downward spiral, as we are also rejecting the pleasure that social interaction can bring. In this case the best advice might be to stop thinking altogether and just go to the event.

The goal of ancient and contemporary methods alike is to break the vicious cycle of persistent thoughts. Wise insights into how such thoughts emerge and develop in us are found in both monastic sayings and medieval writings. In "The Parson's Tale," Chaucer gives a potent description of how acedia starts in mere laziness and develops into full-fledged despondency. The desire to avoid hardship becomes the dread of taking any action at all, and particularly of beginning to do any good thing. Soon we despair, not only of our own efforts but also of the mercy of God. As we grow ever more sluggish, negligent, and careless, we come to a "dull coldness that freezes the heart" and arrive at acedia's threshold. The medievalist Siegfried Wenzel notes that while mystics such as John of the Cross speak of a "spiritual dryness" and "impasse" that share with acedia "such symptoms as the absence of devotion, a feeling of being abandoned by God, depression, inner bitterness, [and] coldness," acedia goes even further, in that the cold and dark do not disturb us. The recently reported fifty-year crisis of faith suffered by Mother Teresa illustrates this distinction. Her inner torment was intense, but the struggle itself implies that she envisioned something better. This is best defined as a classic "dark night of the soul," not a succumbing to acedia.

For Evagrius it is acedia "alone of all the [bad] thoughts" that is "an entangled struggle of hate and desire. For the listless one hates whatever is in front of him and desires what is not there." If we cannot rein in this thought and the depredations it brings, we become, in Evagrius's vivid phrase, the playthings of our demons, no longer able to distinguish between what will enhance our lives and what will destroy us. "Like an irrational beast," he writes, we find ourselves "dragged by desire and beat from behind by hate." As always, however, there is a remedy, and it is close at hand. "Endurance cures listlessness, and so does everything done with much care and fear of God." Evagrius's concluding admonition is exactly what a contemporary spiritual director might advise: "Set a measure for yourself in everything that you do, and don't turn from it until you've reached that goal." But he also exhorts us to "pray intelligently," and with fervor, so that "the spirit of listlessness will flee."

IX. *A Silent Despair*

The Living Water

Punahou School does reunions in a big way. In early June every year, alumni come to Honolulu from all over the world for a four-day celebration with receptions at beach homes for each reunion class, plus an on-campus, all-class luau. This is made possible by the volunteer efforts of a large number of alumni who live in Hawai'i, having returned after obtaining college and professional degrees on the mainland. For years my excuse for not attending the reunion was that South Dakota's weather is at its best in June, and if I could afford one trip a year to Honolulu, it would be in winter. But I was also afraid. While I had a few close friends in high school, I was often ill-at-ease among my peers. And at Punahou the social savagery that teenagers must generally contend with is greatly compounded by the school's unique position in Hawaiian history. It was founded by the missionary Hiram Bingham in 1841 on land donated at the urging of Queen Ka'ahumanu, one of the wives of King Kamehameha I. The school originally educated the children of missionaries and of the *ali'i*, or Hawaiian nobility, and to this day many students are descended from those families as well as from the American entrepreneurs, British ship captains, and Scottish ranchers who settled in the islands in the 1800s, often marrying into Hawaiian royalty and establishing what are now the state's most prominent commercial and cultural institutions.

Over the years the student population at Punahou has reflected the ever-shifting status of immigrant groups in Hawai'i, which as they rise to the middle class begin sending their children to private schools. Only after World War II did Punahou abandon its quota system for admission of Oriental students. A friend who transferred from a public school in rural Oahu in the early 1950s felt as if she had stepped through the looking-glass, from an environment where most students had been Chinese, Filipino, or Hawaiian, to one in which, as a Chinese-American, she was in a distinct minority. Coming from Illinois in 1959, I didn't find it odd that so many of my classmates were white. If anything, the group appeared diverse to me, with a substantial number of Chinese-Americans, and also many Sansei, or third-generation Japanese-Americans. I was slow to comprehend the great societal change that their presence represented, as my classmates included the grandchildren of plantation owners alongside those of the Japanese laborers who had been brought to Hawai'i to work their fields.

While the social standing of one's parents inevitably factors into the competitive atmosphere of any college preparatory school, at Punahou the variables of status are positively byzantine. It did not take me long to realize that the family names of many of my classmates were embedded in Hawai'i as the names of corporations, streets, parks, buildings, beaches, and neighborhoods. Bright students with a lesser pedigree are welcome at Punahou, but they can be treated badly. When my brother was a senior in 1961, he hoped to go to Yale, but was advised by school counselors that he was "not Yale material." A graduate from the 1970s told me that the school refused to send his transcripts to Stanford, presumably in order to secure the placement of less academically solid graduates who had better social connections.

Some of my peers, through the force of their personalities, managed to break through the formidable social barriers. One girl, the effervescent daughter of a military officer, who joined our class during junior year, disturbed the status quo by being voted onto the cheerleading squad. I admired her determination and applauded her success, as I was incapable of anything but retreat. I am still paying the price, for in feeling rejected, I learned to reject, and became far too good at it; I have declined to accept even many of the good things that might have come my way in life. As my fortieth reunion approached, I decided to attend, to see whether I could let go of some of that old baggage. I registered, and soon received notice of a "Celebration of the Arts" to be held on the reunion's first evening, including a "Meet the Authors" event. I had not been invited, and while this did not surprise me, it did not sit well with me, either. I didn't have the energy to be angry, or even to question whether my exclusion was a matter of ignorance or intent. It may have been an open event for which I had failed to register. But that old feeling of being left out had surfaced, and I recognized that I faced a spiritual challenge.

The Gospel passage for the Sunday before the reunion was one in which Jesus says, "Those who are well have no need of a physician, but those who are sick" (Matthew 9:12). Hearing this made me realize that who my classmates were, all those years ago, and who they had become was between them and God. I was the one in need of healing. The story in Matthew is of a woman who has suffered from a hemorrhage for twelve years, a condition that has made her a social outcast. As she reaches out to touch the fringe of Jesus' cloak, believing that this will heal her, he turns to her and says, "Take heart, daughter; your faith has made you well." As my own particular hemorrhage had lasted for forty years, I thought it likely that Jesus Christ was now the only one who could heal it. So I pondered, and prayed, and on Thursday evening I dragged Jesus off to celebrate the arts at Punahou. He has no doubt been in stranger places.

The event was held at the new Case Middle School, built with a major donation from Punahou graduate Steve Case, cofounder of AOL. As people gathered for the presentation of class gifts, I wandered alone through the literary display and found a large table with books from the school library by alumni authors. Barack Obama's memoir was there, and several scholarly, beautifully illustrated works on Hawai'i's flora and fauna. There was a book on dog astrology, many novels and short stories of local interest, and one novel set in Maine. I saw one of William Ouchi's books on business management, and an anthology edited by a friend, Denby Fawcett, of essays by her and other women who had served as war correspondents in Vietnam.

There must have been well over a hundred books, but none of mine. "It does not matter," my monk spirit rose to tell me, and I recalled the emphasis that the ancients gave to being able to accept praise and insult with equanimity. I'll never get there, but I can try. Then, as I turned to leave, I spotted one of my books peeking out from the pile, a long-out-of-print poetry volume, *Little Girls in Church.* I laughed out loud; this was far too weird to be hurtful. And soon things got even stranger. As I slipped into a crowded multipurpose room, a member of a class from the 1940s, a well-known local businessman, was presenting a check to the school president. Representatives of other reunion classes spoke in turn, and when 1965's turn came, I was startled to hear the class representative call my name, and to be hustled to the microphone by another classmate who had noticed my late arrival. In a giddy swirl, I was handed the edge of a blown-up posterboard check amounting to more than $120,000 and asked to pose for photos with several classmates who had doubtless contributed much more than I to the fund. Punahou received more than $1.5 million from its alumni that evening, but I received something, too. Hospitality is doubly blessed when it is unexpected.

As I wandered through the art exhibits, Hawaiian music performed by alumni drifted over the large lanais. I had noticed that one of the authors slated to be signing books was a friend who had written a children's story about her family's participation in the Bon dances held each summer in Buddhist temples. Her family is now Christian but still honors Buddhist ancestors in this way. I had given several copies of the book as gifts. This was turning out to be not such a bad evening after all, I decided, after a pleasant conversation with her and her husband. I also encountered a former editor of the school literary magazine, *Ka Wai Ola*, who reminded me that I had published my first poem there. *Ka wai ola* means "the living water" but evokes something more: "the water of life." As I walked home, I admired the night-blooming cereus hedge, originally planted in 1836 by Mrs. Hiram Bingham, in full, magnificent flower on the school's lava rock wall. A light rain fell, otherwise known as a Hawaiian blessing.

The next evening, my class held a BYOB cocktail party at the Queen Emma Summer Palace in lush Nu'uanu Valley. Upon arrival I deposited my offering, a bottle of single-malt scotch, at the bar; this de-

lighted some former football players, and freed me from trying to recall which boy on the team once called me a dog to my face. In talking with people that night, I found several classmates who had not
been back to Hawai'i since our graduation, and an impressive number
who had been inspired by Punahou's fine English and history teachers to become English professors and historians themselves. Many of
us had fond memories of a teacher who had turned his required art
history course into something important and formative. Socially, some
things remained the same. Several former cheerleaders, still alarmingly
energetic, were amiable, while others looked at me as if I were from another planet. Our aristocrats, now full-blown society matrons, well
maintained and impeccably groomed, mostly kept to themselves and
their kind. The rest of us milled around them, discovering who we
had become as adults. One man, whom I vaguely remembered as a
football player and wrestler, was now a hospice social worker. Another,
the independently wealthy scion of a prominent family, proved to be
just the same as he was as a teenager: unassuming, easygoing, good-
humored. Several women who, like me, had gone from Punahou to
East Coast colleges, compared notes on our culture shock. Two friends
recalled a sleepover that I hosted late our senior year, when my father
had reserved an oceanfront cabin at a military recreation area with a
divine view of the deeply scored Ko'olau Cliffs. We reveled in the memory of our 1960s selves singing "Blowin' in the Wind" on the beach
at dawn.

A memorial service for deceased classmates was scheduled for the
next afternoon. A woman I had known since we were bused to school
with other military dependents, who is now an ordained minister, had

asked me to do a reading. She had chosen 1 Corinthians 13, popularly known as "the love chapter": "Love is patient; love is kind; love is not envious or boastful or arrogant or rude. It does not insist on its own way; it is not irritable or resentful; it does not rejoice in wrongdoing, but rejoices in the truth." I gladly assented, praying that it would prevent me from needing to hate any of these people again. Our service was held out of doors, by the lily pond and spring that give Punahou its name. (*Puna* means "spring of water," and *hou* is "new.") As each deceased classmate's name was read, we scattered vanda orchids over the pond. One alumnus, a surgeon, teared up as he recalled a classmate who had recently died of cancer. He said that as he listened to the Bible reading, he realized that for him, she had epitomized that kind of love.

We moved on to a raucous photo session, and then the luau. A woman who had graduated in the 1920s was honored as the oldest attendee. Two members of the class of 1930, one a neighbor of my mother's, cheerful and spry despite a recent bout with pneumonia, were also honored. Other awards were presented, and speeches given that we barely heard over the din of conversation. The food was good, and the after-luau party was great fun. A classmate, now an attorney, who had been an airline "stewardess" when that term was in vogue, demonstrated that she still had all the moves, doing the ritual dance of pointing up to overhead bins and down to the exit lights, and commenting—as some flight attendants probably wish they could—that if you can't figure out how the seat belt works, we don't want you on this plane. Her display inspired one of our Hawaiian classmates, a comic genius, to do a riff on King Kamehameha I as an airline pilot, giving tourists his version of Hawaiian history as he steers them over the island chain. Any lingering resentment got belly-laughed out of me, and while I suspect that I'll never have an easy relationship with the school, I felt more at peace.

Several of my classmates asked me what I was currently working on. When I said that it was a book about sloth, I heard a range of responses, from knowing laughter and offers to contribute material to a disbelieving and accusatory "What could you possibly know about *that*?" The woman who asked this moved on before I could reply with anything more than ineffectual mumbling. But she had touched on something vital. When we last knew each other, I was a grind, always handing in my papers on time, acing English class. I had no social life to speak of. Over the past decade, as I had churned out a number of books of poetry and nonfiction, I appeared on the surface to be anything but slothful. But acedia, as sloth's spiritual manifestation, is deceptively contradictory, and a compulsive productivity can be one of its masks.

Acedia first came to me on the proving ground of adolescence, becoming my unknown and unnamed companion. To defeat it I learned to keep busy. To forgo the despair that seemed ready to surface and seize me, I plunged into prodigious reading and writing. I also adopted a studied aloofness as a way of easing pain, not comprehending that a refusal to suffer pain is also a refusal to love. It may be that people were created to care, but that does not mean that it comes naturally, and to a maladjusted teenager, caring can seem like weakness. As I left my teens and explored my vocation as a writer, acedia urged another deadly misapprehension on me, the romantic notion that freedom consists of a lack of obligation. The idea that a true artist stands alone, unaccountable to anyone but herself and her art, was attractive to me, but I was being pulled in another direction, toward a religion that insists on the human need for community.

The Sickness unto Death

As a teenager beginning to ask whether religion held life's answers for me, I found Søren Kierkegaard. It was all wrong for me to read *Fear and Trembling* and *The Sickness unto Death* many years before I encountered his sources, including the early Christian theologians, but that is what I did. Kierkegaard's prose absorbed me as I read him, furtively, on the buses that brought me to and from school. Bits of clarity would strike from time to time, only to be lost if I gazed for a moment out the window. If someone had asked me to summarize what I had just read, it would have been like asking me to summarize a roller-coaster ride.

The bite of Kierkegaard's sarcasm was accessible to me, as was his scorn for the complacent Christians of his own day, stupefied in their state-authorized church. I admired the boldness of his claim to both a philosophical and an imaginative license, his calling *Fear and Trembling* a "Dialectical Lyric," for example, and his insertion of a merman (obviously a dig at the "little mermaid" of his sentimental and far more popular contemporary Hans Christian Andersen) into a serious discussion of the story of Abraham and Isaac. I loved the confidence of Kierkegaard's bold proclamations—"Doubt is thought's despair; despair is personality's doubt"—even if I had difficulty following his detailed expositions. I was deeply attracted to the way his keen vision cut like a laser through the superficial. It thrilled me to read that "to be unaware of being defined as spirit is precisely what despair is." That I may have had football stars and cheerleaders in mind is far less significant than Kierkegaard's insistence that beneath our temporal satisfactions, "deep, deep within the most secret hiding place of happiness there dwells also anxiety, which is despair." In a metaphor that delighted me at fifteen, and still instructs me when I am faced with the onset of a despondency whose causes are not easy to discern, Kierkegaard compares despair to "the troll in the fairy story [who] disappears through a crevice no one can see. . . . So it is with despair, the more spiritual it is, the more urgent it is to dwell in an externality behind which no one would ordinarily think of looking for it."

But the question remains: Why Kierkegaard, that sly and most exacting of thinkers, for an adolescent with a spotty understanding of Christian tradition and a constitutional incapacity for philosophical rigor? Kierkegaard could rely on his solid education in the Greek classics and a wide range of theologians. I was an illiterate by comparison. Kierkegaard had read, in the original, the early Christians who had defined despair as sin, as well as Aquinas, who acknowledged that despair often arises out of a fervent desire for the good. But what was I to make of the whirling dervish of Kierkegaard's prose? How could I hope to follow his dazzling array of categories, his atomized language? Under "forms of this sickness (despair)," for instance, he lists: "Infinitude's Despair is to Lack Finitude" and "Finitude's Despair is to Lack Infinitude." Trying to cope with this made my struggle with algebra seem easy.

In Kierkegaardian terms, I gave up on algebra but persisted with the Dane because it was both absurd and necessary to do so. I felt a deep and personal affinity that I could neither explain nor deny. If Søren Kierkegaard was an unlikely companion for a dreamy adolescent girl in Honolulu during the 1960s, he was also a kindred soul. Like me, he had inherited a melancholic temperament, along with a lively sense of the comic element in even the most painful turns of life. Like me, he harbored a hidden self that he felt would never be accepted or understood by others. Kierkegaard could conceal his melancholy by applying what he termed his "gift of dialectical clarity," while I relied on the synthetic powers of metaphor and poetry, but the results were similar: a divided self, which could appear to be one person on the page and quite another in the world. From early childhood, in misguided attempts to communicate my passions to other children, I had frequently encountered what Kierkegaard describes as the "sadness of having understood something true—and then of only seeing oneself misunderstood." Feeling fated to be alone is a common sentiment among adolescents, and it lends itself to an unwarranted sense of superiority. But when one's otherness is repeatedly borne out in experience, another dynamic takes hold, and life choices are made accordingly. For Kierkegaard, famously, it was the decision not to marry, or as he wrote in his journal, the curse of "never to be allowed to let anyone deeply and inwardly join themselves to me." I would not have expressed my sense of aloneness with such encompassing finality, but I did come to believe, at an early age, that I could have no expectation of either marriage or childbearing. I regarded this not so much a matter of choice as a sensible accommodation to my peculiarities.

For years I saw my stance as one of precocious self-awareness. Only lately, as I have come to better comprehend acedia's grip on me, do I understand my adolescent self more truly. Beneath the façade of a free and creative spirit I was fearful. I was afraid to make my bed because it would sadden me to have to do it again tomorrow. I was afraid to risk relationships, because they might demand too much of me. And I was especially afraid to consider pregnancy and childbirth. Haunted by an aunt's suicide in the year that I was born—she had given birth while she was a patient in a state mental hospital, and killed herself a few days later—I unconsciously adopted a defensive "prepartum" depression. When one is running from a demon, the most dubious rationalizations take hold, and I assumed that I could avoid a postpartum depression by not bringing another mortal life into the world in the first place. I now know that what I had considered a realistic assessment of myself as someone who was not cut out for motherhood was, at least in part, a surrender to acedia.

There is more to that story, but when I took up Kierkegaard and clung to him for dear life I was searching for a way to understand what I could not name, a personal confrontation with the noonday demon. It is good to know that even in my adolescent fog I was looking in the right place, for Kierkegaard was a Protestant with an appreciation of early Christian theology as a taproot that still provided nourishment in the mid–nineteenth century. In an 1839 journal entry, he wrote that he respected the "deep knowledge of human nature" that had led the early monks to include aridity and melancholy among the seven deadly sins. "That," he stated, "is what my father called: *'a silent despair.'*"

Despair and Possibility

My early reading (and misreading) of Kierkegaard did spur me to learn more about the history of acedia and despair in the Western tradition. The question of whether despair is a sin, a sickness, or both has been answered in various ways. If the early monks and medieval theologians approached the subject with psychological subtlety, Martin Luther did not hesitate to exhort a melancholy friend to fight like hell. Given his history of debilitating despondency and notoriously combative temperament, it is no surprise to find Luther offering this bracing advice: "You must be resolute, bid yourself defiance, and say to yourself wrathfully . . . 'No matter how unwilling you are to live, you are going to live and like it! This is what God wants. . . . Begone, you thoughts of the devil! To hell with dying and death!' . . . Grit your teeth in the face of your thoughts, and for God's sake be more obstinate, headstrong, and willful than the most stubborn peasant."

A century later, Luther's outburst may have struck the Renaissance humanist Robert Burton as unseemly. Writing in 1621, he spoke not of the assaults of the devil but of the "anatomy of melancholy." Burton's stated purpose in devising this "anatomy" was to reveal melancholy as "an ordinary disease," for if it could be shown to be caused by the physical "humours," a natural remedy might be found. As an Anglican priest, Burton did not discount the religious element in the struggle against despair. His seven-point prescription for healing includes acknowledging that the source of our misery is sin, and that our help comes from a God we approach by the practice of repentance and prayer. Still, his work had the effect of turning despair into sickness. This coincided nicely with the eclipse of theology and the rise of scientific methods as the best, if not only, way of understanding human behavior. The literary historian Reinhard Kuhn speaks of the late Renaissance as a period in which an ennui arose "whose germs had lain dormant in acedia, the monastic sickness," and entered a long, slow process of secularization, becoming today's "nameless melancholy."

The *Oxford English Dictionary* states that "in the Elizabethan period and subsequently, the affectation of melancholy [became] a favourite pose among those who made a claim to superior refinement." To some extent this attitude remains with us today. The psychiatrist Peter D. Kramer believes that "depression is to our culture what tuberculosis was eighty or a hundred years ago . . . a disease with spiritual overtones." The question lingers: Is despair a sin, an illness, or a case of one-upmanship on the sensitivity front? I have witnessed it in all three guises. It may be helpful to regard the matter in another light.

The scholar Mary Louise Bringle notes that while Kierkegaard knew the Latin root of the word *despair* as "that which is opposed to hope," his native vocabulary would have offered another perspective. Some Danish words reflect the sense that despair arises not out of a lack of hope but out of "a fundamental 'doubleness' or 'dividedness' in the human spirit." As Kierkegaard places the individual in a constant tension between "Finitude/Infinitude" and "Possibility/Necessity," he becomes less a nineteenth-century person than a contemporary. Kramer, in his book *Against Depression,* calls Kierkegaard "the meeting point" between the ancient concept of melancholy and "the contemporary sense of personal identity." If Kierkegaard is a classic case of what Kramer terms "the exceptional man who translates his suffering into art," he also "picks out an element of melancholy that has had special meaning ever since, the alienated consciousness, always aware of its distance from authenticity, immediacy, and single-mindedness."

Kierkegaard's bold assertion that "purity of heart is to will one thing" inspired me when I was young, and in midlife I appreciate his rejection of both the romanticizing and the medicalizing of despair. Kierkegaard valued the insight of the Christian ancients in naming despair a sin, even as he presented a new term, "the sickness unto death," that would so accurately describe contemporary humanity. Yet even as we suffer from this malady, Kierkegaard maintains, we are not merely ill but also caught up in "the battle of *faith*." When someone faints, he writes, "we call for water, eau de Cologne, smelling salts; but when someone wants to despair, then the word is: Get possibility, get possibility, possibility is the only salvation . . . for without possibility a person seems unable to breathe."

Many years after I had found my desert monks, who also comprehended faith as a constant battle with themselves, I returned to Kierkegaard, not so much to his phenomenology of despair, which still can make my head spin, but to his journals, where I found him sounding like an ordinary, if remarkably perceptive, human being. A passage from July 1835 moved me so deeply that I copied it into my journal. Describing a seacoast that was one of his favorite places, Kierkegaard summons the creation story in Genesis:

> I stood there one quiet evening as the sea struck up its song with deep and calm solemnity . . . and the sea set bounds to the heavens, and the heavens to the sea. . . . As I stood there, without that feeling of dejection and despondency which makes me look upon myself as the enclitic of the men who usually surround me, and without that feeling of pride which makes me into the formative principle of a small circle—as I stood there alone and forsaken, and the power of the sea and the battle of the elements reminded me of my own nothingness, and on the other hand the sure flight of the birds recalled

the words spoken by Christ: Not a sparrow shall fall on the ground without your Father: then all at once I felt how great and small I was; then did those two mighty forces, pride and humility, happily unite in friendship.

Lucky is the man to whom *that* is possible at every moment of his life; in whose breast those two factors have not only come to an agreement but have joined hands and been wedded—a marriage which is neither a *mariage de convenance* nor a *mésalliance* but a tranquil marriage of love held in the most secret chamber of man's heart. . . . He has found . . . that archimedean point from which he could lift the whole world.

As a teenager I was surrounded not by the waters off the rocky Scandinavian coast but by the bright and variegated blues of the ocean off the island of Oahu. To employ Kierkegaard's grammatical metaphor, if I was sometimes an "enclitic," eager to attach myself to older, more sophisticated friends even if it meant losing myself in the process, I could also be fiercely independent. While many of my contemporaries gladly entered the sea to surf, I tended to stay onshore. It was enough for me to take in the scene, from mountain to ocean, and consider my blessings: loving parents, a few good friends, excellent teachers, and singing in a lively church choir. Most days, I would not have described myself as unhappy but might have admitted to an underlying sense of despondency.

In an 1848 journal entry Kierkegaard writes of his despair: "I must never, at any moment, presume to say that there is no way out for God because I cannot see any. For it is despair and presumption to confuse one's pittance of imagination with the possibility over which God disposes." Here Kierkegaard allies himself firmly with the early monks, who recognized in despair the most vicious and self-defeating temptation of all, that of losing trust in God's providence and love. They also valued humility as a tool for maintaining hope. While today the word *humility* may connote a placid servility in the face of mistreatment, its Latin origins suggest strength and fertility. The word comes from *humus,* as in "earth." A humble person is one who accepts the paradox of being both "great and small" and does not discount that hope which Kierkegaard terms "possibility." We may look to physicians or therapists when our lives go off track, or we may pray the psalms, or seek solace in a favorite novel. But in a sense we are all seeking the same thing. We want to prepare a good soil in which grace can grow; we want to regard the cracks and fissures in ourselves with fresh eyes, so that they might be revealed not merely as the cause or the symptom of our misery but also as places where the light of promise shines through.

When possibility bursts like grace into our lives, changing everything, we might, like Julian of Norwich, envision the world contained in a hazelnut and declare that "all will be well." The question "How can that be?" is one that we can put off, as we experience a profound joy. But we might ask whether this serenity is not the end of all our therapies and potions, and also why it is that we usually settle for less. Although I was helped by a Jungian analyst when I was in my early twenties, and my husband and I benefited on several occasions from marriage counseling, I have found therapy to be of limited usefulness, constrained in ways that religion is not, because it consistently falls short of mystery, by which I mean a profound simplicity that allows for paradox and poetry. In therapy I am likely to be searching for explanations, causes, and definitions, information that will help me change

my behavior in healthful ways. But wisdom is the goal of spiritual seeking, and it is religion's true home.

Mystery penetrates the Bible stories that intrigued me as a child
and still offer sustenance: I pass through turbulent waters dry-shod and
am led by a pillar of cloud or fire. I am refreshed by water that flows
unexpectedly from rock. If I now see through a glass, darkly, I can hope
to one day see face-to-face. Relying on reason yet pointing to truths beyond my imagining, religion always offers me something more than I
can fully articulate or comprehend. And it makes me see that I am not
alone: even Jesus transfigured on the mountaintop required others to
bear witness to what had happened to him. The disciples responded
foolishly at first, and with fear, but their eyes had been opened to the
promise of beneficial change within themselves.

Baby's Breath

Our inner transformations may come upon us like barely discernible
shifts in the wind. But sometimes change seizes us by force. If the dense
prose of Søren Kierkegaard helped me to encompass my otherness as
an adolescent, it took just two words, "baby's breath," to give me a better understanding of my middle-aged self. I was long married by then,
and happily settled in my mother's hometown on the Great Plains.
One day, as David and I were driving through the grasslands on our
way to the Bismarck airport, we were enjoying one of our treasured,
desultory conversations. A wedding we'd recently attended came up. I
couldn't remember the name of the smallest flowers in the arrange-
ment, and David said, "Baby's breath."

The words had a physical effect on me, stirring something that had been buried for years. As I struggled to articulate this, I realized that I would be able to relate it only in a poem. David understood, and we moved on to other topics. I slept restlessly that night, and the next day, in the Minneapolis airport, I began writing in earnest, a poem titled "The Blue Light." I was on my way to New York, to visit my friend Betty Kray, and as I scribbled, I grew determined to finish the poem so that I could show it to her. Betty was always a perceptive reader of my verse, and she had seen me in this enthusiastic state many times. After I arrived at her apartment, she read the poem and murmured approvingly, but as she moved into the last section, she sighed and said, "I begin to lose you here." I had hoped against hope that the poem would stand, and when Betty spotted trouble I knew that this meant work. My ending was off, and just how far off I would not know for well over a year. I would take the poem from its folder and look for a way to fix it. Nothing would occur to me, and I'd set it aside. I had to be patient, not force things; attempting to finish the poem too soon had gotten me into trouble in the first place.

The poem is about a memory to which I have very little access, of an event that occurred when I was a prelingual infant. This seems a curious situation for someone who works with words. The story is this: By the age of six months I had developed severe infections in both ears and was critically ill. When I lay in my hospital crib, I would roll my head from side to side, as if that would ease the constant pain. The doctors at Providence Hospital in Washington, D.C., felt that surgery was my only hope, and wanted to perform a double mastoidectomy to remove infected portions of the bone behind each ear. But they knew that I would need massive doses of antibiotics. It was 1948, and while penicillin had been used successfully on soldiers during World War II, it had never been given to infants in such great quantities as I would require. My maternal grandfather, a physician, took a train from South Dakota, a three-day journey, to authorize this experimental treatment. My mother has told me that I grew so accustomed to the penicillin shots that the nurses could turn me over, inject me in the rear, and turn me over again without waking me up. When I was six years old, just before we moved from Washington, my mother and I visited the surgeon. He took a volume from his bookshelf and showed me the story of my early adventures as "Baby X"—a tiny part of a medical revolution; now physicians treat childhood ear infections with antibiotics instead of surgery. The doctor said something I had already heard from my parents and grandparents, that I had survived in part because I had such a strong will to live. I believed it for years.

My poem came because on hearing the words "baby's breath," I had suddenly doubted that I had fought to stay alive as an infant. People who have come close to dying often describe being drawn toward a tunnel of light. I will never know exactly what happened to me, but isn't it likely that I was attracted to that light and its beauty? And isn't it possible that I would have felt rejected, even angry, when it was denied me? In the first draft of the poem, because the right words hadn't come, at least not as quickly as I wanted them, I had resorted to abstraction: "The love that moved me then / still moves me; / the anger and fear are gone." By ending my poem with this convenient lie, I had shut a door that I then had to work hard to open.

The last stanza originally began with me alone, swimming laps in a pool, the blue light of the water triggering my infant memory. Betty had declared: "You have to get out of that pool." That was enough to make me see that I had implied a drowning, and possibly a suicide, which I did not intend. It was many months before I could determine the crux of my problem. I had not survived in that hospital on my own, and my poem needed other people in it, people my reader could see. Poems come together out of diverse sources, and it was praying Psalm 107 in a monastery choir that helped me grasp another piece of my puzzle. The psalm envisions seamen caught in a wild storm, their souls melting away at the sight of the massive waves and the sound of the howling winds: "They staggered, reeled like drunkards, for all their skill was gone. / Then they cried to the Lord in their need / and he rescued them from their distress" (27–28).

I realized that while the physicians and nurses who had cared for me were professionals with the expertise to save a life, they were also limited in what they could do. I put them into the poem's final version as "the nurse who fed me a bottle / through the operation, / the doctor working helplessly / with all his skill," adding that "it was their world / I learned to want," the world in which mistakes happen and our knowledge can take us only so far. I wanted to convey this, and also to suggest that before I had the words to express it, I had been given a glimpse of heaven and then been tossed back into this painful, messy, and uncertain thing called life. The poem now concludes: "I saw the perfect / backs of angels / singed with light: / I turned from them, / I let them go."

Who knows what I "really" saw? That is not a question a six-month-old can answer. It is clear, however, that I retained strong memories of the hospital. When I was a toddler, certain motor noises and harsh lights frightened me unduly. If the Hoover vacuum with the dark red bag and small headlight was in use, I would flee to another room, my heart pounding. Above all, I distrusted anyone dressed in white. When my favorite babysitter, a neighbor, once came to the door in a white dress, I threw such a tantrum that she went home and changed her clothes. Over the years I have come to suspect that the main effect of my illness and operation was a deep-seated anger: having had to choose life over death, I was enraged and felt lost. It's as if I had entered childhood as Dorothy, forced to live in Kansas after being enchanted by Oz. This experience was locked within me, leaving me a little girl with, as my mother often said, sad and grown-up eyes. My strangeness emerged in many ways. I loved to paint, as most children do, but when a teacher asked me and my classmates to paint our vision of heaven I quickly grew frustrated, because I couldn't make it dark enough. And even before I could read, my favorite song in my family's musical primer, *Fireside Book of Folk Songs,* was "I Am a Poor Wayfaring Stranger." With a dirgelike melody and mournful lyrics, the song envisions life as "a-traveling through this world of woe," on our way to our loved ones who have already crossed over to a world with "no sickness, toil, or danger." I must have been a spooky child, warbling the words in my high-pitched voice: "I'm just a-going over Jordan, I'm just a-going over home."

This is what I carried within me as, in Honolulu, in the turbulent 1960s, I entered adolescence, what the adults around me had a maddening habit of proclaiming as "the best years of your life." I knew this could not be, but had not much vision of what "the best" might entail. I did know that from the time I was an infant I had been set on a quirky and lonely path. Far too soon, before I had language with which to express it, I had been made aware of death. My feet had been set on a pilgrim way, and if I was often dejected and feeling utterly alone, that was all right. I could only hope that a time would come when my skewed perspective would be of use.

I was in my early forties the first time I visited an oncology ward for terminal patients. I was apprehensive, as I was going to the front lines of a battle that our culture labors mightily to keep hidden, but I needed to visit a friend. I did not expect that the ward would be an apocalypse in the literal sense of the word—an unmasking or uncovering. The intensity of misery was overwhelming, yet it did not frighten or repel me, for I had entered holy ground. People my own age, as well as the elderly, were shockingly frail and needed support just to totter down the hall. Still, they were alive, and walking, saying their good-byes to friends, children, and grandchildren. What struck me was that the atmosphere was not merely one of sadness, but also one of beauty deepened by the sobering inevitability of death, and blessed by the presence of a vibrant love. While the relentless activity of New York City surrounded us, here everything unessential had been stripped away. Only life remained, a gift and a joy beyond our understanding. I had arrived in the real world.

The Prayer You Don't Understand

Anthony of the Desert once said that a true prayer is one you don't understand. What I think of as the true prayer of my life came to me on a night when I was in my thirties, on retreat at a Benedictine abbey. It was well after vespers, and I was sitting in a choir stall near a statue of the Black Madonna. I felt too tired to pray, but as a powerful emotion welled up in me, words formed in my belly before they reached my brain. When they finally came—I did not intend them and could not hold them back: *I want to know motherhood*—I began to weep. Whether to bear a child was a question I had decided many years before, and effectively set aside; why had it seized hold of me now? A matter I thought closed was suddenly an open wound—how could I have "known," at fifteen, that I was not meant to be a mother? How was it that this conviction remained steady throughout my twenties and thirties? More than I wanted to admit, I had been fearful of the bodily changes that pregnancy brings, of labor itself, and of the manifold responsibilities of motherhood. My personal fears were supported by the spirit of an age in which a philosopher, E. M. Cioran, could casually refer to pregnant women as "corpse-bearers," and a fictional nihilist in Mikhail Artzybashev's novel *Breaking-Point* could declare, "Whenever I see a pregnant woman, I feel inclined to kill her. If the child lives and begets others in turn, how many thousands of cripples, of scoundrels, of murderers will be among them, how many will perish in war, how many go mad. What a crime she commits against millions of future wretches." As for myself, having sensed that I had an uncertain grip on life, I doubted that I had the moral courage to bring a new life into this world. But that dilemma and decision had been settled in the past, or so I had thought. I had convinced myself that I was not the mothering kind.

I remained sitting in the choir stall for a while and then went to my room, and to bed, only to be awakened a few hours later by abdominal cramps. My menstrual period had begun—another month in which the possibility of motherhood was lost to me. I glanced at the photograph of my youngest sister and her infant daughter that I had placed on the dresser mirror and noted that the child was wearing a red dress and an unaccountably wise expression. It is out of such odd juxtapositions that poems come, and once I began writing, in the wee hours, I didn't stop until it was time for morning prayer. In the poem I termed myself "a useless woman," and in a cruel and literal sense that is how the world might judge any woman who does not bear a child. But the prayer, and the poem, had opened up the possibility of knowing motherhood in other ways. It could be that while I still have breath, while blood flows in me, I can find ways to generate life, and to pass it on. I regard that poem as the first answer to my prayer.

Another answer came months later, when the baby in that photograph was seventeen months old and had a bad case of chicken pox. David and I were in Honolulu for the winter, and I became my niece's companion for most of the day, until her mother came home from work. The child was in a miserable state, so restless that even when she was on the verge of collapse she refused to lie down. I followed her around the house, and when she dropped from sheer exhaustion, I would lie next to her and try to nap as well. If I couldn't take away her discomfort, I might ease it a bit, and be present when she woke. I read her countless stories and fed her prodigious amounts of papaya and poi. When she inevitably drooped over the food and fell asleep, I would gently lift her out of the high chair, wipe her face, and put her on the sofa, in a place I had prepared with a pillow and blanket. Each afternoon, as I gave my niece over to my sister, I stood in awe of the everyday perseverance of mothers. Christian theologians from Anthony to Augustine to Kierkegaard teach that prayer changes not God but the one who prays. I had prayed for something impossible: to "know" motherhood. I did not summon this prayer. It came precisely because I did not know how to ask for it, or even what to ask.

x. The Quotidian Mysteries

A Pilgrim's Progress

I first read John Bunyan's *The Pilgrim's Progress* when I was in my early twenties, a young woman far more aimless than I cared to admit. The seventeenth-century novel gripped me in ways I did not expect, and awakened a dormant sense of conscience. I recently reread the book and was struck anew by its psychological acuity. Early in his pilgrimage, the hero, Christian, stumbles into the Slough of Despond, a swamp fouled by fears and doubts, where he struggles to maintain his footing. His being there has one salubrious effect: he is forced to acknowledge his true condition. He is lost and must pay close attention if he is to reach firmer ground. As our pilgrim soldiers on, he meets a full range of humanity: Mr. Talkative, Mr. Smooth-man, Mr. Facing-bothways, Mr. Anything (in our own day he would be Mr. Whatever), Mr. Money-love, Lord Time-server, and a parson, Mr. Two-tongues. Christian walks with Hopeful, the companion he has adopted, by the banks of a river. When they encounter adverse conditions, they find their way diverging from the pleasant river road and are tempted toward By-path Meadow, seeking a shortcut and an easier passage. What happens then is for me the heart of the story, and reminds me that whenever I attempt to escape hardship and pain by taking what seems a safer route, I only make more trouble for myself. Bunyan's pilgrims soon must seek shelter from a thunderstorm. It is growing dark, and the river waters are too turbulent for them to turn back. They find a small hut and fall asleep.

When they awaken, they see that they are trespassers in the land of Doubting Castle, ruled by a loutish giant named Despair, and his cruel wife, Diffidence. Upon learning that her husband has beaten his prisoners and chained them in his dungeon, she suggests that he urge them to suicide. The giant tells the pilgrims that "since they were never like to come out of that place, their only way would be forthwith to make an end of themselves. . . . 'For why,' said he, 'should you choose life, seeing it is attended with so much bitterness.'" The pilgrims ask only that he let them go, and their innocent presumption so enrages the giant that he falls into an apoplectic fit and is powerless to administer another beating. Christian and Hopeful spend the night in anxious conversation, finally deciding to exercise more patience, but in the morning Despair takes them to the castle-yard to see for themselves "the bones and skulls of those that [the giant] hast already dispatched." The pilgrims spend another unhappy night, while Diffidence tells her husband, "I fear . . . that they live in hope that some will come to relieve them or that they have picklocks about them, by the means of which they hope to escape." The giant promises to search them in the morning.

At daylight, the couple is awakened by an unaccustomed noise, the creaking open of the stubborn iron gate of the castle wall. Christian and Hopeful have escaped, and paralyzed by another of his rages, Despair cannot go after them. In an epiphany just before dawn, Christian had declared, "What a fool . . . am I, thus to lie in a stinking dungeon, when I may as well walk at liberty." He has remembered that he has a key, called Promise, that will open any lock in Doubting Castle. It has been in his possession all along. He has only to recall this and put the key to use. When I first read this passage it delighted me and resonated deeply. I continue to be amazed at how the slightest hope, like a small breeze, will arise when despair seems most invincible. The obstacles it has set in my path prove to be phantoms, and following a faint scent of fresh air, I find my way through the musty castle, run into the open, and inhale.

But this is not the end of my journey, for even as I taste my newfound freedom, I know that I am bound to lose it again. The next time I am feeling beleaguered, it will not be easy to recall that I possess the means of my release. The tools are many: naming my illness, dilemma, demon, or "issue," and once I have recognized my need for help, being willing to ask for it, from a friend, pastor, or physician. It strengthens me to know that, as Evagrius points out, "it is not in our power to determine whether we are disturbed by [the bad thoughts], but it is up to us to decide if they are to linger within us." Whether I call my affliction "sin" or "sickness" matters far less than what I do once I admit that something is wrong. Half the battle is won if I can resist my inclination to acedia, to act as though I were a spectator at life's banquet.

I encountered *The Pilgrim's Progress* at a time when I felt that I was looking at life more than living it. I had drifted away from the religious moorings of my upbringing and was careening between a lack of courage that prevented me from exploring life's possibilities and a recklessness bordering on self-destruction, with casual drug-taking and even more casual sex. Naturally, I thought of myself as sophisticated. The poetry I listened to as part of my job at a New York City arts institution, as excellent as it often was, could do nothing to change my behavior. If I was being asked to live a life of purpose and meaning, I generally managed to be deaf to the call. In her poem "Annunciation," Denise Levertov suggests that the message the angel Gabriel brings to Mary is one that comes to each of us. We receive an intimation of some purpose larger and more challenging than anything we have imagined for ourselves, but all too often those strange and risky times

> when roads of light and storm
> open from darkness in a man or a woman
> are turned away from
> in dread, in a wave of weakness, in despair
> and with relief.
> Ordinary lives continue.
> God does not smite them.
> But the gates close, the pathway vanishes.

Even as a young woman I was good at closing gates and watching pathways vanish with a satisfying sense of release. When I met the man who would become my husband, and committed myself to our relationship, I knew I was doing something scarily bold and new, but I was not at all prepared for the changes that would be wrought in us during our thirty years together.

My marriage is the one thing I kept saying yes to, even when it hurt to do so, and in that sense it was another answer to my prayer to know motherhood, for it is through marriage that I came to understand a bit about labor pains, as suffering willingly, even gladly, for the sake of something much greater. The very nature of marriage means saying yes before you know what it will cost. Though you may say the "I do" of the wedding ritual in all sincerity, it is the testing of that vow over time that makes you married. I hope that I will always have faith in the giddy wonders of romance, but in considering what makes a marriage endure, I am likely to employ such ascetic and unromantic terms as *discipline, martyrdom,* and *obedience.*

The words *discipline* and *disciple* are of course related; the former suggests a teaching, the latter a person who is willing to learn. In the give-and-take of married life, as each person learns from the other, both become, individually, and as a couple, much more than they could ever be on their own. The word *martyr* proves fruitful in the context of marriage. When consulting Eric Partridge's *Origins* for its etymology, one is directed to *memory.* There one finds that the Greek starting point is *martus,* or "witness." Related words include the Latin *memor,* "mindful," and the Old English *murnan,* "to grieve." This is a place to begin. To keep a romantic relationship alive, one must be mindful enough to recognize the danger signs of inattention and sloth. My husband and I were surprised that even in a small town, we could become so busy with our own concerns that we easily lost sight of each other. Just to fail to eat together on a regular basis was to court indifference, or worse. We would snap at each other without knowing why; it took an intentional "date" to set things right again, and a renewed resolve to do more everyday things together. Over time we found that the accumulation of shared experiences provided a storehouse of memory that helped us bear the worst of circumstances. Our situation might be bad in the present, but it had not always been so. If our memories gave rise to grief over what we had lost, they also provided us with the strength necessary to move on together, into an uncertain future.

And what of obedience? It is usually regarded as desirable in dogs but suspect in people, and is a loaded word for women, who for far too long were asked to vow obedience to their husbands in the wedding rite. Even now some women tolerate criminal abuse of themselves and their children in the name of obedience, while others find it a convenient foil; they can dominate their families while proclaiming themselves "submissive" wives. But at its root, the word *obey* means "hear." And listening in that sense, as mutual obedience, is fundamental to marriage. A profound joy comes in knowing that I have been heard, that another person cares to know me as I am. Such intimacy is a great gift, but it also contains the challenge of doing what is necessary, every single day, to maintain the relationship. I am reminded of this truth when I consider that one of the most consoling passages in Scripture (from Lamentations 3:21–22), "The steadfast love of the Lord never ceases, / his mercies never come to an end: they are new every morning," follows a lament that begins, "I am one who has seen affliction."

A Rule for Beginners

I was in my thirties when I first read the Rule of Saint Benedict, and was surprised to find it so helpful in understanding my married life. How could something written in the sixth century to outline a way of life for celibate monks be of use to someone attempting to maintain a monogamous relationship some fifteen hundred years later? In the opening paragraph of the prologue to his Rule, Benedict speaks of firmly embracing "the labor of obedience" as a means of "[bringing] you back to him from whom you had drifted through the sloth of dis-obedience." I was puzzled that sloth was placed so prominently in this context. What did sloth have to do with obedience? But my very un-ease signaled that Benedict's emphasis was worth exploring. For if the acedia I had struggled with for much of my life was a key to the Rule, it was no surprise that I had found it so attractive.

Benedict's suggestion for confronting sloth is deceptively simple: "First of all," he writes, "every time you begin a good work, you must pray to [God] to bring it to perfection." For me that is not an easy habit to maintain, if I admit that "beginning" is something I must do every day, many times a day. Yet I am encouraged by a phrase Benedict employs at the end of his Rule, characterizing it as a "little rule that we have written for beginners." This may come as a shock for those accus-tomed to regarding monks as professionals in holiness, and I am not necessarily comfortable with the idea that a vowed life, whether to marriage or to a monastic community, is less an accomplishment than a pilgrimage for those willing to always start anew. To be always a be-ginner, in our competitive culture, is to be a loser. It is to remain con-tinually vulnerable, and not many of us would care to endorse Abba Isaiah's assertion that "nothing is so useful to the beginner as insults. The beginner who bears insults is like a tree that is watered every day."

Beginnings can be trying for anyone as goal-oriented as I am, for I want to make quick progress and am tempted, like Christian and Hopeful, to take shortcuts to that end. Patience and discipline are re-quired to appreciate beginnings, and those are qualities I often lack. While my impatience can energize me to accomplish a great deal in the course of a day, it makes me susceptible to acedia. If I am not going full-tilt, I am likely to collapse. Impatience also spurs me to eat too rapidly, and the culture colludes with me here, every time a waiter looks at my half-eaten plate and asks, "Are you still working on that?" Not enjoying, but working as fast as I can. The job gets done, but at a cost, for in rushing through a meal, I lose the flavor of the present moment, denying my body both pleasure and the time it needs to properly ingest food. I devour each moment distractedly, hurling myself into the next task, moving toward the next imaginary goal.

Because it impedes my illusory forward movement, having to begin again can feel like failure. It reminds me that work I thought finished must be redone, and I resent being reminded of the transitory nature of all things, including myself: when I dust, I am humbled, because I, too, am dust. As a writer I must begin, again and again, at that most terrifying of places, the blank page. And as a person of faith I am always beginning again with prayer. I can never learn these things, once and for all, and master them. I can only perform them, set them aside, and then start over. Beginning requires that I remain willing to act, and to summon my hopes in the face of torpor. Above all, beginning again means rejecting that self-censurious spirit that will arise to scorn my efforts as futile. Abba Poemen reminds us that *"accidie* is there every time one begins something, and there is no worse passion, but if a man recognizes it for what it is, he will gain peace." I would not claim to have "gained peace," yet in my struggles with acedia I have learned a valuable lesson: Once I have started out, it is crucial that I not rush to the end, but remain where I am for a time. I have to trust that change is working within me, even though I seem to stagnate.

I dislike the use of birthing imagery for the process of artistic "creation." "Maker" is what the word *poet* means at its Greek root, and the poems I make and the personae that fill them are not creatures in the fullest sense, having life and breath. But I do detect in the rhythms of writing and not-writing a stage that might be described as "parturi-ent." It often happens that when daily life seems an inescapable and ap-palling repetition, and I seem dead inside, an inner conviction comes, of its own accord, telling me that what had seemed "dead time" was ac-tually a period of gestation. New writing then begins to emerge.

Repetition, Again

And what of the "dead times" in a marriage, when the romance has faded, and "happily ever after" seems a cruel sham? The rock musician Lou Reed once said that repetition was "fantastic," because it was "anti-glop." His is an aesthetic concern for shunning the mushy and mawk-ish by employing repetitive sound, yet the insight might apply to marriage as well. For repetition resists the glop of sentiment, and also tests the spirit. It is easy to fall in love over a meal in a restaurant, where someone else does the cooking and the cleaning up; it is hard to toler-ate, much less love, the person who shares our kitchen, bath, and bed. How does repetition turn relationships stale and lifeless, so that a once beloved face becomes an object of scorn? What is it about repetitive acts that makes us feel that we are wasting our time? Although it is easy to dismiss our daily routines as trivial, these are not trivial questions, any more than sloth is mere laziness without spiritual consequence.

That repetition can be life-giving is not something I had consid-ered until I experienced the most intense writing period of my life, in which I produced an entire volume of poetry in a matter of months. For some time poetry had been submerged in me as I worked on prose, and I wondered whether I would ever write verse again, as yet another prose project was on the horizon. But as soon as I settled into residence at the Collegeville Institute at Saint John's Abbey in Minnesota and began attending the daily monastic liturgy, the poems came in a rush. The hymns we sang and the psalms we recited were like muses, and to my great surprise I found myself writing nearly a poem a day. Even more astonishing, they were coming out nearly whole, needing very little revision. I had never encountered anything like this, and I feared that this great flow of energy would soon backfire on me, leaving me depressed. It did not happen. I had not counted on the power of routine to provide a protective scaffolding. My joining the monks in church at seven a.m., noon, five p.m., and seven p.m. stabilized me so that the work got done but did not overwhelm me.

Could we regard repetition as a saving grace, one that keeps returning us to essential understandings that we can discover in no other way? The human need for routine is such that even homeless people establish it the best they can, walking the same streets, foraging in the same dumpsters, sleeping in the same spots, in an attempt to maintain basic relationships with people and places. For any of us, affluent or not, it is by means of repeating ordinary rituals and routines that we enhance the relationships that nourish and sustain us. A recent study that monitored the daily habits of couples in order to determine what produced good and stable marriages revealed that only one activity made a consistent difference, and that was the embracing of one's spouse at the beginning and end of each day. Most surprising to Paul Bosch, who wrote an article about the study, was that "it didn't seem to matter whether or not in that moment the partners were fully engaged or even sincere! Just a perfunctory peck on the cheek was enough to make a difference in the quality of the relationship." Bosch comments, wisely, that this "should not surprise churchgoers. Whatever you do repeatedly has the power to shape you, has the power to make you over into a different person—even if you're not totally 'engaged' in every minute."

So there. So much for control, or even consciousness. Let's hear it for insincere, hurried kisses, and prayers made with a yawn. I may be dwelling on the fact that my feet hurt, or nursing some petty slight. As for the words that I am dutifully saying—"Love you" or "Dear God"— I might as well be speaking in tongues, and maybe I am. And maybe that does not matter, for it is all working toward the good, despite myself and my most cherished intentions. Every day and every night, whether I "get it" or not, these "meaningless" words and actions signify more than I know. Repetition *is* "anti-glop." It helps us to be more honestly and fully human. It knows us better than we know ourselves.

Mysteries Great and Small

Perhaps our most valuable mystics are those of the quotidian, people who do not contemplate holiness in isolation, or devote themselves to the pursuit of spiritual arcana accessible only to a select few, or reach for illumination in serene silence. Instead, they search for God in a life filled with noise, the demands of other people, and duties that can submerge the self. They may be young parents juggling child-rearing and making a living, or nuns in a small community who have to wear three or four hats because there are more jobs than people to fill them. And they may find that whatever spiritual strength they have arises out of weariness and frustration. In an essay, the poet Kate Daniels writes of an evening in which she tries to make dinner as her children fret and argue, littering the table and floor with scraps from art projects, and the dog overturns the kitchen garbage can. Like her and her husband, she says, the children are "tired, overstimulated. The events of the day are clamoring inside them." In the midst of this familiar but dangerously charged atmosphere, Daniels senses that they are all at risk: "We have all come home to each other to be healed and hailed, to be soothed if a victim, chastised if a perpetrator, and morally realigned. But . . . we lash out in irritation, frustration, anger." In the act of naming this sorry truth she finds the courage to take a stand: "Try as I may—and I do— I have a hard time browning the ground turkey I'm planning to mix with canned spaghetti sauce for the glory of God. . . . I know that God is here, but in the chaos and the noise, I can't seem to find him." Yet she has: her faith has burst open her kitchen walls as surely as Christ burst through his tomb.

Daniels has seen that it is love they are seeking, this ordinary family on an ordinary evening in an ordinary home. And if they are lucky, they will have to try to find this love all over again the next night, and the next. This is faith, and also the obedience that the Benedictine David Steindl-Rast has termed "an intensive listening," whose opposite is the acedia that recognizes life's absurdity but chooses to remain "deaf to [its] challenges and meaning." We may resist the drudgery that seems to pull us away from what we vaingloriously perceive to be our "real" lives, but we are fools to do so. If we are truly listening, we will see prayer not as a control mechanism or a duty we fulfill so we won't be sent to hell. If we are too proud, bored, or numb to pray, we are already in hell.

Steindl-Rast, echoing the masters of the Christian spiritual tradition, suggests that we endeavor to "make everything we do prayer."

This is no pious nostrum, but the acknowledgment that when we pray, we are not sending out orders expecting that they will be fulfilled. Citing Dante's magnificent image at the conclusion of *Paradiso*, Steindl-Rast defines prayer as a quality of attention, the capacity to attune yourself "to the life of the world, to love, the force that moves the sun and the moon and the stars." Browning ground turkey while your children are arguing in the kitchen, you may not feel connected to this great mystery, but you are. This is the sort of thing that parents, poets, mystics, and monks come to know very well, if they are willing to be always beginners, setting yesterday's burdens behind them in order to recommit themselves to each new day.

We want life to have meaning, and want to be fulfilled, and it is hard to accept that we find these things by starting where we are, not where we would like to be. Our greatest spiritual blessings are likely to reveal themselves not in exotic settings but in everyday tasks and trials. No less a saint than Thérèse of Lisieux admitted in her *Story of a Soul* that Christ was most abundantly present to her not "during my hours of prayer . . . but rather in the midst of my *daily* occupations" (emphasis mine). The twentieth-century martyr Dietrich Bonhoeffer wrote from the illegal seminary he had established in Nazi Germany: "We prevent God from giving us the great spiritual gifts He has in store for us, because we do not give thanks for daily gifts. . . . How can God entrust great things to one who will not thankfully receive from Him the little things?"

One step toward that blessed receptivity for "the little things" is to discern which activities foster our spiritual freedom, and which do not. I cannot watch television, for example, and write a poem. I might be inspired to pray by something I see on a news program, but this is rare. The activities I find most compatible with contemplation and writing are walking, baking bread, and washing dishes. I like the poet Donald Hall's theory that poetic meter originates in the steady, repetitive rhythm of arms and legs in motion, and agree that walking conditions more than my leg muscles; the instinctive movements also loosen my imagination. For me, bread-baking is a hands-on experience of transformation. While the dough is rising I often sit and write, aiming for transformations of my own. And in dishwashing, I approach the moral realm; there are days when it seems a miracle to be able to make dirty things clean.

I may intellectually assent to the notion that such utilitarian chores can open my heart to the world, and appreciate Gerard Manley Hopkins's observation that "it is not only prayer that gives God glory but work. Smiting on an anvil, sawing a beam, whitewashing a wall, driving horses, sweeping, scouring. . . . To go to communion worthily gives God great glory, but to take food in thankfulness and temperance gives Him glory too. To lift up the hands in prayer gives God glory, but a man with a dungfork in his hand, a woman with a sloppail, give Him glory, too. He is so great that all things give Him glory if you mean they should." But when acedia is at work in me, it takes my whole self to know that, like Kate Daniels, or anyone else attempting to sustain a relationship through daily trials, I will have to "mean it" over and over, every night and every morning, cleaning house, running errands, complaining and listening to complaint, and giving those I love the attention they deserve. It is all for the glory of God, and how we perform those often dispiriting duties, from the changing of a baby's diaper to the bathing of an aged parent, reveals what kind of God we worship.

That faith and love operate best through the humble means of boring, everyday occupations is a thoroughly biblical perspective, for its stories repeatedly remind us that God's attention is fixed on what we regard as unimportant and unworthy. The Scriptures depict God not as a Great Cosmic Cop, eager to catch us in minor transgressions, but as a creator who loves us enough to seek us in the most mundane circumstances of our lives. We are asked to remember that we are refreshed each day like dew-laden grass that is "renewed in the morning" (Psalms 90:5). Or in more personal and also theological terms: "Our inner nature is being renewed every day" (2 Corinthians 4:16). In this light, the apparently ludicrous attention to detail in Leviticus, where God is involved in the minutiae of daily life, right down to cooking and cleaning, might be seen instead as the love of a God who desires to be present to us in everything we do.

This is the God who inspires the psalmist to declare, as he wakes from sleep, "I will bless you, Lord, you give me counsel, and even at night direct my heart" (Psalms 16:7). This is the God who speaks through the prophets, reminding us that by meeting the daily needs of the most vulnerable among us we prepare our hearts to welcome the day when God will put to rights our unjust world. Woven together, these threads of biblical narrative provide a revelation of God's love for all creation, with each day offering the promise of salvation. This concept is beautifully summed up in what Abba Poemen said about another monk, Abba Pior: "Every day he made a new beginning."

According to Genesis, this is no more than God has asked of himself. The creation was a daily process, and in relating the story, the narrator repeats at every verse, "And God said," leaving us to imagine what will be revealed on the morrow. If it seems a form of play, it is strenuous play, and after God speaks every new bit of the world into being, he lets it rest until the next morning. Not until the sixth day do the animals come into being, including the humans who are made in God's image and thus are called to honor each day with prayers, just as God honored its creation. We may offer desperate utterances in the den or the bathroom, or at tables around which our family is squabbling, but we can also resort to the "liturgy of the hours," the traditional daily prayer of Christians that is still observed in monasteries. At dawn, lauds reminds us of our need to renew, remember, and recommit our lives to their proper purpose. Those who are not "morning people" know what an effort this can be, and those who are subject to depression know that simply getting out of bed can be the greatest challenge of the day. Noon prayer is a time to briefly rest from our labors, and take stock as we prepare for the demands of the afternoon. As sunset approaches, vespers is a surrendering of contention, a willingness to surrender the day, and let God bring on the quiet, brooding darkness in which dreams will wrestle with and nurture our souls. Every night compline invites us to be like the farmer of the Gospel parable, to admit to the limitations of our consciousness, and submit to the realm of God: "The kingdom of God is as if someone would scatter seed on the ground, and would sleep and rise night and day, and the seed would sprout and grow, he does not know how" (Mark 4:26–27).

Our bodies still reflect the diurnal rhythms of creation, and sleep is still a fundament of mental and physical health. But in our modern society we can stay up late, take one drug to help us sleep a few hours and another to get us going in the morning. We might go for a refreshing walk during our lunch hour, but are more likely to cram in a PowerBar and coffee at our desk, fighting drowsiness as we work. When the Dalai Lama was asked for advice about how people could improve their spiritual lives, he laughed and said that it was obvious: Eat less, don't stay up so late, and sleep more. If his realism shocks or even offends us, it may be because it is so easy for us to lose our place in the world. I once heard a woman say that she didn't like the island of Kaua'i, because "there weren't enough places to shop." The tragedy of her hubris goes deep: she is the sort of consumer the tourist industry avidly courts by inserting generic shopping malls into breathtaking tropical valleys. How is it that we can grow so insensitive to the world around us? Acedia is at work in us when we prefer buying things to witnessing the beauty of nature, "reading" catalogues instead of books, or lingering in a museum store instead of touring the museum itself. These are not insignificant choices, for in making them we risk losing our capacity for wonder. When acedia has so thoroughly possessed us, making life seem so dull that only artificial stimulation can get our attention, it may be crazy to suggest that the ordinary rhythms of time, the passing of day and night, have something to teach us, or that there is a world to be revealed when the mall is closed, the electric power has failed, and it is too dark to see anything but shadows and stars. Cast back on our lonely, raw, and wounded selves, we may find that nobody is at home.

If monks have always insisted that each hour of the day and night has its own distinct message for us, the rapid pace of contemporary life leads us to believe that it is otherwise. We are "free," it seems, to have anything but a nurturing leisure. "I have so little time," goes the frequently heard lament, which conveniently ignores the fact that everyone is granted exactly the same twenty-four-hour round. As these hours pass, we rush from one task to the next. To those who can't cope, we snarl, "Get a life." But the question remains: Do we use our time to really live, or do we allow time to use us up? I remember hearing a woman ask, in all seriousness, at a tightly scheduled conference: "Do I have time to go to the bathroom?" She decided that she did, if she could take her BlackBerry with her into the toilet stall. Her question could be posed only in a fallen, post-Genesis, world.

At Play

Is it not a good jest that when God gave us work to do as punishment for our disobedience in Eden, it was work that could never be finished, but only repeated, day in and day out, season upon season, year after year? It is another kind of joke that being rendered temporarily mindless as we toil can be a welcome invitation to forget utility and enter into play. I was once a teacher's aide at a kindergarten, and I remember that one of the most popular sites was a sink in a corner of the classroom. A few children at a time would take turns filling, emptying, and refilling plastic bowls and cups, watching bubbles form as they pressed objects deeper into the sink or tried to get others to stay afloat. This privilege was so highly regarded by the children that they took great care not to abuse it by squirting water at one another or at their teachers. Whenever I resent having to wash dishes, I recall the faces of those children.

I often fail at converting drudgery into play, for even as the contemplative in me recognizes the sacred potential in the mundane task, the busy go-getter resents the necessity of repeating it. Kierkegaard reminds us that "repetition is reality, and it is the seriousness of life . . . repetition is the daily bread which satisfies with benediction." After reading a story such as *Peter Rabbit* to a child, how lovely it is to hear a small voice summon the authority to say, "Read it again." I once observed a girl about four years old find a coin on the floor of a post office. "Look, Momma, a penny," she said. Her mother, busy with the clerk at the window, mumbled an acknowledgment. The girl put the penny back on the floor, in a different location. "Look, Momma," she said again, "I found another one!" She kept at it until she had found five pennies, each of them "new."

Adults may appreciate the innocent wisdom of children, but we are expected to forgo indulging in such foolish games. As we approach work that must be done and redone, we feel the dread weight of tedium. But we can still be surprised. I have grasped poetic inspiration from the common experience of doing housework in a distracted state, finding myself at the foot of my basement stairs, with little idea of what I was doing there, and no memory of having descended the steps. My hands held clues, in the form of a piece or two of dirty clothing, several books, a dustpan and whisk broom, a box of crayons, a coffee mug, and an old plastic pitcher. Operating in housewife mode, I had conceived of a place, the "right place," for all these items in the basement, and I was about to set them there, in a finely tuned sequence of events that had now slipped my mind. This struck me as comical, but I knew it could be otherwise. When my husband spent those weeks in the psychiatric ward, a woman there, an abused wife, spoke of such an event as the precipitating cause of her hospitalization. She had been cleaning house in a frenzy, to escape the next beating, an attempt she knew to be futile. She stopped, suddenly, and stood in her basement for more than an hour, unable to move. She eventually crawled up the stairs and asked a neighbor to call an ambulance. Serious play, indeed.

And what is the point of it all? Both housework and poetry require that I pull disparate things together, sort through the odd pieces of my life, and try to make a whole that is greater than the sum of its parts. But envisioning such wholeness is increasingly countercultural, as fragmented people are better consumers. It is the aim of advertising to make us anxious, doubting that what we have is enough, or enough of the best and latest stuff. It also engenders a low-level but treacherous dissatisfaction that makes us susceptible to acedia and its handmaid, narcissism. How wonderful that the advertisements are all addressed to me, personally. So many pleasant voices, speaking as if I were the only person in the world, driving the only car on the road. Why should I allow any other voices to interrupt my reverie? Thus it is that mere things become spiritual impedimenta.

From my lofty perch on the status pole, how am I to respond to the pure democracy of the necessary and menial work that I must either do myself or hire others to perform? The word *menial* derives from a Latin word meaning "dwelling" or "household." It is thus a word about connections, about family and household ties. That it has come to convey something servile may explain why in this country we consistently pay garbage collectors much more than those who care for our precious infants and toddlers in day-care centers. Tending small children was once done without remuneration in the confines of the home. Precisely because it is so vital, and so close to us, so bound up with nurture, it is often considered to be of less importance than that which is done in public.

It is easy to imagine that by devaluing the bonds that connect us to the everyday we can rise above them. But not one of us can escape our daily, bodily needs. If they were not vital to our spiritual as well as our physical well-being, we would not live in fear of being incapacitated by illness or old age, and in need of assistance with activities we once could take for granted: eating, bathing, dressing. Like daily liturgy, such work draws its meaning and value from repetition. But how distressing to have to always begin again. How playful, and yet how practical, of Mary Magdalene to have harbored seven demons, one for each day of the week.

And how difficult to hold in our hearts the reason that we labor in the first place: to know and to love ourselves, the world, and one another. John Bunyan may have helped when I was young and heedless, but now, although I share the medievalist Barbara Newman's reluctance to "take even a day's journey into the savage wood of Dante criticism," I must turn to the poet, who was midway through his life when he found himself "in dark woods, the right road lost," and discovered that his journey had only begun. In daring to view the human condition from the perspective of eternity, Dante asks us to witness to the power of love. As love takes us on a harrowing journey, even to hell and back, we may find the path arduous but remain convinced that it is the only one worth taking. I am intrigued that Dante, like Aquinas before him, discerns in the sin of sloth a refusal to do what love requires. Acedia renders us unable to live committed to another person and to the changes the relationship with that person demands of us when it no longer offers the enticements of a new romance but has been scarred by pain, loss, and the passage of time.

XI. *The "Noon"*
of Midlife

"How Is It That We Choose to Sin and Wither?"

When I was nearing fifty, the person I had thought myself to be disappeared. Like Eugène Ionesco, who in a memoir described midlife as "a reverse metamorphosis [in which] I became a caterpillar," I found myself asking, "Whatever became of the person I was, the person I must still be?" Where was the dutiful, deadline-driven girl, who had been an accomplished multitasker before I knew the word? In eighth grade when I was first assigned a research paper requiring notes on index cards and an outline, which were to be given to the teacher in advance, I panicked upon discovering that I was unable to provide an outline until I had written a first draft of the paper. Instead of confessing to this weakness, I worked in double time to pretend that everything was in order. My hyperefficient system worked well for me for years, and in college, because I always had my papers done early, I was in great demand on the nights before my friends' papers were due. It did not occur to me that I paid a price for this way of working, that the bill would one day come due. I think of the girl in Randy Newman's song "Lucinda," who does everything expected of her, and after graduating from high school parties all night on the beach. In the early morning she refuses to obey (or hear) another order, won't move a muscle, and is run over by a beach-sweeper. I used to laugh over Lucinda and her fate; now I can identify with her. Being flattened by a beach-cleaning machine? In finding a suitable metaphor for midlife, one could do worse.

I am consoled anew by my friend Evagrius, who notes that while young monks contend with lust, or the impulse to pull others toward them, the middle-aged have to fight the desire to push others away. As the young struggle with a raging appetite for more experience, their elders are tempted to grow angry and regretful over experience thwarted or denied. Columba Stewart contends that Evagrius regarded aversion as a much more serious and "larger problem . . . than misdirected desire." Either might be seen, Stewart adds, as "a flammable gas that can be used constructively. But they are always vulnerable to ignition by demons, memory, or bodily appetites." Aversion was more likely than lust to engender a scorn for others that would cause the monk to abandon his community and his vocation.

Acedia, it seems, is not only the demon that lobs an assault at midday but also the bad thought that afflicts us in the middle of life, when it seems impossible to care about so many things that used to matter. Do I have to care, if it means having to acknowledge the contradictions and dissonances by which I survive? The pose of indifference is far more appealing. I may be in dire need of rest, but if I fall asleep in this unsettled condition, I'll still be uneasy when I wake. It will be as if I hadn't slept at all, and I won't know where, or who, I am. I should know by now, for more than half my life is gone. It is time to consult Dante, who, at the outset of his great journey, had to work against "the old fear stirring" as he tried to "tell what I saw, though how I came to enter / I cannot well say, being so full of sleep / Whatever moment it was I began to blunder / Off the true path." If Dante finds himself in midlife only half awake at the edge of hell, the scholar Reinhard Kuhn tells us, it is "not because of any specific evil act" he has committed, but "because of . . . the sin of omission, acedia." It is the careless and deadening sleep of acedia that sends Dante on his journey.

Just after he crosses the threshold of hell, Dante learns the cost of his ill-timed drowsiness. Beset by "strange languages, horrible screams, words imbued / With rage or despair, cries as of a troubled sleep," he witnesses a mirror image of his own recent unrestful state, but now the confusion is loud and the pain palpable. Many sounds rise "in a coil / Of tumult . . . in a ceaseless flail / That churns and frenzies that dark and timeless air / Like sand in a whirlwind." He asks his guide, Virgil, who these tormented souls are who are making such a dreadful noise, and learns that they are those who "kept themselves apart" in life, regarding the world with a studied disinterest. Their passions were so lukewarm that it is as if they never lived at all, and now neither heaven nor hell will accept them. After this first contact with those who manifest the vice of acedia, Dante moves on, past "Minos, great connoisseur of sin," who "discerns / For every spirit its proper place in Hell." In the third circle Dante is drenched, like the gluttons who reside there, by a cold, heavy rain. He enters the fourth circle, asking, "How is it that we choose to sin and wither?" The question presumes the freedom to choose; if I am truthful with myself, I recognize that in midlife, there are many days in which I indeed choose to sin and wither. Even if I can think of ways in which I might rouse myself from lethargy, I resist acting on them.

Continuing his journey, Dante encounters the overly contentious, engaged in endless brawling. Moving toward the fourth circle's farthest edge, he finds a dark and roiling watercourse that discharges "into the marsh whose name is Styx." Here the angry are denied the mercy of forgetting. They stand, naked and muddy in the bog, striking one another with their heads, chests, feet, and backs, tearing with their teeth. Virgil explains the bubbles rising to the surface of this foul marsh by pointing out the slothful, barely visible under the surface of the murky water. In a mournful tone, they say, "Once we were grim / And sullen in the sweet air above, that took / A further gladness from the play of sun; / Inside us, we bore acedia's dismal smoke. / We have this black mire now to be sullen in."

Here Dante ties anger, which entails caring too much about the wrong things, to acedia, which is caring too little about the right ones. To someone in the grip of acedia, the beauty of sunlight, and of life itself, can only reinforce a bitter ingratitude. In recognizing that despondency is frequently the flip side of anger, Dante agrees not just with modern psychologists but with the ancient monastics as well. When unexpressed anger builds up inside, people perform even legitimate duties carelessly and resentfully, often focusing on others as the source of their troubles. Instead of looking inward to find the true reason for their sadness—with me, it usually involves having my plans thwarted, which shatters my illusory control—they direct it outward, barreling through the world, impatient and even brutal with those they encounter, especially those who are closest to them.

I recognize all of these stages in myself, and I know that there are some days when such unfocused anger makes me of little use to anyone. When I am in this state, the popular notion of fixing things by "talking it out" is counterproductive. If I bristle with irritability, and if my anger is out of proportion to any cause, fear and despair are my real enemies, and talking will lead me to rant aimlessly or awaken a self-pity that sends the poison deeper within. If "poison" is too strong a word, I can admit to feeling soured on life. Dom Bernardo Olivera, abbot general of the Cistercians (or Trappists) wrote his 2007 circular letter, "The Sadness Corroding Our Desire for God," on acedia. He explains, in a self-described "home-grown etymology," that in Latin "there is a family of words related to acedia, such as *acer* (sharp, bitter), *acetum* (vinegar), and *acerbum* (harsh), which, taken figuratively, [make] us think that persons suffering from acedia have received a high dose of acidity," and thus are incapable of appreciating the sweetness of life. Just as spoiled wine becomes acid, he writes, "so the joy of [love], when it sours, becomes acedia." As I age, it is easy to feel that my very capacity for love is withering, along with my bone density and muscle tone.

The "Inborn Freedom" and the "Urge for Good"

Love is the whole purpose of Dante's journey, and also its goal. In purgatory he again encounters the slothful, and significantly, as he approaches their terrace in canto 18, he asks Virgil to teach him what love is. Virgil speaks of "an inborn freedom" that is found "at the roots of things." But, he warns, "even if we allow necessity / as source for every love that flames in you, / the power to curb that love is still your own. / This noble power is what Beatrice / means by free will: therefore, remember it, / if she should ever speak of it to you." Dante's response to this existential challenge is to withdraw, becoming apathetic and drowsy. Half asleep, he harbors "random visions" until an approaching crowd commands his attention. It is the slothful, who, to atone for their previous lassitude, are now in constant motion. "Quick, quick," they cry, "lest time be lost." They are trying to compensate for the negligence they once showed "in doing good half-heartedly."

These days we might be tempted to consider these people as sick, not sinners, and wish that Dante had been able to diagnose their "dismal smoke" and attention-deficit disorder accurately. But works such as *The Divine Comedy* continue to offer us profound insight into ourselves. It is still true that there is nothing more cold than betrayal, and that sloth can submerge us in a stew of anger. It is still true that those who do not appreciate the beauty of the "sweet air" of life are ill equipped to find beauty anywhere. But we must ask: Is it "do not," "will not," or "cannot"? Who would truly choose to wither? Perhaps it is more critical to ask what it would mean to be whole in the full sense of the word: hale and holy. If Dante is to point me to an answer, I need to trust that his view of sin is not a primitive remnant of a more conventionally religious time that is embarrassingly present in a literary masterpiece but is, in the words of the theologian Linda Mercadante, an integral part of a worldview that "exhibits a sensitivity to the human predicament that has largely been forgotten."

Understood properly, the Christian doctrine of sin is a vision of wholeness, and Dante represents this tradition at its best. He does not label people as evil because they've fallen short of some ill-conceived, perfectionist goal. Dante's understanding of sin is far more subtle than that, and more humane. These days, we are likely to say to people struggling with addiction or mental illness that their hope lies in a perpetual state of recovery. Imagine for a moment that this is much more severe than anything Dante, or the desert monks for that matter, had in mind. Their ultimate concern was how, as we deepen our relationship with God, we become more free to love, and more free to choose the good. The idea that one would be defined forever by one's sin or sickness would have seemed to them excessively cruel, more likely to engender hopelessness than hope.

The "noble power" of a free will partakes of something even greater than hope, and that is grace. The kingdom of God within us is not something we gain through training, wit, or skill. It comes to us as pure gift, and we are free now, as in Dante's time, to nourish it, curb it, or ignore it. Given the power and resilience of this grace, it is a terrible irony that the despairing so often feel rejected by a distant and uncaring God. When we are convinced that we are beyond the reach of grace, acedia has done its work. John Cassian states that acedia's whole purpose is to "sever [us] from thoughts of God." John Climacus speaks of it as "a voice claiming that God has no mercy and no love for [us]." Thomas Aquinas describes acedia as a "wanton, wilful self-distressing that numbs all love and zeal for love" and makes us unable "to rest in God." Even worse, it divides us against ourselves and our better instincts, "[setting] itself in irreconcilable antagonism to that love which is inseparably linked with the divine indwelling." When so fierce an alienation has me in its grip, I need something more powerful than affirmation and self-esteem. I need that outcast word, *sin*.

Sin for Grown-ups

In *The Seven Deadly Sins*, his study of the concepts of virtue and vice in Judaism, ancient Greco-Roman philosophy, and Christianity, the psychologist Solomon Schimmel reminds us that "the deadly sins are not arbitrary, irrational restrictions on human behavior. . . . On the contrary, [they] . . . concern the core of what we are, of what we can become, and most importantly, of what we should aspire to be." He regards these sins as directly relevant "to a host of problems addressed by clinical and social psychology," related to our capacity for evil. For me, the most basic definition of sin—to comprehend that something is wrong, and choose to do it anyway—is still the most useful. It frees me from the narcissism of fretting over my more trivial failings, even as it forces me to admit to those actions that have hurt others. The point is that I knew they would and I didn't care enough to stop myself. Sin in this sense is definitely for grown-ups; very small children, who can't yet distinguish between fact and fiction, are not capable of sin. A three-year-old can say, in all sincerity, "I didn't break it," when you have seen her send a glass crashing to the floor, and she knows that you saw.

Such fervent wishful thinking can be charming in a toddler. It is less so in an adult who, when convicted of sexually assaulting a ten-year-old, explains himself by saying, "It was my inner child." The penal system will probably reject such an excuse and exact a severe penalty for the crime. As a society we are less certain of how best to change this sort of behavior. Will counseling and psychotherapy be effective? Or will drugs alleviate the compulsive urges of known sex offenders? These are matters under current discussion in this country, as we attempt to sort out what are medically treatable conditions and what are not. What is heard less is any useful discussion of temptation and sin, let alone the monastic perception of the eight bad thoughts. The desert monks understood the great difference between a harmful action and the temptation to do it, and they maintained that while we can't control whether or not the bad thoughts come to us, we can learn how to respond to them. But attempting to stop harmful behavior is a serious challenge. Any monk, or any participant in a twelve-step program, can tell you that it requires daily recommitment.

Our task is not made easier when we find that even as we more clearly understand our primary temptations, we become more vulnerable to them. With acedia, as the seventeenth-century cleric Bishop Joseph Hall noted, the mind may be "sufficiently convinced of the necessity or profit of a good act." But once the thought of toil and tedium are "annexed to it, in a dangerous spiritual acedy, it slips away." Many who have tried to maintain a basic exercise regimen know this syndrome well: just the thought of getting to the gym is enough to keep them from going. For me, the same syndrome applies to attending church, and it can be a major victory over acedia to walk through the sanctuary doors on Sunday morning. We do not require religious faith to experience what Dante calls an "urge for good," or to savor the grace that infuses the still center of the soul. I do find, however, that the religious vocabulary is an inexhaustible source of renewal, reminding me that when I do bad things I need not be stymied by guilt, and reassuring me that something more is possible. An ordinary service can spark with words that ignite my imagination, shore up my resolve, and tell me that I am something more than I had thought myself to be when I awoke that morning. A prayer said after receiving communion, for example, is a bold plea to "ever perceive within ourselves the fruit of thy redemption." If, an hour later, I am tempted to slough it all off in mean or angry behavior, those words still reside in me, as a call to be more compassionate and kind. The point of the eucharist, after all, is not merely to change the bread and wine into Christ, but to change me as well.

If the dynamics of worship continually remind me that such change for the good is possible, I must still pay close attention to my temptations and thoughts. The poignant words of a hymn may move me, a Scripture passage may summon tears of compunction, and I may be struck with a vigorous desire to do things differently from now on. How easy it will be, I think, to change my habits, to be more attentive and prayerful. Yet if I am not careful, this little surge of vanity will dissipate into nothingness in the daily grind. When I fail, as I must, I can only recall the desert monk who told his disciple, "Brother, the monastic life is this: I rise up, and I fall down, I rise up and I fall down, I rise up and I fall down." But in this repeated ebb and flow, the danger is that I will grow weary and more easily discouraged, less able to appreciate that grace is as real, and as available to me, as acedia. If I am inspired by some good thought, if I aspire to do better next time, I am not a fool. I am only being the person I was created by God to be.

Image and Likeness

In the Book of Genesis, I find that I was created in the image and likeness of God. Monastic people have always been concerned with the practical application of this doctrine in a world they perceive to be saturated by God's love. In this context the attempt to reclaim the divine image by pursuing "purity of heart" is not a sentimental or perfectionist endeavor but the very purpose of life. It is a command to act and to appreciate, as the Cistercian Gail Fitzpatrick expresses it, the critical importance of recognizing that "whatever dilutes, falsifies, or blocks this love . . . does not belong in our heart."

Our efforts alone, however, are not enough to undo the blockage, and the monastic tradition is replete with warnings that placing too much faith in ourselves and our spiritual practice will further obscure our integral goodness, even as we grow more satisfied with our presumed holiness. We never lose our need for what John Cassian terms the "Lord's protection"; he gives as an example a farmer who must labor to till and seed his fields. Until rain comes, the seeds remain dormant, and without sunlight their seedlings cannot grow. Cassian's metaphor is an ancient one: in the Book of Isaiah (55:10–11) the word of God is envisioned as the rain God sends to earth, and the prophet declares that it will return not empty, but bearing good fruit. If we are made in God's image, perhaps we are also words of God in this sense, and our life's pilgrimage is to determine what our particular word is and how we are to bring it to fruition. Within this frame of reference, we can envision the whole of our life as a journey home.

The image of rain as grace may seem quaint in an urban and postmodern era. But we ignore the workings of nature at our peril and are wrong to imagine that we are not a part of them. In a recent essay, John Eudes Bamberger, a monk who is also a physician and a member of the American Psychiatric Association, seeks to reassess the ancient doctrine of "image and likeness" in the light of current findings in psychology and biology. He believes that both the theology and the practical experience of monastic people have much to contribute to our understanding of "the neurochemical basis of the emotions, the dynamics of the passions, and the neurological pathways that relate perception to memory."

This is not such a stretch. In his *Chapters on Prayer,* Evagrius speaks of a monk who is so disciplined that he can "pray purely without being led astray." Even so, Evagrius observes, the monk may be tempted by demons who "no longer come upon [his spirit] by the left side but from the right." With great prescience Evagrius states that this phenomenon is due not merely to the bad thought of vainglory, but also to "the influence of a demon who stimulates a specific section of the brain and thus agitates the cerebral circulation." Bamberger finds this passage interesting "for the awareness it reveals [of a connection] between the emotions and the physiology of the brain. Only in very recent times," he comments, "have the details of this relation been worked out in considerable detail through the discovery and description of the Limbic pathways."

For early monks such as Evagrius, Bamberger writes, "God was the horizon within which their concern for the genuine in the human heart and behavior was examined." They wanted their daily lives to reflect "this higher, vaguely perceived implicate order" and remain centered on the love of God. If this seems like religious twaddle, it is not.

As science grows more focused on wholeness and process rather than on the mechanical workings of what were traditionally regarded as "separate parts," it enters the realm of mystery. In discussing the behavior of quarks, for example, physicists can sound more like theologians than the sober guardians of a rigorous "hard" science. Religious mystics and scientists alike point us toward the understanding that nothing is really separate: the hologram best reflects this reality, as any one of its elements contains within it the totality. Our world, it seems, partakes of a wholeness that we can glimpse but not fully comprehend, as nothing is merely the sum of its parts. This is borne out by microbiologists and other scientists, who, Bamberger notes, have discovered that "[higher-level] emergents cannot be completely accounted for by [lower-level] components."

The monastic endeavor, now as in the fourth century, is to purify one's heart so as to better reflect God's creation. Ultimately this is a goal for all Christians: to conform oneself to the mercy, peace, and love exemplified by the Jesus of the Gospels. Monks go about this in a particular way, and sometimes speak plainly about mysteries that seem impenetrable, even to many Christians. I recently heard a homily by a Benedictine monk that, except for references to Darfur and global warming, could have been preached in a monastery centuries ago. "Naked we come into this world," he said, "and naked we shall return. But not quite: our hope is that when Christ receives us, he will recognize his own image in our hearts."

This hope is both a grace and a challenge, and acedia's response is to turn away, clouding Christ's image with indifference. It will always ask that we settle for something less, a life of more limited meaning but one over which we retain a satisfying autonomy. Even taking into account the reductionist view of human beings as little more than an assortment of chemicals, neurons, and electrical impulses, we might view an inner willingness to confront at the outset an aberrant thought like acedia as an impulse in the right direction. Something to build on and help effect a beneficial change. Now more than ever, as psychiatry is increasingly technological, a matter of manipulating the chemicals in our brains, we need symbolic language, the nuances of poetry and the free spaces of story, myth, and faith to help us understand who we are and why we consistently do things that wound ourselves and others. We need John Bunyan's pilgrim to remind us that we have access to the tools that will set us free. We need Dante to lead us through the dark wood, and beyond.

Labor Pains

Beyond, for me, means taking another look at motherhood. At sixty I find that my regrets at being childless are few. But I do wonder why, since I had excellent models for mothering in my own mother and maternal grandmother. The more conflicted models of motherhood provided by my paternal grandmother and her daughter, my aunt Mary, certainly gave me pause. For my grandmother Norris, motherhood was mixed with sadness and regret: while one of her sisters became a medical missionary in the then Belgian Congo, she settled for being a wife and mother on the Great Plains, and justified her marriage to a Methodist pastor and then child-rearing as her form of ministry to the church. She was determined that her sons become pastors, but neither did. My aunt Mary's mental illness (she was diagnosed, probably correctly, as schizophrenic) proved fatal when combined with an out-of-wedlock pregnancy, and her example made me fear that becoming a mother would be too great a strain on my own psyche.

I assumed early on that I would never marry, and with one notable exception, whenever I asked myself whether I should set my sights on motherhood, the answer was no. Only once, when I was in my early twenties, did I fantasize at length about having a baby. The temptation came as a love affair was ending. I should have been glad to be free of an unhealthy relationship—the man was married, much older than I, and, I had discovered, a habitual philanderer—but was transfixed by the notion that I should have his child. Although I was then unaware of the monastic understanding of bad thoughts, I did recognize the idea as insane, if not demonic, and that bit of reasoning was my salvation. When, a few years later, I met the man who would become my husband, I was ready for marriage. The slothful path had proved false, and I no longer imagined that an adulterous relationship would be easier and safer than a fully committed one. My experience is one small instance of what Christian theologians regard as the paradoxically auspicious nature of sin. For only when I became aware of how badly I was acting, selfishly undermining a marriage and shortchanging my capacity for love, could other, better possibilities emerge. It is, as Henri de Lubac has stated, a fortunate "self-consciousness [that] awakens in sin," for it welcomes God to exercise a divine prerogative and derive good from evil. But even as we take that first, conscious step toward our deliverance, we still have work to do and labors to endure.

I may never fully understand why I perceive the Christian doctrine of sin as a blessing and not a curse, and why my sense of promise is so firm. From childhood I have loved the music of worship and the words of Scripture; but more important, my ancestors in the faith, my grandparents and parents, handed down a religion centered on love, not fear. They raised me to believe in a God who loves me, a God who loves us all. The grace I have known as a healing force in my life has little to do with whether I feel happy or sad. I know it as a presence, even when it is invisible or seems inaccessible. It is, in the biblical phrase, "honey from the rock," the unwarranted gift that comes when I least expect it. If I find in the doctrine of sin a joyful sense of the human that keeps me accountable for what I do, but never robs me of hope or self-respect, I am only grasping for what Dante expresses in canto 3 of *Purgatorio*: "Despite the Church's curse, there is no one so lost that the eternal love cannot return—as long as hope shows something green." And of course, when such bounty graces my life, I remain free to reject it.

Despising the Pleasant Lands

When I lived in South Dakota, I inevitably became depressed as winter shifted into spring. The longed-for moment arrived when the air was gentle and inviting and I could again walk out of doors without heavy clothing. But that also meant stirring things into life that had grown comfortably dormant. Every year I was severely tempted to stay inside, hosting an internal winter and allowing my garden to languish as the perennial flowers and herbs contended with encroaching weeds. My mood always passed, yet in the meantime I would hug my dusty old house around me like a shell. Many people in the Dakotas seek help for SAD, or seasonal affective disorder, which comes with winter. Given the tendency in our culture toward what one philosopher has called "dynamic nominalism," or inventing a category and then placing people in it, I am surprised that no one has yet coined "FOS syndrome" for the fear of spring. I have generally counted my seasonal affliction as a typically perverse manifestation of acedia.

I once wrote a poem about my springtime blues, in which I depicted Persephone as a pawn between her mother and the husband who had abducted her and taken her into the underworld. Finally speaking for herself, she says:

... I learned to eat
what was put before me,
and became a wife.

My mother raged, my husband
capitulated. When the deal was struck
no one thought I'd be torn in two.

Now I have my pied-à-terre,
and the inner darkness ...

Now spring is a blind green wall.

These days family responsibilities require me to spend much of the year in Hawai'i, which exists in a more or less perpetual spring. There are other seasons, but their signs are subtle. Surf patterns shift, as the northern shores that receive mammoth waves in winter become in summer as calm as a pond. Winter brings more rain and cooler temperatures. But because of the subtropical climate, the temperature range is small when compared with Dakota extremes. No ice, and except on the uppermost elevations of Mauna Kea (13,700-plus feet) on the island of Hawai'i, no snow. From my kitchen window I view the Ko'olau Mountains that rise above Honolulu, and in any season I can watch rainbows form and dissolve there, and wisps of cloud that seem to catch on the trees of the watershed.

While I am often a grateful observer of this beauty, there are times when I cannot see it at all. I am not alone. Many people stationed in Hawai'i with the military or large corporations come to feel a nagging contempt for the place. They hate the ocean because it reminds them that they are living on an island in the most isolated island chain on earth. They dismiss paradise as "the rock" and refer to their sad condition with a perverse pride as "rock fever." The willful rejection of loveliness has often served as a metaphor for acedia, and I find it true to my own experience. It is all too easy for me to despise the pleasant lands, and choose alienation over connection because it promises to preserve my vaunted independence. Sometimes it is necessary to remind myself that I am not self-sufficient, and never have been.

When my oldest niece was three years old, my brother would drive her to day care in the morning, and her mother, who worked as a stockbroker and financial planner, would pick her up in the afternoon. She always brought an orange, peeled so that her daughter could eat it on the way home. One day the child was busying herself by playing "Mommy's office" on the front porch of our house in Honolulu, and I asked her what her mother did at work. Without hesitation, and with a conviction that I relish to this day, she looked up at me and said, "She makes oranges."

My niece could wait without anxiety for this daily ritual, a liturgy of the delicious orange, bright as the sun, sweet with the juice that is the body and blood of this world. The child thus fed learns to trust in others, and in God. The fruit we are given is not always what we expect or want; it may even be bitter, but we are secure in knowing that it is given to us out of love. The capacity for trust engendered in such ordinary encounters as those between mother and child has a deep significance not only for individuals but also for the human community. It grants us joy in the present and hope for the future. It allows us to believe in love more than in hate and to love life all the more because it comes to an end.

To Wait and to Hope: At Play with Etymology

We live our lives not at the end, but in the meantime, in the interval between birth and death. The word *interval* originally referred to a space between walls or ramparts; now it commonly implies a period of time. But a hint of its physical origins remains as we rush through our nights and days, constructing fortifications against the assaults of time and circumstance. In our younger years we seek our vocations and begin our families, and it is easy to ignore our position on time's continuum. As we age and face the press of mortality, we can drown in ceaseless activity, or retreat into the false calm of inertia. Yet as our defenses grow more rigid, they are also more likely to crack wide open.

Our language provides a glimpse of a better way. In Eric Partridge's *Origins,* I find that *interval* leads to *wall.* I can visualize the sense of that, an inter- or internal wall. But when I look up *wall* and am instructed, "See 'voluble,'" I pause, wondering what strangeness is afoot. *Wall* is a solid noun, while the adjective *voluble* signifies something fluent, even fluid. I rejoice at the hidden wisdom contained in words; this contradiction helps me break out of the closed circle of my thoughts and the self-defeating strategies of middle age. How might I be solid as a wall yet alive with movement? How might I build on all that I have learned yet not resist new challenges and transitions? Two vows that are unique to the Benedictines are of use to me here, the vows of stability and conversion. Even as one promises to remain in a particular community for the rest of one's life, one commits to being open to change.

I may be loath to give up the piece of turf on which I feel most secure. But the revolving motion suggested by volubility allows me to remain where I am, and still take in a 360-degree view. In relinquishing what I believed to be essential, I have discovered something even more valuable and gained not only a new perspective but also a new life. I will have struggled and no doubt suffered in the process, yet my pain is not without meaning. Andrei Voznesensky has expressed it: "The water in living wells / does not stagnate; / the more you tear from your heart / the more of it you keep."

Still, it is not an easy task to make our home in the middle, where we all must live, and to truly live each day, even as we know we are dying. Days are all we have, though, as Philip Larkin reminds us, asking, "Where can we live but days? / Ah, solving that question / Brings the priest and the doctor / In their long coats / Running over the fields." For some of us the steady passage of time becomes unbearably cruel, an endless round of pain that wears us down. My husband was convinced that most suicides come out of sheer exhaustion, and I sense acedia, bringing all of its cruel anguish to bear, in the words of a letter Charles Baudelaire wrote at the age of twenty-four, intending them to be read after he had committed suicide. (His attempt failed.) "I am *killing* myself—without *grief*. . . . I am killing myself because . . . the fatigue of falling asleep and the fatigue of waking are unbearable."

There is a good psychological basis for the impulse, borne out in many of the world's religions, to pray at the hinges of time, at morning, noon, and night, when we might be most open to God but are also susceptible to acedia and its attendant despairs. The psalmist asks us to place our hope in a God who will not grow weary of watching over us at these risky moments, who will "guard [our] going and coming / both now and for ever" (Psalms 121:8). If we cannot find reassurance here, we may, like Baudelaire, find only horror.

To live in the meantime is our common lot, and it is waiting that tests us, as we recommit to whatever mundane tasks are required with each new day and night. When we are very young, time moves far too slowly, leading many an exasperated child to declare, indignantly, "I am *not* six! I am six-*and-a-half!*" But in middle age, as we begin to lose the friends of our youth, the hours rush like a river in flood, carrying us helplessly away. Perhaps it is a mercy that in old age many of us lose our sense of time altogether.

If time is perceived as an enemy, to insist that there is value in waiting is foolish. Advances in technology such as e-mail and instant messaging all presume the question "Why wait at all?" When I started using computers, in the mid-1970s, I noticed that while the programs with which I kept track of the finances of several small businesses made my work much easier, they also made me more impatient. I went from being grateful for how quickly new software could do the bookkeeping to snarling at the machine for being so slow. While I knew that my desktop Apple was many times more powerful than the first UNIVAC, which had filled a huge room in the 1950s, I failed to be grateful for the inventiveness and skill that had made it possible. Instead, I sighed each time I had to wait while the machine checked a record, made a computation, or saved to disk the work I had done.

One day, when I timed one such annoying delay and found that it constituted all of ten seconds, I felt as if I had been slapped in the face and warned: *Pay attention—watch yourself.* And when I did, I saw an idiot groaning with impatience over a tiny increment of time. Technology had made a fool of me, for a few seconds of "waiting" in computer time is no longer than seconds spent "waiting" on a magnificent, rocky beach for the sun to rise over a pearl-tinted ocean; it is only my perception that makes them seem different. And how I perceive such things is a matter of spiritual discipline.

Our perception of time is subject to technological revision, and increased speed has generally translated into a subtle diminishment of our capacity to appreciate our immediate surroundings. In his 1849 essay "The English Mail-Coach," Thomas De Quincey noted that while the new, high-speed coaches of his day offered much faster travel than had been thought possible a few years before, they also distanced passengers from the countryside. The simple pleasures available to the stroller or the wanderer on horseback—the scent of wild roses, a glimpse of a fox with her kits, an exchange of greetings with other travelers or with people resting from their labors in a field of sweet-smelling, new-mown hay—had been traded for increased efficiency. In our own time Wendell Berry has written eloquently of pulling off the high-speed world of an American interstate highway into an Appalachian campground, and needing more than an hour to slow down and adjust to the rhythms of his own body and the world close at hand.

Waiting seems at odds with progress, and we seldom ask whether it might have a purpose in and of itself. Etymology helps us here, for when we look up the word *wait* we are instructed to see *vigor*. Waiting, then, is not passive but a vigilant and watchful activity designed to keep us aware of what is really going on. Isaiah evokes this radical waiting as a source of vitality: "Those who wait for the Lord shall renew their strength, / they shall mount up with wings like eagles" (Isaiah 40:31). Such waiting is meant to engender a lively hope rooted in the physical as well as the psyche. It is an action, the "hop" contained within the word. To hope is to make a leap, to jump from where you are to someplace better. If you can imagine it, and dare to take that leap, you can go there—no matter how hopeless your situation may appear.

Hope may seem a flimsy thing in the face of acedia's cold assurance that nothing matters and that waiting is unmitigated hell. In midlife, waiting can seem a barren thing indeed. What are we waiting for, except the increasing disability and inevitable indignities of old age? But hope has an astonishing resilience and strength. Its very persistence in our hearts indicates that it is not a tonic for wishful thinkers but the ground on which realists stand. For thousands of years the psalmist and the prophets have been a source of strength for people facing plague, warfare, massacre, imprisonment, execution, and exile. This is the sort of hope that matters, for it can conquer not just acedia and despair, but death itself.

Christians have a powerful model for waiting in the face of certain death. On the night before his crucifixion, as Jesus prays in the garden of Gethsemane, he feels abandoned by his friends, and by a God who remains silent, seemingly unmoved by his suffering. It is a situation many of us know all too well. We may not face imminent death, but we are haunted by betrayal and loneliness, and know the pain of the wee hours, when the dark of night matches the state of our souls. In "The Garden of Olives," a poem reflecting on the Gospel story, Rainer Maria Rilke comments on the normality of this experience: "The night that came was no uncommon night; / hundreds like it go by. / Then dogs sleep, and then stones lie. / Alas, a sad night, alas any night / that waits till it be morning once again."

Both mental and physical pain are often worse at night, and sometimes it is the waiting for dawn that is worst of all. The theologian Dorothee Soelle, in her book *Suffering*, quotes the letter of a young Danish sailor who knew that he would soon be put to death by the Gestapo. He had already been tortured, and this led him to identify with the agonies of Jesus on the cross. But it was Gethsemane that drew him into "a new understanding of the figure of Jesus. The time of waiting, that is the ordeal. I will warrant that having a few nails driven through one's hands . . . is something purely mechanical. . . . But the waiting in the garden—that hour drips red with blood."

We do not know what will happen. Disasters will strike, and great blessings will come. Our difficult and glorious task is to live through it all. Paying attention is essential, as is remembering that, as Soelle writes, "the experience that Jesus had in Gethsemane goes beyond . . . destruction. It is the experience of assent." In that gruesome and interminable night, waiting revealed itself as a true ally, a bulwark against fear. And Jesus became the most radically free and dangerous man of all, the one who embodies hope in the face of death and is afraid of nothing.

XII. *Day by Day*

Our Dying Life

Consider a scene from my marriage: A man sipping a drink in a restaurant coughs, stops breathing, and begins to turn blue. In that instant, everything changes. Strangers drop what they are doing. One phones 911, another places him on his side to help him breathe again. When he opens his eyes and responds, however feebly, to a question, everyone cheers. It is as if time had been suspended, waiting for this moment. When the EMTs arrive, the rescuers drift back to their lunches. Having been shocked by the real—forcibly reminded that life is both precious and precarious, a tenuous matter of heartbeat and breath—one will order a stiff drink, another will phone her husband to tell him that she loves him. A man will go back to his office and stare at the family photographs on his desk until tears well up. Eventually he will turn to the blinking cursor on his computer screen.

One of Saint Benedict's "tools for good works" is to "day by day remind yourself that you are going to die" (Rule 4:47). This may seem a morbid preoccupation, but it will not remain so if we allow the thought of our own mortality to engender a greater compassion for other mortal beings. Yet even as we grow more keenly aware of the fragility of our existence and begin to believe that each moment of what Karl Rahner terms our "dying life" is a gift of unfathomable beauty, it is too much for us to bear. If we were constantly enraptured by gratitude and awe, we wouldn't get much done. It's easier and far more efficient to go about our daily tasks as though we were the sun around which the earth is spinning, and devote our attention not to divine mysteries but to whatever comes along: deadlines, e-mail, rush-hour traffic. And all of this is oddly comforting. While we complain about the stress, it reassures us to know we're busy—it means we're essential. We convince ourselves that we are far too important to die, and this is how we live from one day to the next. But for many of the thirty years my husband and I were together, we could not indulge that particular delusion, because we were so often up against life-threatening illness. We had been through so much by the time David was diagnosed with lung cancer that he startled his oncologist by saying, "You know, for us, this is just one more thing."

Our past travails with illness and recuperation did act as a primer that helped us learn to live with the cancer, which meant learning to cope with whatever hardships the treatments would bring. Chemotherapy had made David skeletally gaunt and weak, and even though he eventually regained much of his weight, the damage was done. After a pulmonary blood clot had further sapped his strength, this man who for years had enjoyed walking many miles a day was confined to a wheelchair when we went out. Then he fractured a hip in a fall and became so afraid of falling again that he used a walker even to get around our apartment. Repeated infections in his lung made him ever more dependent on supplemental oxygen. On bad days it was an accomplishment for him to walk the few feet from his living room chair to the front door of the apartment and back. On good days we were able to go to family gatherings, movies, and dinners at favorite restaurants. On occasion we went to a brew pub at Honolulu harbor to watch the activity in the port. Once, a three-masted sailing ship, a training vessel for the Italian navy, was docked nearby, and David enjoyed conversing with the young cadets in his spotty but apparently adequate Italian.

When David was exhausted, or when Kona winds (from the south) made the air heavy with volcanic ash, he stayed indoors. He slept, read, or watched movies that I rented for him, delighting in the French films, newly available on DVD, that we had last viewed as college students in the 1960s. He sometimes worked on the poems he had written in the South Pacific when he'd had a writer's grant with a travel allowance. It was a great joy to him that he had made a pilgrimage to the grave in Western Samoa of Tusitala (storyteller), as Robert Louis Stevenson is known to Samoans, and that he had paged through Stevenson's manuscripts in the rare-book room of a library in New Zealand. When friends our age, just retired, would write of their world travels, we felt more sharply our confinement to a few rooms. Now and then a sense of loss would swell and wash over us like a rogue wave. But all in all, the last five years that David and I had together were a blessed time that I would not trade for anything. Anyone who has not endured this may find it hard to comprehend, but what looks like a hopeless and depressing situation from the outside can feel very different when you are living it.

David occasionally commented, without bitterness, that the medical treatments that were saving his life were also killing him. I once asked if he would rather not have known that he had the cancer until it was too late for medical intervention, or if he would rather be living with full knowledge of his condition. "It's better to know," he quickly replied. "Absolutely." I had to marvel that I, who had remained child-less out of fear that I was incapable of giving a child the care and at-tention it would need, was now a full-time caregiver. My prayer to know motherhood was being answered anew, and David and I con-tended with many role changes. He had always been the cook in our household, and now he directed me, step by step, as I prepared our meal. At times I was so exhausted I could barely stand, and if it had been up to me I would have gone to bed. But David needed to main-tain his weight, so I cooked as well as I could. A curious transition took place: as David withered physically, his depression diminished and mine increased. A water aerobics class helped keep me sane, yet my primary consolation lay in knowing that I could provide so much for David. That he was obviously living on borrowed time made us sad; still, we could enjoy the time we did have. Though I would not describe these years as happy, we often felt a deep contentment that we could not explain, but only accept in a grateful spirit.

As my husband's health declined, I became something of a warrior in his defense. I kept a bag packed with a computerized list of David's medications and other pertinent data that we would need if we had to rush to a hospital. I made the 911 calls giving the readings on our home oximeter, a device that registers the oxygen level in the blood—vital information for ambulance crews. During these crises David was usually in too much respiratory distress to speak, so I dealt with the firemen who were often first responders, as well as EMTs, ER doctors, and nurses. What was increasingly difficult after each such episode was to descend from crisis mode and lay down my arms. When I compared notes with other caregivers, we agreed that having to be on constant alert was our most debilitating challenge. During David's last five years, when he was hospitalized more than a dozen times, I learned more than I ever wanted to know about how hospitals function and how much all patients need someone to advocate for them. I would often take my work—an editing project, a book review—and set up shop in David's room, staying for most of the day. The nurses became used to me and gladly assigned me chores to do. The wards were usually short-staffed, and I could give David more personal service, as if we were at home. By default I became my family's hospital go-to person: my mother phoned me on the night when my father, who was then approaching the last stages of aplastic anemia, had to go to an emergency room.

When I thought about my writing at all, I had to ask myself why I had chosen to do a book about acedia when I was losing so much of what had shaped my life and given it meaning: the loving presences of my father and my husband, both good-humored and decent men. I had indeed taken on "the devil himself," and was being shown that in order to write about acedia, I had to experience it big-time. I had to witness the ebbing of my father's life as he became more helpless, quiet, and gentle, even as my husband was living more precariously. One of my sisters also became gravely ill, and required a lengthy surgery on her esophagus, three weeks in an ICU, and six of recovery in a nursing home. For a time I visited her on one floor of the hospital, then my husband on another.

While I was able to perform the basic duties required of me, I was often numb. It helped that David and I saw the same internist, who was fully aware of our situation. When the proverbial backbreaking straw came, and it seemed likely that we would lose our group medical insurance, both David and I recognized that I had reached the limits of my endurance. I consulted the doctor for help, and she characterized my condition as perpetual posttraumatic stress syndrome, precipitated not by one crisis but by a never-ending string of them. She offered me samples of an antidepressant, which I was glad to accept. The doctor advised me that the medication would require at least two weeks to take effect, but I felt that a weight had been lifted in having consulted her. A friend had told me that for her taking antidepressants had been like going from night into day. Though I did not undergo so dramatic a shift in mood, I thought the pills were worth a try. On most days I harbored no ambition but to let each day go, content with the Gospel truth "Sufficient unto the day is the evil thereof" (Matthew 6:34, KJV), and praying that I would wake with the strength to face the dawn. Well aware that many people in the world contend with far greater burdens, I also prayed for the ability to better accept the measure of suffering that was mine.

The Comedy of Grace

Throughout this distressing time I did have plenty of occasion to laugh at myself. Once, when I was sunk deep in lethargy, I received a copy of an article about my writing in which the author termed me "a docent of hope." How strange it was to be reminded that the books I had written over the past decade—*Dakota, The Cloister Walk, Amazing Grace,* and *The Virgin of Bennington*—were out there in the world, proclaiming good news while I sat stupefied, unable to write even a postcard. The disparity was grim, but funny: God's grace working despite my weakness, or maybe because of it. I was tempted to regard myself and my work as a fraud, which, as Dorothee Soelle notes, often happens when "that which gave life its meaning has become empty and void." One decides that it has all been "an error, an illusion that is shattered . . . a void. The paths that lead to this experience of nothingness are diverse, but the experience of annihilation that occurs . . . is the same."

Although I felt like a big nothing, I realized that the thoughtful letters I continued to receive from readers did mean something, and that my work could be considered fraudulent only if I bought into the myth of spiritual celebrity. By that I mean the notion that people who write books on spirituality do so because they've got it all figured out, and have somehow "succeeded" at the spiritual life. Jesus reminds us, however, that it is not proficiency that heals us, but faith, and faith does not traffic with success or failure. It does know comedy: how else to explain the fact that my most "spiritual" activity during the last year of my husband's life was cleaning out his urinals and commodes? I even came to welcome this task, because it signified that part of my husband's battered body was still functioning normally. On waking each morning I loved to hear the sound of David's breathing, as it held the promise of another day with him. I already had enjoyed far more time with him than I had any right to expect. If praying the psalms had become impossible, I could thankfully rest in this moment before getting to work and making the prayer of the commode.

The comedy of grace is that it so often comes to us as loss, sorrow, and foul-smelling waste; if it came as gain, gladness, and sweetly scented flowers, we would not be grateful. We would, as we are wont to do, take personal credit for the unwarranted gifts of God. It is easy to be attracted to the idea of grace—which one dictionary defines as "divine love and protection bestowed freely on people"—but much harder to recognize this grace when it comes as pain and unwelcome change. In the depths of our confusion and anger, we ask: "How can *this* be God's love? Where is God in this disaster?" For grace to be grace, it must give us things we didn't know we needed and take us to places where we didn't want to go. As we stumble through the crazily altered landscape of our lives, we find that God is enjoying our attention as never before. And maybe that's the point. It is a divine comedy.

"The grace of aridity," a phrase in Graham Greene's tragicomic novel of acedia, *A Burnt-Out Case,* articulates for me this all-too-human situation. Greene's story is of a renowned architect whose worldly success—in his profession and in his personal life, as a womanizer—has left him cold. He can feel nothing except boredom and disgust with himself and with others. Even laughter has become incomprehensible to him, as offensive as a bad odor. As the novel begins, the man is traveling to a remote African leper colony run by a religious order. He seeks "an empty place, a place where no new building or woman would remind me that there was a time when I was alive, with a vocation and a capacity to love—if it was love." The colony's physician suspects that the man is "a burnt-out case," like a leper in whom the disease has run its course. He may be cured, and no longer contagious, but his mutilations—in this case, wounds of the soul—will prevent him from feeling at home again in society. Like the other burnt-out cases, this accomplished and cosmopolitan man will be content to do odd jobs at the clinic if it means that he doesn't have to return to the demands of living in the outside world.

The architect, wishing there to be no mistake about this, insists that he has lost any capacity for religious faith. But this only makes the priests and brothers at the mission admire his humility. To them he seems a great man, whose decision to help them build a hospital in such a lowly place must be divinely inspired. The more the man denies any spiritual motives for himself, the more the others see God at work in him. In one bitingly comic scene—comic because two people are talking at cross-purposes, yet both speak truly—a priest says to him, "Don't you see that perhaps you've been given the grace of aridity? Perhaps even now you are walking in the footsteps of St. John of the Cross." The man replies that the ability to pray has deserted him, but the priest (who is half burnt-out himself, and terribly lonely) replies that he senses in him a deep "interior prayer, the prayer of silence." As this anticonversation ends, each man retreats into his isolation. When the priest asks, "You really do understand, don't you?" the architect responds with "an expression of tired despair."

Acedia contains within itself so many concepts: weariness, despair, ennui, boredom, restlessness, impasse, futility. Spiritual dryness is the state explored by the sixteenth-century Carmelite John of the Cross, a patron saint of poets, in his long poem *Dark Night of the Soul*. His characterization of the signs of this condition is easily recognized by anyone who has ever felt stymied, whether in writing, art, prayer, marriage, or parenting. At the first sign of difficulty or obstruction you try to think of ways to move past it, but at every turn you defeat yourself, shooting each fresh idea down as unlikely to work. How foolish of you to have ever believed in that person, that project, that God. You tell yourself that whatever may have worked in the past won't help now, and you grow cynical in your despair. At the second stage, you are severely tempted to abandon whatever once gave your life joy and meaning. This is a time of great spiritual aridity, when desire itself seems dead, and forsaking hope seems the only adult thing to do.

But John detected a third sign, and it is tricky. Evidently, desire for the good does not die easily in us, and upon discovering that we are unable to flee our dilemma we grow anxious and obsessed. "The most confusing and damnable part of the dark night," notes the Carmelite Constance Fitzgerald, "is the suspicion and fear that much of the darkness is of one's own making." Adding this load of guilt to the burden we are carrying, we further undermine our sense of purpose. There seems no way out, no access to the inner fortitude we would need to stay the course. Fitzgerald reminds us, however, that we can trust in the assurance of "the psychologists and the theologians, the poets and the Mystics" who over many epochs and in diverse cultures have insisted that "impasse can be the condition for creative growth and transformation if the experience of impasse is fully appropriated." In other words, the dark night must be entered and endured. There are no shortcuts, only the passage through.

We can, of course, turn to spiritual mentors—friends, a spouse, a trusted physician or pastor—for counsel. We can ask for psychotropic drugs that might ease our passage through the roughest parts of the journey, and clear our vision enough so that we are able to see our way past obstacles and fears. We can learn to believe in ourselves again and trust in the world. We can look for messengers who will point us toward the good news we have been unable to find on our own. On one occasion when I was both physically and spiritually exhausted, feeling at my wit's end, I took a walk and noticed a bumblebee entering a hollyhock flower. It surprised, touched, and cheered me in such a way that I was compelled to write a poem about it, "Body and Blood," in which I compare the bee at its labors, its whole body quivering with effort, to an infant's mouth at the breast. If a bee could find sustenance in a patch of weedy roadside hollyhocks, perhaps I could as well. If, as the gospel hymn reminds me, "His eye is on the sparrow," it is also on the bee.

I find that John's "signs" or stages of impasse are likely to present themselves whenever I am on the verge of making a new commitment. As I head into the unknown, self-doubts emerge, along with the temptation to settle for less than I had believed possible. If things go wrong, I at first attempt to place the blame anywhere but on myself. Finally I am forced to admit that the new venture will come to fruition only if, as Fitzgerald says, I can "make the passage from loving [and] serving . . . because of the pleasure and joy it gives . . . to loving and serving regardless of the cost." This requires great resolve in the face of a crushing acedia; but having witnessed how both my marriage and I were transformed as I more fully embraced what caregiving required of me, I feel that I have learned a little about what it can mean to see this process through. I also know that I am likely to come up short in the future. Commitment always costs, and there is a particular burden in loving another person, if for no other reason than the fact that this beloved will one day die. This is the true strength of a woman willing to give birth, despite the odds. This is the love demanded of any husband, wife, or parent. It is the freely chosen love Virgil spoke of to Dante, and the love that Dante came to realize moves the moon and the stars.

Elvis, Augustine, and the Nonnegotiables

This vast and beautiful love is also practical, and I serve it best not by keeping my head in the clouds but by remembering that my feet are on the ground. My Benedictine friends, who understand that genuine asceticism consists of learning to live with and love other people as they are, have taught me the value of what my friend Sister Judy calls the "nonnegotiables" of stability, community, and prayer. For many years I found my community in marriage, and my husband and I had stability of place in western South Dakota. David served two terms on the Lemmon town council, and I worked for many years at the small public library. I gardened, David cooked. We worked odd jobs; we wrote. When my first book was a national success, not much changed for us at home. In a small town, or a monastery, everyone is a known quantity, equally famous or infamous as the case may be. David and I were the only people in town who subscribed to the Sunday New York Times, so we were the only ones who knew that my books were on the bestseller list, and we did not mind that, had they known, this fact would have been far less important to our neighbors than the price of spring wheat or cattle.

David and I still enjoyed visiting cities, and seeing friends and family in Boston, Chicago, New York, and San Francisco. But we had come to appreciate small-town life, and it was a real blow when David became too ill to travel back and forth between Honolulu and our beloved prairie lands. Hawai'i was not a bad place to be stranded, as my immediate family was there. Yet he and I were accustomed to quiet, and the stillness of true dark at night, and we uneasily readapted to urban life. Honolulu is an exceptionally lovely city, but it is also con-

gested and noisy. We would have sought out a more serene rural area
had David not required good access to medical facilities. Our displacement had been sudden—we left home in the middle of the night for
an emergency room many miles away—and it came to seem endless:
two months of David's recuperation in Bismarck, North Dakota, and
several more in a short-term winter rental in Honolulu, when we still
could hope that we might go home for the summer. Soon, though, it
was clear that we would need a more permanent place. We got a welcome break, hitting the Honolulu real estate market at a twelve-year
low, yet even that was disorienting, if only in a liturgical sense. I spent
most of Holy Week one year with a companionable Jewish real estate
agent, looking for a condominium. I signed for one, naturally enough,
on Good Friday. David and I couldn't move in right away, and we spent
the next few months living in a four-hundred-odd-square-foot hotel
room with a microwave, mini-refrigerator, and glorious view. Just
below us was the Ala Moana Beach Park, and we could see past downtown and the airport, out to the Wai'anae range west of the city. We
watched airplanes take off and land, and ships coming and going in the
port or at Pearl Harbor. Every Friday evening we enjoyed the colorful
sailboats that left a nearby yacht harbor for a *pau hana* (after-work)
cruise, making a large circle in the water. Courtesy of a friend in the
hotel's management, we had this room for a nominal fee.

David continued to have pulmonary crises with all of the attendant
drama: ambulances, ER, ICU. But most of the time, for up to eighteen
hours a day, he slept, recovering from the blood clot in his lung. In the
morning I worked on *The Virgin of Bennington,* and in the afternoon
I shopped for household furnishings. By a quirk of fate—in New York
we had sublet, and in South Dakota we had moved into a furnished

home—I found myself in my early fifties having to furnish a place fully for the first time in my life. We needed a bed and mattress, cookware, towels, clothes hangers, drapes, a dining room table, and the dishes to put on it. I didn't enjoy all the shopping, but it had to be done. I clipped discount coupons from the Honolulu papers and became a regular in the kitchen, bath, and furniture sections of the department stores. David happily occupied himself, and helped me a great deal, by making scale drawings of furniture on graph paper so that I would avoid buying anything too large for our new place.

I tried to keep in mind that I was working to make a pleasant space for David to enjoy in what we both knew would be the last years of his life. Although this was an uncommonly stressful time, we could rely on the stability of our marriage. But other fundaments of my life were shaken. Once I had finished *The Virgin of Bennington,* I found myself unable to write or pray. I tried to meditate on Scripture, but foundered in my attempts to make it a daily practice. I was not yet part of a faith community in Honolulu; I had convinced myself that this could wait until we had settled into our apartment. With my writing and my spiritual life diminished, I was stunned when friends sent me copies of an article by an otherwise reasonable theologian, Ronald Rolheiser, who had called me "an Augustine for our time." This seemed more than faintly ridiculous: Augustine was highly educated, I am not; he was a systematic theologian, and I am reluctant to put the two words together in a sentence. If we both have confessed our sins publicly, I can only hope I have treated the men in my life better than Augustine treated the women in his. Around the same time that the Rolheiser article appeared, a journalist wrote that I had "introduced many American Protestants to Catholic monastic prayer the way Elvis Presley introduced white Americans to black rhythm and blues." Well, take that to your cell and smoke it: Augustine *and* Elvis! I suppose this means that I can now die happy, having done it all.

While I was surprised that my literary reputation had a vitality all its own, it was heartening to be reminded that my presence was still required for life's nonnegotiables. And despite the dislocations, weariness, anxieties, and fears of that time, I never felt abandoned. When a friend asked whether I had lost my faith, I replied, "Of course not." I believed in the reality of God's providence and love, even when I did not sense its presence in my own life. And I could appreciate as never before the gift of Christian community: If God did not seem to be there for me, it was enough to know that God was active in the lives of others. If I could not pray, I knew that the Benedictines were praying. Throughout the world, in whatever time zone, all day long, every day, they were expressing and honoring the utter stability of God's love.

XIII. *And to the End Arriving*

A Church That No Longer Exists

My husband used to describe himself as "a member of a church that no longer exists." Having been raised a Roman Catholic in the pre–Vatican II era, he was disoriented by wedding or funeral services in the contemporary Church. He heard the Mass as a not particularly inspired translation from the Latin, and was indignant that a gender bias had sometimes been imposed in English where none existed in the original. He was glad to see altar girls alongside altar boys, but it annoyed him that many of the kids could not recite the Nicene Creed from memory. He'd mutter, darkly, "When I was an altar boy, we had to know it in Latin." The schmaltzy hymn tunes, some lifted from Broadway musicals, made him laugh. At times he would remark, "My mother would not recognize this place as a Catholic church."

David's relationship with the Church was never less than a complex blend of love and loathing, yet he remained grateful to the Jesuits for his education. When he attended Regis High School in Manhattan, four years of Greek and Latin were required, as well as two of a modern language. David often expressed affection for his philosophy, literature, and mathematics teachers, and was grateful that an eminent classics scholar had agreed, after retiring from teaching graduate students, to take on a bunch of teenage boys. Both the school and New York City gave David a wealth of formative opportunities. With a classmate who went on to become an art historian, David frequented the Metropolitan Museum of Art; with other students he attended doublebilled films in the aging movie palaces around Times Square. A Regis teacher with a brother in the theater business often gave students tickets to Broadway shows. Because he was free to explore so wide a cultural range, David's tastes were eclectic: he would attend a performance of Bach's B-Minor Mass at an Upper East Side church, but also go to the Brooklyn Paramount to see Screamin' Jay Hawkins emerge from a coffin to sing "You Put a Spell on Me." A regular at the 92nd Street YMHA, he heard readings by W. H. Auden, T. S. Eliot, and Marianne Moore. For his fourteenth birthday, David asked his parents for tickets to a Nina Simone concert.

The Church had always been an essential part of his family's life. His father had been with the Jesuits for nearly ten years, leaving just before he would have made his final vows, and many of his friends were Jesuits. When David was a boy, he cooked many meals for these "black robes"; on one occasion Bishop Fulton Sheen, whose televised homilies had made him a national celebrity, was among the guests. But when David was a teenager, the Christian religion lost its meaning for him. He could still get A's in theology classes, because he knew the material, yet he no longer took it seriously. Though he would joke about this— and about the time an elderly priest fell asleep when David was making a heartfelt confession—his pain was real and enduring. He used to say that the Jesuits at Regis seemed well aware that when it came to religious faith they would win some and lose some. While several of his classmates became priests, David counted himself among the lost. He told me of once waking on the living room sofa at a classmate's house, after a night of drinking and arguing philosophy, to see the classmate's little sister bound down the stairs, dressed for church. "Are you going to a later Mass?" she inquired brightly. David could respond only with a bleary "Much, much later."

By the time I met him, David had not been to confession in many years, but he often said that this was the one sacrament he really missed. His was a lonely faith that is shared, I suspect, by many former Catholics. Despite his disavowals, David seemed very Catholic to me, and while I never urged him to attend Mass, as it usually depressed him, I did sometimes remind him that while he had rejected the Church, God had not rejected him. God had many ways of finding him through the beauty of the things he loved: nature, poetry, music, and higher mathematics. David appreciated my certainty, and the faith of others could cheer him. He proudly repeated to friends what an emergency room nurse told him after she and a physician had labored to stabilize him when he was in severe respiratory distress. This middle-aged, red-haired woman with a breezy, maternal air had said, "Take care, honey, God isn't done with you yet."

We seldom spoke of it in these terms, but in David's last years I observed the positive attributes of his Catholic upbringing coming to the fore. I marveled at the grace with which he incorporated his increasing frailty, so that laughter, joy, and hope were always a part of his life. And I credit David's Catholic faith for his ability to live fully in diminished circumstances, accepting with grace what Dorothee Soelle terms "unavoidable suffering." For the last five years of his life, that included severe pain from a broken shoulder. The original injury from a fall years before had alerted doctors to David's osteoporosis; a man in his forties, they told us, should not have had such a bad break. David quipped that this condition might be a punishment for his having employed an elderly woman, his beloved Ariana, as his primary muse. The break had been repaired surgically without a pin, and although David had only a limited range of motion in that arm, it did not become a problem until years later, when the surgeon removing his cancerous lung had to raise his arm in such a way that the shoulder broke again. There was no fixing it after that; he had to live with the pain, and remind people not to grab him by the left arm. Of the six oxycodone pills per day he was prescribed, David generally took only two or three; two to help him sleep at night, and one during the day if the pain was worse than usual. David never called his many afflictions his share of the sufferings of Christ. But ultimately that is what it was for him, and this gave him strength.

Some of the saints of David's childhood regained significance for him, particularly Thérèse of Lisieux. He had been impressed that at the Easter before her death, her radiantly confident faith had turned barren: "[God] permitted my soul to be swamped by the thickest darkness," Thérèse wrote, "so that the thought of heaven which had been so sweet to me became nothing but a subject of bitterness and torment." David greatly admired her determination to regard this experience as a grace, a gift from God that enabled her to identify more fully with unbelievers; he felt that this made her his saint. Upon discovering a volume of the dramas she had written to be performed in her convent, he decided to translate them into English. He approached the Carmelites for permission, and found out that they were looking for such a translator; they hired him on the spot. David loved the little plays, and he made a valiant effort with them, visiting a Carmelite convent in North Dakota and lugging the manuscript with him—twice— to the South Pacific. But he had begun so much in his life that had turned bad—college, graduate school, his first marriage—that he tended to expect failure, even sought it out. As with so many of his projects, he procrastinated terribly. The Carmelites were desperate to meet a publishing deadline, and he somehow managed to destroy the computer files on which he had worked for years. Though he was able to submit several dramas in hard copy, he apologized, returned the small advance he'd received, and felt extremely guilty, as if he had let down not just the Carmelites but the saint herself. "You know," I told him, "that she has already forgiven you." David burst into tears and said, "Yes. I know." *That* is a Catholic.

David died at age fifty-seven, after the sudden onset of an infection that quickly turned into pneumonia. His pulmonologist, like all of his physicians in the last years of his life, had been astounded at David's recuperative powers. Here was a man with one lung who had survived a large pulmonary edema, repeated episodes of bronchitis and pneumonia, including aspiration pneumonia, and surgery for a broken hip. After the hip replacement, David had required nearly a year of intensive physical therapy; his surgeon said, "You're not just one of my success stories, you're a walking miracle." But the pulmonologist warned us that with David's weakened lung he would one day get an infection he would not be able to shake. The doctor promised that when that happened he would do everything possible to make David comfortable, and went on to say, "Given your condition, if your heart ever stops, you don't want us to start it again." "Good to know," David replied quietly, and it was. It allowed us to feel that when the time came we would know what to do. And it turned out to be exactly what I needed when that moment did arrive, to help my husband have a peaceful death.

David counted among his favorite prayers the final utterance of compline (from the Latin for "complete"), the prayer service that ends the day: "May the Lord grant us a peaceful night, and a perfect end." Where he was concerned, I understood that prayer as a duty to be fulfilled, to the best of my ability, and with God's help. And it was not at all what we expected. In the months before his death David had been doing well, and we were heartened when his oncologist said that as he had passed the five-year mark with no recurrence of the cancer, it was highly unlikely that it would return. On a routine visit to his internist David responded to the usual question—"How are you feeling?"—by saying that, all things considered, he felt good. We attended a Labor Day picnic with my family, and in early October, a wine-and-Champagne-tasting dinner at a hotel restaurant. David was pleased that he had been able to enjoy the evening without resorting to the oxygen tank I had brought along in a canvas bag.

The end began with a cough in the wee hours of a Tuesday morning in October. I had gone to bed while David stayed up to watch the news and some late-night television. He was addicted to the inspired silliness of Conan O'Brien. When he came to bed, at around two a.m., his cough worried me; I asked if he was all right. "I'm not sure," he replied, which was not his usual response. Alert to a potential crisis, I got out the oximeter and found that his oxygen level was much too low. I upped his intake, but that didn't help. "We're going in," I said, and David didn't argue. I called 911, and the ambulance arrived within minutes. All of this was routine for us—one EMT remembered us from an earlier call—but David was uneasy. As he was being placed in the ambulance, he grabbed my hand and said, "I'm afraid."

The physician on duty thought at first that he could treat David and send him home in an hour or two. And initially David responded well to the practiced ministrations of the medical staff. But then he became delirious from having too much carbon dioxide in his system that he could not expel. That had never happened to him. I was holding his hand and looking into his eyes when a shadow passed over his face, and I thought, "This is death." David nearly did die at that moment, according to a nurse who was present. She had been shocked, she later told me, because his descent into a critical state had been so rapid.

When suctioning David's lung did not produce the desired result, the doctor wanted to put him on a ventilator that would breathe for him until the crisis passed. This also was new: David had never needed such a drastic measure. I agreed to it because I did not want him to have to labor so hard just to breathe. I had seen him recover from apparently impossible things before. Still, the decision troubled me, because he had not wanted to be kept alive on a machine if there was no hope. The doctors assured me that once he was able to breathe again on his own they would remove the device.

It took many hours to get David out of the ER; his doctor insisted that he be placed in an intensive care unit rather than a regular room. David had no recollection of the move but was conscious again late on Tuesday night, and for all his exhaustion he was in a good mood. I spent the night in his room, sleeping on a windowsill that I promised his nurses I would vacate by six a.m., when the supervisor would make her rounds. In the morning David rallied, amazing his doctor. The medical news was sobering; he still couldn't breathe on his own, and his heart was weakening, but he seemed unaffected. He wrote me notes: he wanted me to thank the nurses for their help, and he wanted the morning newspaper.

The pulmonologist, a man with a blessedly calming presence, said that things could go either way. "If you come through this," he told David, "you will face a long recovery." That was nothing new to us, but the medical situation was serious enough that I phoned David's brother and sister; even if he could not talk to them, he could hear their voices. I also told my family to come if they wanted to see him. "Tonight and tomorrow," the doctor said, "we'll see if he's going to pull through." Later in the day another physician making rounds was upset to find David on the ventilator, for we had spoken to her previously about his desire not to be kept alive artificially. But when asked whether he wanted the machine turned off, David shook his head and scrawled a note: "Not yet." A group of student doctors arrived with their professor, and as David slept they asked me a slew of questions about David's medical history that I was glad to answer. I can only hope that I will never be so interesting to medical students.

David slept for most of that day and well into Thursday, but he squeezed my hand when I spoke to him. I left for supper and a nap, and when I returned later that night, I found that he had a new nurse, a pleasant Irishwoman named Maureen. I told him that, and also that she had suggested I remove his wedding ring because his hand was swelling. I promised to keep it safe for him and told him I loved him. He made no response, which troubled me. Early the next morning when I entered his room, I asked the day nurse how David was doing. "He's been on a downward trend for the last twelve hours," the nurse replied. My heart sinking, I said, "I guess that's all I need to know."

David's body was shutting down, and only a heart medication and the ventilator were keeping him alive.

I asked the nurse what would happen if we removed the ventilator now, and he said that David would gasp for breath for anywhere from two to twenty-four hours. My decision in the emergency room had not been such a bad one, after all. I consulted with David's pulmonologist, who promised to come soon. He authorized the nurse to stop administering anything but pain medication, which allowed David to die on a Friday morning, a good Catholic boy to the last. Before he died I had more than an hour alone with him, except for a nurse who came in occasionally to read the monitors registering his vital signs. I spoke to David and recited some poetry. He responded only once, when I said the Kyrie Eleison. Lord, have mercy, indeed. I could not recall the Latin for the requiem hymn "In Paradisum," which David had told me he loved, but hoped that the English would do: "May the angels lead you into Paradise." David muttered something incomprehensible, and I felt a faint pressure on my hand.

I watched the monitors as his heart rate slowly declined. The nurses had told me it could take an hour or more for him to die, and asked whether I wanted anyone with me, whether I would be all right. I told them that I needed this time with my husband. I hadn't requested a chaplain, but one appeared at the door and asked if he could pray with us. I couldn't refuse, and was grateful that the man had a gift for spontaneous prayer. He asked whether there was a Scripture passage I'd like him to read, and I said Psalm 27. But, casting a suspicious eye on the Bible in his hands, I asked, "What translation is that?" It was the New International Version. "That's not acceptable," I told him, and explained that my husband was a poet and needed more beautiful language. As I did not want to let go of my husband's hand I asked him to dig out the Book of Common Prayer from my purse. It had been a gift from David, many years before. Hospital chaplains must receive many odd requests, but the man proved reluctant to root around in a woman's handbag. This is becoming quite a spectacle, I told David, but I am only trying to find you a decent translation. I am certain that he heard me. I would not let go of his hand, but I did take my eyes off him for a moment as I attempted a one-handed retrieval of the book from the depths of my bag. While I was thus occupied, the nurse told us, "His heart has stopped." I could only sigh and say that David was always doing this to me in airports, too. The minute my back was turned, he'd be off somewhere, and I'd have to go look for him. "See," the nurse replied, "he was being himself, right up to the end."

I asked the chaplain to read the psalm, and after a brief but moving prayer of blessing on us and our marriage, he and the nurse departed. I stayed with David to honor the deep silence in the room and say a few final loving words. When I could let his hand go, I went to the nurses and told them that I wanted to help with the body. I find this an admirable Benedictine practice: in at least one community I know, it is the job of the prioress to wash and dress the corpse of a sister. The nurses hesitated, but by now they knew that I was not likely to become hysterical. The body bag they brought was white—the color of mourning in Japan, I thought idly—as I helped them wipe David's body, now heavy with edema, and move it into the bag. The sound of the zipper was horrid, final.

I wanted to stay with David for as long as I could, so I asked to accompany him to the morgue. A nurse warned me that this was a grim process; I said I didn't mind. I did gasp at the table brought by the attendant, which is cleverly designed to disguise the fact that there is a human body inside, perhaps to avoid frightening other patients and their families. "Now, that is cold," I said, as my husband's corpse disappeared inside the contraption. The nurse nodded. It was strange to pass down the hallway hearing talk and laughter, as if this were a normal day. At the morgue door I could only sigh, thank the orderly, and depart. I went to find my mother and sister, who had arrived at the hospital shortly after David had died.

Doing Nothing, Gallantly

One week after my husband's death, to the day and the hour, I accompanied my other sister to a hospital, where she was to begin post-surgical treatment for breast cancer. She is officially designated as "developmentally disabled" and refers to herself as "special." She had wanted my company, she explained, because I knew all about this hospital stuff. It was Halloween, and the costumed nurses gave the ward a festive air. I was impressed that even without the holiday decor the place had clearly been designed to lift the spirits. Each treatment chair faced a window overlooking an expansive view, allowing patients to feel as if they were floating, not under a fluorescent glare but out of doors, in natural light. The two chemotherapy wards I had been in with David and my father had been grim by comparison, with curtained cubicles crowded like afterthoughts into windowless rooms; the patients probably felt like afterthoughts as well.

My sister's prognosis was excellent, and as this hospital primarily serves women and children, it is a place more concerned with birth than with death. The lobby and elevators are full of pregnant women, and young parents with infants and toddlers. On a stroll later that fall I discovered the pediatric oncology ward and witnessed a bald child happily pedaling a three-wheeler with a laughing aide in hot pursuit. I also found a little chapel nearby, which was decorated with a Christmas tree on which grieving parents had placed photographs and other mementos of the children they had lost. I returned often, finding comfort in a place where grief was so openly attested to and shared.

My sister has always been full of surprises, and she charmed the nurses and her oncologist with her positive attitude and good cheer. It was not feigned: she looked forward to her chemo sessions, as they got her out of the care home where she lives, and the staff showered her with attention. She enjoyed deliberating over her lunch order and receiving all the juice, soft drinks, and snacks that she wanted. Best of all was a small personal television set, on which she could watch reruns of *Leave It to Beaver, Gunsmoke,* and *Bonanza.* At home she shares a set with four other women. Her side effects were minimal, and she didn't even mind the hair loss. She got to don a striking wig and announce to anyone who would listen, "I'm her only blonde sister."

I was still numb with loss, but I was glad to help my sister navigate the medical territory. It took me out of the void I had been experiencing, and brought a sense of familiarity to a life that with David's death had become foreign. Of my three nonnegotiables, stability, community, and prayer, the first two had toppled, and the third was on an uncertain footing. I had lost both the place I had called home for a quarter-century and my identity as a married woman. The community of two that had constituted my marriage was no more, and I had no idea how I would inhabit that devastating word, *widow.* As for prayer, I was not surprised that acedia's mocking spirit was alive within me, or that when I most needed the consolation that prayer can bring, I was unable to pray. Even the insight of Saint Augustine and Thomas Merton that the very desire to pray can be our most meaningful prayer was of little comfort.

I was touched by the concern of the older widows at the Episcopal church I'd been attending, who gave me sensible advice: "Be good to yourself." "Don't make any major decisions for a while." When one elderly woman whose husband had died many years before told me, "You will never get over it," I realized that in no way did I want to "get over" a relationship that had been the center of my life for so many years. "But," she added, taking my arm, "it does get easier, over time." A man told me about his own mother, recently deceased, who had lingered with Parkinson's and dementia. As she neared death, he reminded her that she was loved by many people. "Of course people love me," she replied sharply, then softened as she slowly named her children and grandchildren, and her husband, who had been dead for nearly forty years. Love never ends.

But how terrible the absence of our beloved dead, and how beautiful their continued presence in memory. When I missed David most acutely, the pain washing over me in thunderous breaking waves, I would remind myself that I could not wish for him back, because that would mean his having to endure more suffering. All of that was over for him, the gasping for breath, the pain of that accursed cracked shoulder. I did not know what to hope for, but I knew that I needed to pray again. I set aside something from the Book of Common Prayer that had been a mainstay in the years of David's decline, the Prayer for the Sanctification of Illness. This decidedly old-fashioned supplication fortunately had survived the 1979 revision of the book, and I had prayed it often for David: "That the sense of his weakness may add strength to his faith and seriousness to his repentance; and . . . that he may live with you in everlasting life." David's response, when I read it aloud to him, was, "That's lovely."

Sanctification may appear to have little to do with illness, and as the Dominican Paul Philibert has written, "[Even] many Christians interpret their suffering and frustration as distractions from and impediments to" their life of faith. Yet Christianity teaches that the trials in our lives can be linked to Christ's suffering and "redemptive gift" if we intend that they should. As a poet I rejoice in discerning correspondences and connections between my everyday life and a deeper wisdom, but what Philibert calls "an intentional symbolic life" is not just for poets or priests. He reminds us that "what binds . . . together the random experience of day-to-day reality with the experience of faith is symbolic imagination." We are all endowed with such an imagination. It is part of what makes us human.

I did feel fragile and disconnected after David died. But I found a prayer for myself—also among those intended for the sick—that proved suitable for my mourning and my continuing struggle with acedia: "This is another day, O Lord. I know not what it will bring forth, but make me ready, Lord, for whatever it may be. If I am to stand up, help me to stand bravely. If I am to sit still, help me to sit quietly. If I am to lie low, help me to do it patiently. And if I am to do nothing, let me do it gallantly. Make these words more than words, and give me the Spirit of Jesus. Amen."

Doing nothing, gallantly. Awake, not asleep, and not trying to escape. If "Rumpelstiltskin" provides a useful metaphor for the naming of acedia, another folktale, "Sleeping Beauty," has an even deeper resonance for me. Acedia is like the bad fairy who is not invited to a royal christening, and in her indignation exacts a terrible revenge. The spell she casts out of spite—a deathlike sleep—falls on not only the princess but the king and queen as well, and all of their attendants, right down to the scullery maids. Vines and thickets grow up to hide the castle from view, and it is soon forgotten. There are stories about what once was there, about a beautiful young princess. Only a foolish young man would set out to find her, and his love alone can break the spell.

I picture acedia preening in fancy dress, then snarling at being excluded from the party. With what fierce determination she casts her shadow on the festive scene. And I picture myself as a young woman, all too willing to sleepwalk through my life instead of daring to live it fully. And then a foolish young man came along, and his quiet persistence changed everything.

Raphael, God's Medicine

More than twenty years ago, when I became a Benedictine oblate, I had to choose an oblate name. I selected Raphael, because he is the angel named in the Book of Tobit, a charming if cautionary tale of wedlock. It contains a bracingly comic domestic spat, the old man Tobit and his wife, Anna, going at it as one suspects they have for many years. There is also a young couple in the story who face a major obstacle in attempting to marry. The young woman has had seven bridegrooms, but each has died on the wedding night. Understandably, she is despondent, and she is ridiculed by her household staff. When Tobias, son of

Tobit, seeks to marry her, he is aided by the angel Raphael, who has been sent from heaven, disguised as a traveler. The pathos of the tale is mixed with a heady dose of the ludicrous: Raphael and Tobit concoct an exorcism by means of the heart, liver, and gall of a fish, and ancient Israel's version of a hibachi.

The abbey's director of oblates, Father Robert West, presided at the Mass where I made my oblation. He had set aside the lectionary for the day and instead preached on the passage from Tobit in which Raphael blesses Tobias before returning to heaven. "Do not be afraid," the angel says, which is what all angels say when they reveal themselves to humans. "Bless God forevermore," he adds. "Write down all these things that have happened to you." Well, I have tried. But there is more to this story: with God, there is always more.

A few weeks after my husband died, I looked up the date of his death, October 24, in a book about patron saints, *Saints Preserve Us!* The cover evokes the Dick-and-Jane readers of my childhood, depicting a cheerful boy and girl in 1950s attire playing with their dog while Dad, sporting a fedora, sits at the wheel of a two-toned sedan in the driveway of their home. Towering over this scene is a saint in white robes and a halo with a cheesy, Velveeta-like glow. I had bought the book for David in fun and once had nearly donated it to a church auction. In its pages I discovered that October 24 is traditionally the feast day of Raphael, patron of lovers, travelers, and pharmacists. I was still missing David terribly, caught in that bind of wanting his presence but not all the pain that it would mean for him. It was possible for me to imagine that when I had to let him go, Raphael was there to catch him. The thought will console me for the rest of my life.

David and I had chosen our wedding day, September 29, for purely practical reasons and were resigned to believing that the only notable thing about the date was that it marked the birthday of the cowboy actor and singer Gene Autry. We were later stunned to learn that September 29 is the feast of the archangels Michael, Gabriel, and Raphael. Flannery O'Connor once referred to Raphael as the angel of "happy meeting," and for many years David and I treasured the thought that this angel had brought about our chance meeting, two troubled souls who surely needed each other. From our first date, which had been arranged by a friend who was also a poet, we were never apart for more than a few weeks, and that suited us fine. But there were also many difficult times over the years of our marriage, when the belief that it had been "made in heaven" was about the only thing that kept me committed to it. Our relationship was nothing that David and I could have planned for, envisioned, or accomplished on our own. It was such a great gift that I could not refuse it even during the worst of times, when that seemed the only sensible thing to do. This final encounter with Raphael was pure blessing, and I choose to regard it as a promise of a "happy meeting" yet to come.

Raphael is the least known of the three archangels, at least by the standards of Western art. In many great paintings and sculptures, as well as a host of kitschy ones, Michael is a warrior doing battle with Lucifer. Gabriel is in every painting of the Annunciation, as the messenger announcing to Mary that she will bear the savior. Images of Raphael are harder to come by in the United States, unless you head to the Southwest. It is easy to recognize the angel when you enter a church: he's the winged fellow carrying a hobo sack and a dead fish, taking a stand against futility and the devil's wiles, ever ready to fight for the radical possibilities opened by hope, love, and the judicious use of hibachis.

David often grumpily disparaged the Christian faith, saying to me "Doesn't it bother you that none of it is true?" As an amateur mathematician he was fascinated with how very little can be known for certain, and came to find the proofs of mathematics more compelling than the surmises of religion. He took spiritual sustenance from the arcana of binary codes and from the idea of numbers so huge as to be unfathomable, including "inaccessible cardinals"—a term that can give Roman Catholics a turn. David once compared exploring the big numbers to climbing in an ice field, shivering with cold but standing in awe of the beauty, moving in small leaps or climbing ice walls, until unable to go any further. I replied that my impassable ice cliff had come to me in third grade, when I was faced with the multiplication tables.

Late one night as we were conversing about such matters at our kitchen table, it occurred to me that what David called "big numbers" and I called "angels" might well be the same thing: after following our different paths to get there, we might come around on the circle and meet in the place Keats glimpsed when he equated truth with beauty. David was delighted. I think he would love a simile that seems fitting for our marriage: it was like the differential equations the mathematician Bernhard Riemann insisted he had not invented; he had found them in the universe, where God had hidden them.

A few months after that late-night conversation, David handed me a new poem he had written. When I read it now, I realize that if he did have to "go away," I have to learn to live with that. But I can always find him present in these words:

THE HIGHER ARITHMETIC
by David J. Dwyer

In heaven, I do not know that there are angels,
but I know there are numbers there, and light.
(Arithmetic and heaven are both uncountably
full of light.) Inaccessible cardinals, there,
will lord it over mere infinities;
the naturals will dance among the reals. . . .

Apart from numbers, how little we know.

*There is no largest prime. The Halting Problem
is formally undecidable. Every subset
of a well-ordered set is well-ordered itself. And so on . . .*

Such things are true, even easy to prove.
Are there uncountably more, unknowably other
true things about the world?

I had to go away. A woman I love
(and this is true, too) put an icon
of an archangel into the glove-compartment
of my car. I haven't looked, but I know it is there,
as I know there is no largest prime.
                                        Raphael,
she said. *His numberless wings cloak all of us
poor travellers who do not know, but are not lost.
The angel,* she said, *of happy meeting, after all.*

XIV. *A Widow's Uneasy Afterword*

Heaven, Again

As my husband's heart was failing and he neared death, I felt a sudden and ferocious temptation to doubt. Echoing David's habitual question, I thought: What if none of this is true? What if there is no God, no Christ, no angels to sing him to his rest, no meeting again in heaven? The Christian spiritual tradition had prepared me for this moment, teaching that it is when you most need your faith that it is likely to be shaken to its foundations. I have been told that this is the reason why nearly every icon of the nativity includes Joseph in a lower corner, usually the left, in a posture of despair. Sometimes a hairy little man who represents the devil is there as well, but often it is Joseph alone, slouched, head in hands, graphically depicting the anxiety and despondency that might come to any man who is taking on a new identity as a father. But the image also reflects religious doubt, a demon, hairy or not, telling us that there is nothing holy or even meaningful about what we are experiencing. When the thought came to me at David's deathbed, I kept a firm grip on my beloved's hand and sent the thought packing.

I relish the contemplative poet Robert Lax's response to the question of whether growing old—he was then in his eighties—had led him to fear death. "When the time comes," he said, "we pick up our duds and return to where we came from. We're all brought into this life because heaven loves us, and back to that love we go." Were I asked to sum up my marriage, with all of its ups and downs, I would respond with a similar certitude: It was a gift from God. Beautifully, comically, and against the odds—David a classic depressive, me harboring an equally classic acedia—we were able to make it work. But while my store of memories helps me grieve, it cannot diminish the reality of my loss. My husband was a man who believed that kindness always matters, who had no enemies but himself. I could not make him want to live, but I could be his companion in making a life worth living. When he said in a dejected tone, as he sometimes did, that he wanted to be lost at sea, I was there to respond: "What makes you think you're not?" It was an honor to be with him as he dealt with addictions, a crippling guilt, and the many difficulties caused by his chronic procrastination. When I think of all that David did accomplish, contra his "well-defended neuroses" and his melancholic bent—two pilgrimages to the South Pacific; two volumes of verse as well as a host of unpublished poems; wide-ranging interests that led him to produce translations of French literature, articles on random access codes, and several well-made and sturdy bookshelves; many long-lasting friendships; and of course our marriage—I am filled with joy. David was an uncommonly grateful person, and if he felt himself unable to pray, he appreciated the prayers of others on his behalf. "I need all the help I can get," he would say, with a shrug and a smile. I don't think that he would mind if I used an epitaph for him that Coleridge wrote for himself, asking of any who might pass by his grave:

O lift one thought in prayer for S.T.C.;

That he who many a year with toil of breath

Found death in life, may here find life in death!

Mercy for praise—to be forgiven for fame

He asked, and hoped, through Christ. Do thou the same!

Let Me See Again

On the Sunday after my husband died, I went to church and heard a story from the Gospel of Mark, in which Jesus asks a blind man, "What do you want me to do for you?" The man replies, "Let me see again" (Mark 10:51). As these words penetrated my fog of grief, I had to admit that Jesus' question was now critical for me. But if I needed to reinhabit a life that was now barely recognizable as mine, I did not feel up to the task. There was that horrid chasm of a word, *widow*, with its connotations of emptiness, separation, and division. There was the dread weight and awful persistence of sunrise and sunset, and all the daily necessities that seemed so incongruous and painful now that David was gone. If Christ were to be a part of my healing, I could not see how.

I found it difficult to believe that Christ cares, or despite what the Gospels attest, that he prays for me even when I am unable to pray for myself. It hurt to hear the passages in which Jesus says such things as: "I have to go away; and it is for your good; and if I go, I will send you the Advocate, the Holy Spirit. I have many things to say to you, but you cannot bear them now" (John 16). "If not now, when?" I wanted to cry out. For me these words had become mixed with David's having to go away. I could not see past the pain, and the numbness of acedia appealed to me. Loss and death are worthless from a secular perspective, and my faith that they might have meaning was worn thin. I recalled the difficult period, many years earlier, when I had begun to reclaim my religious roots. My struggles had been so intense that even the pastors who were my friends and mentors wondered whether I should give it up; at the very least, they suggested, give it a rest for a while.

I had not regressed to that sorry state, but I desperately needed a metaphor, and found one in a book on prayer by Karl Rahner: "the rubbled-over heart." When one's life is dusty with ruin, it can seem reasonable to bury oneself in the wreckage rather than expose oneself to more suffering. Rahner reminded me that it would be all too easy for me to "slowly die to [myself] each day, without commotion and without rhetoric," so quietly and unwittingly that, ultimately, "no one will notice, not even [myself]." That would be acedia's victory, but one tool I can employ to defeat it is the Lord's Prayer, which Gregory of Nyssa recommends as a way to "remember that the life in which we ought to be interested is 'daily' life. We can, each of us, only call the present time our own. . . . Our Lord tells us to pray for today, and so he prevents us from tormenting ourselves about tomorrow."

This is not an easy prayer when I am tempted to give up on both today and tomorrow, dwelling in the shadows like a wounded animal in its den. Yet even if this is a necessary stage of grief, there is also a time to emerge and attempt to find a place in the new and alien landscape. The prayer of my heart, offered when I was too worn out to pray, offered silently and beneath any conscious level, was for the strength to hazard this transition. But the word *transition* cannot convey my struggle with the rigors of grief, a residual exhaustion from years of steadily increasing adversity, and the promptings of acedia to respond to all of this by not caring.

The grieving person undergoes a kind of death, and on many days my grief has readily attached itself to my propensity to acedia, making me feel as if I were barely living. Even as acedia tempted me to see life as flat and meaningless, I could recall the monastic teaching that temptation itself is a form of spiritual progress. And I could remind myself that God had not brought me this far only to abandon me. If I was haunted by the anguished question the Israelites asked at the shores of the Red Sea—"Was it because there were no graves in Egypt that you have taken us away to die in the wilderness?"—I also had the reply of Moses: "Do not be afraid, stand firm" (Exodus 14:11, 13). For me this "standing" meant appreciating my past even as I looked for ways, however small, that I might enjoy the present again.

Such enjoyment would need a good foundation, and I hoped to build it on the significant transformations I had undergone on my life's journey. What does it mean to have learned how to love, rejecting the fleeting pleasures of infatuation for the deeper satisfactions of commitment? Or to have apprenticed myself to the discipline of writing, so that I now crave the desert journey of revision as much as the initial burst of creativity and flow of words? Or to have undergone a religious conversion, replete with fervor and gladness in its early stages, and now marked by aridity and pain? If I find myself starved for the merest hint of spiritual ardor, I know I have arrived in a place where many others have been. The monks and mystics of my faith all teach that persevering in a spiritual discipline, especially when it seems futile, is the key to growth. The wisdom of such spiritual masters as Saint Ignatius Loyola is of use to me whether I suffer from grief, depression, or acedia. When "one is completely listless, tepid, and unhappy, and feels separated from our Creator and Lord," he writes in his *Spiritual*

Exercises, "one should never make a change." Ignatius recommends patience, and also urges the despondent person to a fresh perspective. "Desolation is meant to give us a true recognition and understanding," he states, "that we may perceive interiorly that we cannot by ourselves bring on . . . great devotion, intense love, tears, or any other spiritual consolation, but that all these are a gift and grace from God."

In my present state, while I have gained some perspective on who I have been, my challenge now is to ask: Who am I in that precious "today" that Gregory of Nyssa speaks of as the only time I can call my own? I can scarcely name what it is that I want anymore, let alone answer the Christ who asks, "What do you want me to do for you?" I, who have always been so goal-oriented, now resist thinking in such terms, and if practical matters loom large, I am content to set them aside. There is the house in South Dakota, where my mother's toys gather dust in the basement, and books, icons, and abandoned knitting projects clutter my study. My grandmother's trousseau lies folded in tissue paper in its cedar chest, and my husband's cookware sits on the kitchen shelves he built, as if he might walk in the door any minute and prepare a batch of his renowned tomato sauce. While this is a life that is no longer mine, my life in Honolulu feels haphazard and temporary. I am not sure where my home is, and that which has long been essential to my identity—prayer, poetry, love itself—seems dormant within me.

My adolescent bugaboo, a disdain for boring and seemingly fruitless practice, remains a hindrance when I am confronted with the task of prayer, which, like anything worth doing, requires effort if it is to become habitual. Anyone can pray—"If you are a theologian, you will pray truly," Evagrius wrote, "and if you pray truly, you will be a theologian"—but it is one thing to pray when you feel like it, and another to make it as much a part of you as breathing. Paul Philibert tells us that "we don't always have to *say* a prayer, we can *live out* a prayer"; this is how the "ceaseless prayer" extolled in the Christian tradition "comes to be achieved in [one's] life." Given my temperament, I was not surprised to find that in my grief, prayer seemed out of reach. Still, it was a painful discovery, and I am grateful for any reminder that in my displacement and distress I am on the right track. "The touchstone of God at work," writes the Carmelite Ruth Burrows, "is the ability to recognize that God is trying to get us to accept a state where we have no assurance within that all is well . . . where no clear path lies before us, where there is no way; a state of spiritual inadequacy experienced in its raw, humiliating bitterness." Only when we admit that we have "no way" do we have any hope of finding one. Out of what seems desolate a newly vigorous faith can arise, a certainty that is not subject to changes in moods or feelings, or the vicissitudes of life.

This corresponds to what I have learned as a writer about seeing "dry spells" through: it helps considerably if one has developed writerly habits. People often remark that they would write, or paint, or sculpt, if only they had the time. But this is pure fantasy: the artist does whatever is necessary to arrange her life so that she will have the time to make her art. Even as I fret over juggling responsibilities to my aging mother, my disabled sister, my friends, and my art, I have to admit that it is not obligation I fear, but my distressing eagerness to squander the precious time I do have in running from the emotional demands that writing will make of me. I may gripe about the inescapable chore of revision, of laboring over what I have written until I get it right. But in my current state, revision is less my problem than a reluctance to allow the flow of words to come in the first place. In my grief I dare not be as open as I once was, and my sadness increases as I am less able to see the world as I know it to be: ablaze with significance, potent with meaning. Yet I know that even if I am too exhausted to see them, the images, correspondences, connections, and metaphors that would free me are there, to be discovered, and to live as a poet means not to abandon my search for them. Such insights may come as gifts, but it is the prepared and fertile heart, not the one dulled by acedia, that is best able to receive them.

As with prayer and poetry, so with love; it has not ended for me because I have lost the love of my life. How chilly that casual phrase, as if the possibility of enjoying love, and life itself, were irretrievably gone. In my grief I have encountered the full blast of what Evelyn Waugh called the "malice of Sloth," which "lies not merely in the neglect of duty (though that can be a symptom of it) but in the refusal of joy." Knowing that my husband wanted me to enjoy the rest of my life without him does not make it any easier to do so. Thomas Merton describes acedia as the temptation to reject experience itself as "wearying and narrowing," and being a caregiver only reinforces one's capacity for limiting life to the pitifully small spaces of bedroom, bathroom, doctor's office, and hospital room. How cruel that it is death that has freed me from these confines, and acedia that now makes it difficult for me to emerge from this diminishment. In ways I could not have intimated when I first read his words, I share with Søren Kierkegaard the sense that "my soul has lost possibility. If I were to wish for something," he writes in *Either/Or*, "I would wish not for wealth or power but for the passion of possibility, for the eye, eternally young, eternally ardent, that sees possibility everywhere."

Medical evidence suggests that the death of a spouse is among the most severe traumas a person can undergo. Now, more than ever, I need to know both love and possibility as constant and even eternal presences within me, and in the world around me. One safeguard against the callousness of acedia is accountability: I try the best I can to be there for my family, friends, and church community, and try not to be too hard on myself when I fail. Above all, I need to recall, even if the culture has forgotten it, the spiritual wisdom that correctly opposes acedia not to laziness but to love. It is a matter of common sense that I keep a close watch on myself during this critical time, discerning whether I am having what a psychiatrist might classify as the "normal sadness response" of grief, or harboring a virulent acedia, or becoming clinically depressed.

The Hard Questions

Over the years I have learned what generally helps me navigate life's more treacherous passages, but I have little idea of what might work for someone else. I have seen people blossom and mature with the help of therapy, and others become infantilized by it. I have witnessed people who had been all but crushed by despair be restored to life with the right combination of medication and counseling. And there is my young friend who reached all the way back into the fifth century to find healing in John Cassian's description of the "spirit of sadness," often a precursor to acedia, that can arise suddenly, and with no apparent cause, making us irritable and intolerant even of those who are dearest to us. She had not rejected contemporary psychological treatment, but found in Cassian a religious element that had been missing, which she desperately needed.

The early desert monks distinguished between natural illness and the "illness of the demons," which was not considered demonic possession but, as the scholar Andrew Crislip notes, was "understood as a somatic and psychic manifestation" of bad thoughts and temptations. Acedia in particular was known to foster physical symptoms such as headaches that would quickly dissipate if challenged. The monk Pachomius, suffering from weakness and lack of appetite, determined that "the illness was not physical," rallied, and was soon able to resume his place at table and at prayers. A similar distinction is made in some African-American churches today, when people are "prayed through" their problems. In some circumstances, however, while prayers are offered, the petitioners are also strongly encouraged to consult a counselor or physician.

Illness is a sensitive subject, and to ask whether the causes of depression remain largely unknown—let alone to assert, as does the philosopher Gordon Marino, that "whether or not depression is best understood in biochemical terms remains an open scientific question"—is to invite a harsh and judgmental response. Some people believe that if a person is tough enough, she can (and should) will her way out of despair; while others advocate antidepressant drugs at any sign of sadness or distress. Marino criticizes the intractability of "pharmaceutical fundamentalists" and of religious fundamentalists who "try to pray their way out of psychological squeezes that could be treated effectively by medication."

In *The Noonday Demon*, Andrew Solomon cites a psychoanalyst who laments that "psychiatry has gone from being brainless to being mindless," in that therapists "who once neglected the physiological brain in favor of emotionality now neglect the emotional human mind in favor of brain chemistry." Solomon regards both perspectives as essential, and one senses that, like Evagrius, he is speaking from experience. "Psychoanalysis is good at explaining things," he writes, "but it is not an efficient way to change them. . . . When I hear of psychoanalysis being used to ameliorate depression, I think of someone standing on a sandbar and firing a machine gun at the incoming tide."

Writers such as Solomon, William Styron, Art Buchwald, and the poet Jane Kenyon have given valuable witness to the ravages of depression. When I read the harrowing descriptions of what they have endured, I recognize that I have never suffered anything so severe. I once described to a physician what I felt was a manic episode; she replied that I wasn't even close, and she was right. As a writer I have sometimes manifested what I think of as "controlled" mania. Once, when I was finishing a book, a peculiar sleep pattern established itself: I slept well every *other* night. On the "sleep" nights, I got in a good seven or eight hours of rest. On the others, I would wake periodically, as often as every fifteen minutes, having thought of revisions to the text. They often proved to be significant improvements, and I was grateful for the inspiration. But I was relieved that once the project was completed, my sleeping stabilized. If it had not, I would have needed medical help.

I seem to have an inner stability that keeps my extremes in check. I come by it honestly, by maternal inheritance. And from both of my parents I received an uncommonly strong and saving sense of humor. When I am feeling listless or "down" and the biblical words I have placed on my refrigerator door—"Be still and know that I am God (Psalms 46:10); "When you search for me you will find me" (Jeremiah 29:13)—are dead to me, I can usually manage to laugh at the postcard next to them, an artist's depiction of an interstate highway in which the standard green directional signs read: "Depressed for No Reason," "Depressed for a Good Reason," and farther on, "Still Depressed." My favorite, probably because it is the lane I most frequent, is a small orange sign in the foreground that sports a right-turn arrow: "Just Depressed, Don't Want to Analyze It."

When I am in a spiritual desert, whether or not it is depression or acedia that has led me there, the last thing I need is the false assurance of either/or thinking. I would be foolish to reject out of hand new and scientifically based understandings of the human brain. But I also believe that both science and religion have a legitimate place in the conversation. Unexamined things that we just "know" to be true are essentially self-limiting. You're either saved or damned; addicted or in denial; depressed or too dumb to know it. Such deterministic thinking is useless to me, and I must endeavor to stretch my mind beyond orthodoxies of any sort. I may be more willing than most to employ the language of religious discourse, but it helps to have more than one language at hand. It humbles me to recognize that even words considered archaic can still reach us at the deepest level. A woman who had lost her premature infant, and to whom a diagnosis of "postnatal depression" was of little help, was inexplicably drawn to the title of Kierkegaard's *Fear and Trembling*, because, she says, it so clearly described "what seemed to be my emotional plight." The book taught her that "anxiety has spiritual significance leading us to faith and healing"; in it she found the freedom to stop "[running] away from my trouble . . . [and to] drop it into the hands of God."

God talk may not be your fancy, but it is what worked for this woman. My inclination at the first sign of trouble is to turn to the brief prayer recommended by the early monks, still said in monasteries several times a day: "O God, make haste to my rescue, / Lord, come to my aid!" (Psalms 70:1). And I regularly consult the stories and sayings of the desert mothers and fathers. Experiential in tone, they help me resist the culture's bent toward polarized ideologies, and toward putting too much faith in my own convictions. A prophetic saying of Anthony the Great cautions that "a time is coming when men will go mad, and when they see someone who is not mad, they will attack him, saying, 'You are mad, you are not like us.'" This sums up for me the psychologizing hysteria of the current era.

But I also recognize that we have come a long way in sixteen hundred years, and that the increasing reliance on pharmaceuticals to alleviate the effects of despair forces on us some hard questions, not the least of which is: Do antidepressant medications work? Now that antidepressants are the most commonly prescribed medications in America, we need to know, but the evidence at hand is spotty. A 2002 article in *Prevention & Treatment* reported on a study in which approximately eighty percent of the response to six antidepressants that became popular during the 1990s was duplicated in control groups who got a sugar pill. A more recent National Institutes of Health study, the largest, non-industry-sponsored test of antidepressants to date, revealed that the drugs failed to cure the symptoms of major depression in nearly half the people taking them. Although the drugs tested—

Celexa, Wellbutrin, Zoloft, and Effexor—work in different ways, they had roughly the same effectiveness or lack of it.

Some scientists were discouraged by the results of the latter study. Nevertheless, the director of the study recommended that people still seek professional help. "The glass is half full from our perspective," he said, but it is also "half empty in that we need to come up with better treatments." A *Newsweek* cover story summarized the latest research into the genetic causes of depression, suggesting that "molecular tests" one day will enable doctors to provide more individualized therapies than are now available. Biologists are looking at a "mutation in the serotonin transporter gene," for example, which makes people more susceptible to depression brought on by stress; and at "beta-arrestin-1," a protein that exists at low levels in depressed people.

While such technologically advanced medications may be available in the future, we have immediate evidence that a substantial number of people in our society could be helped greatly by adequate treatment for mental illness now. It should give us pause to recognize the extent to which, as Andrew Solomon writes, "depression cuts across class boundaries, but depression treatments do not." In a disturbing chapter of his book titled "Poverty," he relates the story of several physicians who set out to bring treatment for mental illness to underserved rural areas and inner-city neighborhoods. The results were "surprisingly consistent," as everyone involved "believed that his or her life had improved at least a bit. . . . They had been introduced to agency and had begun to exercise it; even when they were up against nearly insurmountable obstacles, they progressed." Unfortunately, he reports, the pilot programs that had brought about these beneficial changes ended once the funding ran out. The question here is not whether or not treatment works, but why our society is willing to regard so many people as not worth bothering about.

On the flip side of the issue of access to medical care is the tendency of the affluent to purchase all the drugs and therapy they can afford. One friend compares her periodic visits to a psychiatrist to adjust her medication to the daily flossing she gives her teeth. For her it is preventive medicine, an unpleasant but necessary chore. Kind of how I regard going to the gym. How far we have come since Søren Kierkegaard spoke confidently of despair as evidence of our "superiority over the animal." We seem to have lost a sense of the reverse, that it could be hope rather than despair that sets us apart. Today we are likely to take our depressed pets to veterinary psychologists.

And what of our depressed infants? A *Wall Street Journal* article, "Sending the Baby to a Shrink," describes parents seeking to treat the depression, anxiety, and eating disorders in their nine-month-old children. Another newspaper piece, "Major Depression at Age 5: Researchers Say It Can Happen," adds yet another term to our prodigiously expansive therapeutic lexicon: PMDD, or preschool major depressive disorder. The reporter comments that after studying three-, four-, and five-year-olds diagnosed with depression, researchers "have far more questions about depression in preschoolers than they do answers." Thank God for small mercies. Even as I want these children to be respected, loved, and listened to, I don't want us to presume that there are easy answers here.

Kathryn Schulz, author of the *New York Times Magazine* article "Did Antidepressants Depress Japan?" quotes a Japanese psychiatrist: "Melancholia, sensitivity, fragility—these are not negative things in a Japanese context. . . . It never occurred to us that we should try to remove them." Consider this a litmus test: Is this anathema, or a legitimate expression of cultural diversity? Depression, of course, fuels a multibillion-dollar industry, and pharmaceutical companies see Japan as an emerging market. "Between 1998 and 2003," Schulz writes, "sales of antidepressants in Japan quintupled." (A similar increase has been noted in the United States, in antipsychotic drugs prescribed for children and adolescents between 1993 and 2002.) Schulz interviewed one man who obtained a prescription in the hope that adjusting his brain chemistry would help him have a more stable life. Side effects drove him to seek a more traditional Japanese remedy, a fasting retreat in the mountains, followed by a soak in a hot spring. He would not recommend this as a cure to anyone else, he says, and he still sees a psychiatrist. But he is off medication, and his cycles of depression have ended.

As Schulz had any number of medical professionals at her disposal, I was touched that she concluded by citing a mere novelist, Thomas Hardy, who said that what we often gain by science is sadness. Despite the great medical advances we have made since Hardy probed the depths of the human spirit, we are still asking, What does it mean to be human? And what does science offer to the current discussion? Would we strike a blow for sanity by erasing sadness? Or love, which can hurt, or grief, which pains us terribly when we lose those we love? What about ecstasy, or joy, which Christian theology regards as one of the fruits of the Holy Spirit? Could we modify what seems a universal, the longing for belief itself? Would the excising of our religious impulses make us more free or more humane? This popular fallacy strikes me as the ultimate in naive and wishful thinking.

Fighting Back

Where my own mental health is concerned, I will try to shun false polarities in favor of balance. I can readily accept what Thomas Merton said to a group of monastic novices, in relating John Cassian's teachings to their lives as contemporary monks. While we are tempted to "think sadness is a mood, an emotion," he told them, in truth it is "a passion which easily leads to sin." Merton's admonition that *"the causes of our sadness are not to be sought . . . in other people, but in ourselves"* is an essential for surviving in the rock tumbler of relationship, whether one is within a place of business, a monastery, or a marriage. *"It takes real courage,"* Merton insists, *"to recognize that we ourselves are the cause of our own unhappiness."* The trick is to maintain a nuanced view as we attempt to discern what trouble we have caused and are responsible for, and what is truly beyond our control.

Such discernment is necessary for contending with either depression or acedia, as we try to determine what might help us, a personal "molecular test," if you will, to probe the particulars of our situation, and reveal where remedy may be found. I appreciate the writer Jeffery Smith's observation that it is all too easy to succumb to the dangerous notion that only our despair truly knows us as we are, even as it mocks any desire we may have to improve our condition. Echoing Evagrius, who was speaking about acedia, and not depression as it is currently understood, Smith writes that when one loses oneself to any present joy, the future comes to look "like nothing other than an endless loop of now." As to whether depression is due to one's temperament or is an illness, he notes that this has been debated for well over a thousand years, and warns that because "hard and fast clinical boundaries are new to mental illness," we would do well to allow for flexibility in our thinking. We might even rejoice at the equanimity of Abba Paul, who embraced the "endless loop of now" as a precious gift, even though he knew that one day he would have to burn the baskets he had worked so diligently to make.

I respect the down-to-earth wisdom of Andrew Solomon, who in an *O* magazine interview dispels some myths about depression, for example the idea that to tough out a bad spell will strengthen your character. Citing scientific evidence that repeated bouts of untreated despondency actually change brain physiology, he stresses the importance of getting help early. He also discusses the many ways that people can combat depression, including keeping up basic daily habits: eating a healthful diet, exercising, practicing a religious faith. "When you're depressed," he says, and "begin to feel that your life has no purpose, religion can give . . . some very specific goals and objectives."

"Goals and objectives" are not what I have in mind when I go to church on Sunday morning, but I'll let that pass. Sometimes I persuade myself to go because I know I'll receive a blessing, or because I need to listen to the words of Scripture and give them a chance to work on me. I may desire to sing hymns with others, or be cheered by the sight of children perched on their favorite "climbing tree" before and after services. If I go to church feeling depressed, a congregation, by its very nature, reminds me that I am not in the struggle alone. But even as I acknowledge by my presence that I am accountable to this faith community, I can expect that people will listen and offer something worth its weight in gold, accepting, in Solomon's words, "that [my] statements, no matter how distorted they may seem, are [my] truth for the moment."

Above all, Solomon encourages us to enlarge our capacity for enjoying the good times in life and to expect that rewards will come after pain. "Don't give in to your depression," he says. "Don't accept it as the norm. Dig up from somewhere within you the will to fight back." This is sound advice. Starting with what you know of yourself, you can find what works and claim it. I am less likely to consult a physician than a spiritual director, and while I have used medications on occasion, I have found them less helpful than my lifeline of prayers, psalms, and monastic spirituality. When I detect acedia beginning in myself, I do well to muster my resistance, even if it is only to let John Cassian remind me where I am headed if I do not. "From acedia," he writes, "[are born] idleness, somnolence, rudeness, restlessness, wandering about, instability of mind and body, chattering, [and] inquisitiveness." If I allow myself to reach this stage I will be a distracted tourist rather than a pilgrim, and am likely to turn away from the very things that might bring me to my senses. I have learned that nothing will erase my susceptibility to acedia, for it is a part of who I am. But this does not mean that I am helpless. I can look for the seed of hope in my despair, and pray with the psalmist: "Bring my soul out of this prison, / and then I shall praise your name" (Psalms 142:8).

Time with Tears

I continue to be inspired by the ways in which the ancient monastic story intersects with and informs my own, orienting and directing me in ways I could not have anticipated. If discovering Evagrius when I was in my thirties helped me understand an experience that I had at the age of fifteen, as I enter my sixties I find him illuminating an aspect of my attraction to monastic prayer that I had never fully understood. I responded to the psalms as poetry, but this did not explain the depth of my desire to keep returning to them in prayer, or the sense of peace and purpose I find in praying them. The psalms are available to me when I worship in any Christian church, but they are likely to be snippets chosen for their suitability as Sunday-morning praise. They tend to disappear in the service, a little dose of poetry to be rushed through and soon forgotten. One can attend church for years and never perceive the psalms as both a primary inheritance from Judaism and the core of Christian prayer. To the Benedictine Luke Dysinger, the psalms are "a vision of the whole of creation" and "the training-ground of the Christian contemplative." What I discovered in monasteries was a fresh and meaningful way of reading and hearing them, all one hundred fifty, joyful, vengeful, lamenting, grateful, angry, and awestruck. Every emotion is expressed, as humanity is laid bare before God and everyone.

By reciting the psalms slowly, and surrounding them with silence, the monastic liturgy allows their words to penetrate my thick skull and hard heart. Often when I am sitting in a monastery choir, the words of a psalm will strike with a physical impact: tears come to my eyes, and I see myself and my life in a new light. The moment passes, as it must, but when I feel both regret over my failings and the certitude that they need not define me, I am inspired anew to believe that not despair but hope will have the last word. When I return home I will face the same old battles with restlessness, impatience, and anger, and acedia will urge me to discount my monastery retreat as a shipboard romance. I may be less able to feel the psalms' power when I pray them on my own, accompanied by the sounds of traffic on the street outside instead of the reverent stillness of a monastery choir. Yet over the years my most potent encounters with the psalms have had their effect, enabling me to believe that tears can indeed melt away my wickedness, my own Wicked Witch. And this, I discover, is exactly what the monk Evagrius believed the psalms are intended to do.

Not long ago, in a dry-as-dust journal of monastic studies, in an article on compunction and tears in Evagrius, I found something that helps me understand both my attraction to monastic prayer and my struggles with acedia. The Benedictine Jeremy Driscoll maintains that for Evagrius, both tears and the psalter itself are the monk's essential tools for living a grounded spiritual life. The psalter is not merely a collection of prayers; it is meant to be a song that resonates in the monk's soul, accompanying him on life's journey and illuminating his path. Even more, it is a particularly effective weapon against the bad thought of acedia. I seem not to have a monastic vocation in any traditional sense, but that is not the point. If acedia is my primary temptation, and praying the psalter a tried-and-true means of battling it, then it is no wonder that I have kept returning to monastery choirs for so many years. From the first time I stumbled onto morning prayer at an abbey, when I barely knew what an abbey was, and did not know what the monks were reciting, I was handed one of the greatest gifts of my life.

Evagrius writes that "if, weary from our toil, a certain acedia overtakes us, we should climb up a little onto the rock of knowledge and *converse* with the psalter" (emphasis mine). He is discussing Psalm 49, which contemplates an unjust world and "evil days" in which the rich prosper, trusting only in their wealth. The psalmist hopes that in poetry itself he will find the enduring truths behind society's façade: "I will turn my mind to a parable, / with the harp I will solve my problem." He reflects that he need not fear the powerful of this world, for "they cannot buy endless life, / nor avoid coming to the grave" (Psalms 49:1, 10). In conversing with this psalm he comes to realize that power and status are illusions that fade in the glare of mortality.

Luke Dysinger, who is a physician as well as a Benedictine monk, finds in Evagrius the suggestion of "a reciprocal relationship between spiritual progress and biblical exegesis." He agrees with Evagrius that the psalms can have therapeutic value for the monk who prays them, and suggests that we regard such prayer as something much more than an ascetic discipline. As psalmody and prayer interweave, Dysinger writes, "the monk perceives in the mirror of the psalter his need for reform," and in the words of God (and in Christ as the Word) can find the strength to undertake the process. Every day, if necessary. Or, if one is stubbornly unregenerate, as many monks admit to being, several times a day.

In a section of *The Praktikos* that deals with fighting the eight bad thoughts, Evagrius makes an intriguing suggestion: "When we meet with the demon of *acedia*," it is "time with tears to divide our soul in two. One part is to encourage; the other is to be encouraged." He recommends Psalm 42 as a way to "sow seeds of a firm hope in ourselves." The psalm opens with a poignant image that must have resonated with a desert-dweller such as Evagrius: "Like the deer that yearns / for running streams, / so my soul is yearning / for you, my God. / My soul is thirsting for God, / the God of my life." If another verse brought to mind his former life in Constantinople, and the success he had enjoyed as an up-and-coming churchman and theological prodigy, it would be difficult for him to recite without nostalgia or regret: "These things will I remember / as I pour out my soul: / how I would lead the rejoicing crowd / into the house of God, / amid cries of gladness and thanksgiving."

The opulent churches of the great city were a far cry from his Egyptian cell, and Evagrius no doubt felt keenly the lament "With cries that pierce me to the heart, / my enemies revile me, / saying to me all the day long: / 'Where is your God?'" But if his harsh experience of exile is not to sever him from the love of God, this is a question he must constantly ask himself. Conversing with this psalm, then, means contending with paradoxical forces within the self that can conceive of God as "my rock" and in the next instant ask, "Why have you forgotten me?" Early in the psalm is a verse in which two distinct voices emerge. One asks, "Why are you cast down, my soul, / why groan within me?" and the other responds, "Hope in God; I will praise yet again, / my savior and my God." These two verses are repeated at the end of the psalm.

Who has not heard these voices within, at one moment expressing hope and joy, and in the next reflecting doubt and sorrow? This psalm challenges me, even as it allows me a safe harbor where I might remember and give thanks for all the good gifts that, as I now recall them, bring both joy and pain. The two cannot be neatly separated in grief, or in life itself. There is the bad news of a cancer diagnosis that comes with a small bit of hope attached: it may be operable, and your lung capacity will allow for surgery. There is the chance meeting with an old friend that becomes a true and immeasurable blessing because she dies soon after. For a seed to propagate it must rupture, and in the words of the prophet Isaiah, only those who truly mourn are able to receive "a garland instead of ashes, / the oil of gladness instead of mourning, / the mantle of praise instead of a faint spirit" (Isaiah 61:3).

Looking at the difficult passage life sets before us, which will take us over rocky ground and through steep valleys before we can approach the heights, we may feel our spirits sag. It's enough to make one cry, and valuing tears as a weapon against acedia was a well-established tradition in the monastic desert. Evagrius's choice of this psalm also suggests that tears work best with praise and affirmation. This may seem a contradiction, but as the contemporary Benedictine Mary Forman points out, the monastic tradition holds that there is such a thing as "godly sorrow," which comes when a person recognizes that she is at fault and in need of forgiveness, and at the same time realizes that forgiveness is possible. As one ancient monk put it, "*Penthos* [the sorrow of repentance] without thanksgiving would be despair . . . while thanksgiving without repentance would be a presumptuous illusion."

As I age, I find that the strategies employed by Evagrius in his *Antirrheticus* are of more use to me than ever. My best weapon against despair, what he terms "the thoughts of acedia that demolish my hope," is a line from Psalm 27: "I am sure I shall see the Lord's goodness / in the land of the living" (27:13). Or, as I struggle "against the thought of acedia that sets before [my] eyes a lengthy period of old age, a bitter penury that goes unrelieved, and illnesses capable of killing the body," Evagrius recommends this cold plunge into Job: "Inquire now of bygone generations, and consider what their ancestors have found; / for we are but of yesterday, and we know nothing, for our days on earth are but a shadow" (Job 8:8–9).

If acedia is a distorting mirror, we might look for a truer reflection of the soul in what Evagrius calls "apatheia." This has nothing to do with apathy, but is a blessed state of equilibrium, free from distraction or regret. I doubt that I will ever know apatheia as Evagrius describes it, but no matter: just the thought of it is enough, especially as he suggests that it might serve to inspire anyone who seeks sound physical, mental, and spiritual health. "The proof of apatheia," he writes, comes when "the spirit begins to see its own light, when it remains in a state of tranquility in the presence of the images it has during sleep, and when it maintains its calm as it beholds the affairs of life." If acedia has so stupefied us that we cannot care about anything, even that we are unable to care, apatheia restores us to alertness, and our better selves. Evagrius warned, however, that as we approach apatheia our vanity and pride will tempt us to imagine that we have reached a state of superior spiritual accomplishment. If we succumb to this seduction we will soon become more susceptible to assault by the bad thoughts. The contemplative life, for Evagrius, is one of remaining constantly aware of what will either hinder or help us in our quest, and taking nothing for granted. In these circumstances a healthy dose of skepticism about ourselves and our motives need not be seen as a stumbling block or a sign of weakness, but may be valued as a prerequisite for spiritual progress.

A proof of apatheia's power may be discerned in the life of Evagrius himself. I would be wary of anyone who claimed to have attained such a state, but the scholar Christoph Joest reports that Evagrius's fellow monks attested to his gentle and peaceable nature. As he lived a quiet and humble life in the desert, he won a new kind of renown, demonstrating in himself "the perceptible exterior fruits" of an inner peace seeded, rooted, and fulfilled in love. Clearly this was a man who did not allow the bitter circumstances of his life to make *him* bitter, and if I am to take inspiration from his example, I must keep love at the center, a love that can endure even the hard exile of widowhood. If I find myself lonely—the word suggests a place not only unfrequented but desolate—I will need to seek in solitude a deeper relationship with God. I will also need to nurture my relationships with others. This is much easier said than done, for I know that acedia will tempt me as I struggle to grasp each day as a blessing, and to regard the lowly twenty-four-hour round as not nearly time enough to offer my thanks.

Lowering My Standards Can Help . . .

In an article in *Cistercian Studies Quarterly,* the French monk Placide Deseille quotes at length a passage from an eighth-century monk of the Syrian East, Joseph Hazzaya, whose ability to pray had suddenly abandoned him:

> Once when I was sitting silently in my cell, that accursed demon of acedia rose up against me and refused to let me celebrate the office both night and day. I lay on the ground for a week under the massive weight pressing down upon me, in such a way that the remembrance of God could no longer well up within my heart. . . . Being stuck all this time in this distressing situation, I began to despair of my life, saying to myself: "It would be better for me to leave for the world rather than to wear the monastic habit; I am doing nothing at all, save being lazy and thinking vain things."

When Hazzaya was preparing to leave the monastery as a failed monk, he suddenly received what Deseille calls "an interior inspiration that advised him to stay in his cell, and for each hour of the liturgical office, to recite only Psalm 117, the shortest of all the psalms, consisting of only two verses. This remedy," Deseille writes, "soon brought his trial to an end."

On reading this I laughed out loud, and I suspect that many monks and nuns would do the same. What a lazy fellow, to content himself with so little: "O praise the Lord, all you nations, / acclaim God, all you peoples! / Strong is God's love for us; / the Lord is faithful for ever." But in contending with acedia, one is wise to grasp any tool that works. Hazzaya's story reminds me of what the late poet William Stafford used to say about writer's block. He claimed never to have experienced it, because as soon as he felt it coming on, he lowered his standards.

Writing is like fishing, Stafford would say. A nibble will always come, but all too often we dismiss the little nudge as not worthy of the great works we vaingloriously imagine we will write. In a similar way we block our spiritual progress. The message of salvation that begins as a whisper is easily missed in the noise of passions such as envy, pride, anger, and acedia. Citing a Jesuit psychologist, Deseille comments that Hazzaya's struggle is a common passage in the life of the human spirit, when we must "grasp in the darkness the divine help that cannot be felt" or clearly seen.

. . . But It Is Not Enough

How can I find my way in this impenetrable darkness? How can a few words from a psalm that I say upon waking be all I need to begin again, after I have been worn down to almost nothing by acedia? The danger in lowering one's standards, with acedia, is that one might accommodate oneself to less and less, until one is lowered right out of existence. So I will attempt a bit more, and turn to Psalm 90, which poignantly addresses my present condition. Now that my beloved grandparents and father are gone, and my mother is ninety years of age, I need more than ever the solace of its opening verses: "O Lord, you have been our refuge / from one generation to the next. / Before the mountains were born / or the earth or the world brought forth, / you are God, without beginning or end."

I also need the psalm's shift from exultation to ultimate realism: "Our span is seventy years, / or eighty for those who are strong. / And most of these are emptiness and pain. / They pass quickly and we are gone." Savoring this stark truth in a holy book, I am better able to confront my acedia, and ask myself why I am so willing to waste time, as if it were not a gift, mindlessly consuming and discarding my precious mortal life. I can pray, with the psalmist: "Make us know the shortness of our life / that we may gain wisdom of heart." I may feel lost and weary, but these words provide sustenance. If the life of faith, like depression, is a cycle of exile and return, I am a prodigal become a pilgrim, if only I can remember to turn toward home.

The Christian spiritual tradition employs a number of biblical metaphors for acedia: the Israelites' wandering through the desert and despairing of God's continued guidance; the disciples' falling asleep in the garden of Gethsemane, thus abandoning Jesus on the night before his death. Each of these stories holds meaning for me, but another has becor more significant, that of the childless woman, seemingly barren, whose unexpected motherhood becomes an essential part of salvation's story. It is as a childless widow that I embrace these women of

Scripture—Sarah, Hannah, Leah; Elizabeth, the mother of John the Baptist; and Mary, the mother of Jesus—with their harsh circumstances and apparent dead ends. We encounter each woman at a time when she is certain that she is incapable of being a mother. Yet each becomes a bearer of the promise, carrying within herself the mystery of transformation as Thomas Merton described it: "Prayer and love are learned in the hour when prayer has become impossible and your heart has turned to stone."

A way where there is no way; this is what God, and only God, can provide. This is salvation, which in Hebrew means widening or making sufficient. As we move from death to life we discover grace, a force as real as gravity, and are reminded of its presence in the changing of the seasons, and in the dying of seeds from which new life emerges, so that even our deserts may bloom. It permeates the very language we use, and we are fortunate indeed that our words are far wiser than we are. Any poet knows that they can spark with new meaning, even years after we have written them, and tell us what we most need to know. Poetry might not seem like much in an unjust and violent world, in which acedia tempts us to give up on the fight for something better. But poetry—psalms and hymns—can be a remedy for the human tendency to take refuge in indifference.

Many years ago, after I had settled with my husband in my South Dakota home, I evoked the biblical Sarah in a poem about housekeeping. At the time I was delighted to have made a connection between myself and this woman who had laughed at the absurdity of God's promise to her. Now I find that my old words have taken on a meaning that I could not have intended when I wrote them. We have reason

to celebrate, and to sing, if even one person can find a measure of recourse and hope, if even one voice is lifted on a cold spring morning:

My barren black cat rubs against my legs.
I think of the barren women
exhorted by the Good Book
to break into song:
we should sing, dear cat,
for the children who will come in our old age.
The cat doesn't laugh,
but I do. She rolls in dust
as I finish sweeping.

I empty the washer
and gather what I need for the return:
the basket of wet clothes
and bag of clothespins,
a worn, spring jacket in need of mending.
Then I head upstairs, singing an old hymn.

XV. *Acedia:*
A Commonplace Book

PSALMS 61:3
From the end of the earth I call;
my heart is faint.

PSALMS 91:5–6
You will not fear the terror of the night
nor the arrow that flies by day,
nor the plague that prowls in the darkness
nor the scourge that lays waste at noon.

LUCIUS ANNAEUS SENECA (c. 4 B.C.–A.D. 65),
"On Tranquillity of Mind"
All are in the same case, both those who are afflicted with fickleness
and ennui and continual shifting of aim, who are always fondest of
what they have given up, and those who are languid and yawn.
Subjoin those who turn from side to side like insomniacs trying to
settle down, until they find rest in weariness. . . . Subjoin those who
are immutable by excess not of constancy but of indolence; they live

not as they choose but as they have begun. The malady has countless symptoms but its effect is uniform—dissatisfaction with self. . . . They are unstable and vacillating, [and] regret for what they have begun possesses them, and fear of beginning again, and [their vacillation] can find no outlet. . . . And so, when the entertainment which busy people find even in business is withdrawn, their mind cannot endure home, loneliness, walls, and cannot abide itself left to itself.

ANTHONY THE GREAT (b. c. 251)

When the holy Abba Anthony lived in the desert he was beset by *accidie,* and attacked by many sinful thoughts. He said to God, "Lord, I want to be saved but these thoughts do not leave me alone; what shall I do in my affliction? How can I be saved?" A short while afterwards, when he got up to go out, Anthony saw a man like himself sitting at his work, getting up from his work to pray, then sitting down and plaiting a rope, then getting up again to pray. It was an angel of the Lord sent to correct and reassure him. He heard the angel saying to him, "Do this and you will be saved." At these words, Anthony was filled with joy and courage. He did this, and he was saved.

EVAGRIUS PONTICUS (345–399), *Eight Thoughts*

A waterless cloud is chased away by a wind, a mind without perseverance by the spirit of acedia.

SHENOUTE OF ATRIBE (b. c. 348), Canon 3

Let us . . . not fall ill with the illness of the demons and lie down secretly out of sloth lest God be wroth with us and commit us to a base heart.

JOHN CASSIAN (360–435), *The Institutes*

[Acedia is] a wearied or anxious heart. It is akin to sadness and is the peculiar lot of solitaries and a particularly dangerous and frequent foe of those dwelling in the desert. . . . Once [acedia] has seized possession of a wretched mind it makes a person horrified at where he is, disgusted with his cell, and also disdainful and contemptuous of the brothers who live with him or at a slight distance, as being careless and unspiritual. Likewise it renders him slothful and immobile in the face of all the work to be done within the walls of his dwelling: It does not allow him to stay still in his cell or to devote any effort to reading.

AMMA SYNCLETICA (late fourth–early fifth centuries)

There is a grief that is useful, and there is a grief that is destructive. The first sort consists in weeping over one's own faults and weeping over the weakness of one's neighbors, in order not to destroy one's purpose, and attach oneself to the perfect good. But there is also a grief that comes from the enemy, full of mockery, which some call *accidie*. This spirit must be cast out, mainly by prayer and psalmody.

OXFORD CONCISE DICTIONARY OF THE CHRISTIAN CHURCH

Accidie (Greek for "negligence," "indifference"). By the early 5th cent. the word had become a technical term in Christian asceticism, signifying a state of restlessness and inability either to work or to pray. It is accounted one of the "seven deadly sins."

BENEDICT (c. 480–547), The Rule, 48:1
Idleness is the enemy of the soul.

GREGORY THE GREAT (c. 540–604), *The Book of Pastoral Rule*
For the slothful one is as it were awake in that he feels aright, though
he grows torpid by doing nothing: but slothfulness is said to cast
into a deep sleep, because by degrees even the wakefulness of right
feeling is lost, when zeal for well-doing is discontinued.

JOHN CLIMACUS (579–649), *The Ladder of Divine Ascent*
Tedium is a kind of total death for the monk. A brave soul can stir
up his dying mind, but tedium and laziness scatter every one of
his treasures.

HUGH OF ST. VICTOR (1096–1141), *De sacramentis christianae fidei*
The rational soul in its health is a strong and sound vessel. . . . When
the vices enter into it, they spoil . . . and corrupt it in this way:
through pride it becomes blown up, through envy it dries out,
through wrath it cracks, through *acidia* it breaks.

GILBERT OF HOYLAND (d. 1172), Sermon 38:6
The spirit attacked by boredom knows with what boredom it
endures being bored with the good life. How it disdains the disdain!
With what bitterness it wrestles against bitterness, against that
violent bitterness which intrudes uninvited into the unchanging
round of regular discipline. . . . The spirit is worn out both by its
boredom and by loathing for this boredom. Both feelings are

repugnant: to have no taste for what you have chosen, and to experience what you loathe. Each is a trial: to protect discipline and put lethargy to rout.

THOMAS OF CHABHAM (c. 1160–c. 1236), *Poenitentiale*
Acedia is a most grievous sin, and yet it is hardly known to anyone. The sin of *acedia* is called by the Apostle "the sorrow of the world which works death" [2 Corinthians 7:10]. On account of this many have killed themselves when they are so absorbed that they have no joy in God.

DAVID OF AUGSBURG (d. 1272), *Formula novitiorum,* 51
The vice of *accidia* has three kinds. The first is a certain bitterness of the mind which cannot be pleased by anything cheerful or wholesome. It feeds upon disgust and loathes human intercourse . . . [and] inclines to despair, diffidence, and suspicions, and sometimes drives its victim to suicide when he is oppressed by unreasonable grief. The second kind is a certain indolent torpor which loves sleep and all comforts of the body . . . [and] flees from whatever is hard, droops in the presence of work, and takes delight in idleness. This is laziness proper. The third kind is a weariness in such things only as belong to God, while in other occupations its victim is active and in high spirits. The person who suffers from it prays without devotion. . . . He hastens to rush through the prayers he is obliged to say and thinks of other things so that he may not be too much bored by prayer.

THOMAS AQUINAS (1225–1274), *Summa theologica*
We might say that all the sins which are due to ignorance can be
reduced to sloth, which pertains to the negligence by which a man
refuses to acquire spiritual goods because of the attendant labor.

DANTE (1265–1321), *Inferno*, canto 7
Once we were grim
And sullen in the sweet air above, that took
A further gladness from the play of sun;
Inside us, we bore acedia's dismal smoke.
We have this black mire now to be sullen in.

PETRARCH (1304–1374), *The Secretum*
I act like a man stretched out on a very hard bed who often seeks
relief by changing positions although he never finds a good one.
Tired of the place I live in, I go to another that is no better, although
its newness makes me find it better [for a while]. But then I leave in
order to search elsewhere.

GEOFFREY CHAUCER (1340–1400), "The Parson's Tale"
For envy blinds the heart of a man and anger troubles a man; and
acedia makes him heavy, thoughtful, and peevish. Envy and anger
cause bitterness of heart; which bitterness is the mother of acedia,
and takes from a man the love of all goodness. Then is acedia the
anguish of a troubled heart; and as Saint Augustine says, "It is the
sadness of goodness and the joy of evil."

WILLIAM CAXTON (c. 1422–c. 1491), *Order of Chyvalry*
A man that hath accydye or slouthe hath sorowe and angre the whyle
that he knoweth that an other man doth wel.

BLESSED PAUL GIUSTINIANI (1476–1528), *Rule of the Eremetic Life*
If either the days or the nights begin to seem overlong . . . [the hermit]
will soon . . . waste his time, which must be considered most precious,
on superfluous sleep. Or else through gadding about and profitlessly
chatting, he will make himself and the others lose many opportunities
for doing good. . . . [But] even in the cell itself [the hermit] must
willingly remain in one place and steadfastly and immovably at one
work. For those who are less eager for stability can sometimes, while
staying in the cell, be driven about all day long as if by a . . . demonic
impulse and spirit of wandering. They go around the different
workplaces of the cell and in the same hour begin and leave off
various tasks. This is truly the most wretched form of the vice.

IGNATIUS OF LOYOLA (1491–1556), *Spiritual Exercises*
I call desolation . . . darkness of soul, turmoil of spirit, inclination
to what is low . . . restlessness rising from many disturbances and
temptations which lead to want of faith, want of hope, want of love.
The soul is wholly slothful, tepid, sad, and separated, as it were, from
its Creator and Lord.

JOHN OF THE CROSS (1542–1591), *Dark Night of the Soul*
It is evident that . . . disgust and dryness do not come from slackness
and tepidity; [because] tepidity is characterized by not caring much

or having an inner solicitude for the things of God. . . . There is
a great difference between dryness and tepidity. . . . The state of
tepidity implies great negligence and slackness in will and mind,
without willingness to serve God; but purgative dryness is
accompanied by . . . willingness, with concern and sorrow . . .
that one does not serve God.

JOHN DONNE (1572–1631), "A Nocturnal upon St. Lucy's Day"
> For I am every dead thing,
>> In whom love wrought new alchemy.
>>> For his art did express
> A quintessence even from nothingness,
> From dull privations, and lean emptiness;
> He ruined me, and I am re-begot
> Of absence, darkness, death; things which are not.

BISHOP JOSEPH HALL (1574–1656), Sermon, v. 140, 1623
Though the mind be sufficiently convinced of the necessity or profit
of a good act; yet for the tediousness annexed to it, in a dangerous
spiritual acedy, it slips away.

BLAISE PASCAL (1623–1662), *Pensées*, 622
Boredom. Man finds nothing so intolerable as to be in a state of
complete rest, without passions, without occupation, without
diversion, without effort. Then he faces his nullity, loneliness,
inadequacy, dependence, helplessness, emptiness. And at once there
well up from the depths of his soul boredom, gloom, depression,
chagrin, resentment, despair.

ANNE FINCH, COUNTESS OF WINCHILSEA (1661–1720), "The Spleen"

What are thou, Spleen, which everything dost ape?

Thou Proteus to abused mankind,

Who never yet thy real cause could find

Or fix thee to remain in one continued shape.

Still varying thy perplexing form

Now a Dead Sea thou'lt represent,

A calm of stupid discontent,

Then, dashing rocks, with rage into a storm . . .

Through thy black jaundice I all objects see

As dark, as terrible as thee,

My lines decried, and my employment thought

An useless folly or presumptuous fault;

Whilst in the Muses' paths I stray,

Whilst in their groves and by their secret springs

My hand delights to trace unusual things,

And deviates from the known and common way;

Nor will in fading silks compose

Faintly the inimitable rose,

Fill up an ill-drawn bird, or paint on glass

The Sovereign's blurred and undistinguished face,

The threatening angel and the speaking ass.

MARIE DU DEFFAND (1697–1780), letter to Voltaire, 1759

All conditions and all circumstances seem equally unfortunate to me, from the angel to the oyster. The grievous thing is to be born.

MARIA EDGEWORTH (1767–1849), *Ennui*

Whilst yet a boy, I began to feel the dreadful symptoms of that mental malady which baffles the skill of medicine. . . . I felt that something was the matter with me, but I did not know what: yet the symptoms were sufficiently marked. I was afflicted with . . . a constant restlessness of mind and body; an aversion to the place I was in, or the thing I was doing, or rather to that which was passing before my eyes, for I was never doing any thing; I had an utter abhorrence and an incapacity of voluntary exertion. Unless roused by external stimulus, I sank into that kind of apathy, and vacancy of ideas, vulgarly known by the name of *a brown study*. If confined in a room for more than half an hour of bad weather or other contrarieties, I would pace backwards and forwards, like the restless *cavia* in his den, with a fretful, unmeaning pertinacity. I felt an insatiable longing for something new, and a childish love of locomotion.

ÉTIENNE PIVERT DE SENANCOUR (1770–1846), *Obermann*

I shall no longer look for better days. The months pass, the years come and go. All things are renewed in vain; I am ever the same. . . . I have found nothing, I possess nothing; weariness consumes my years in unending silence. . . . I am forever encompassed by an empty void, which, as the seasons pass in long procession by, spreads in ever-widening circles around me. . . . Springtime came for nature; for me it came not. The days that brought the vital spark of life awakened every being; yet their unquenchable fire did not revive me, but filled me with lassitude. I was an alien in the world of gladness. . . . Season of joy! For me the beautiful days are profitless, the soft nights are full of gall. . . .

Miserable man that I am! The heavens are on fire, the earth brings forth fruit, but the waste of winter still keeps its watch within me.

WILLIAM WORDSWORTH (1770–1850), "Preface," *Lyrical Ballads*
The human mind is capable of excitement without the application of gross and violent stimulants; and he must have a very faint perception of its beauty and dignity who does not know this. . . . It [appears] to me that to endeavour to produce or enlarge this capability is one of the best services in which, at any period, a Writer can be engaged; but this service, excellent at all times, is especially so at the present day. For a multitude of causes . . . are now acting with a combined force to blunt the discriminating powers of the mind, and unfitting it for all voluntary exertion to reduce it to a state of almost savage torpor.

SAMUEL TAYLOR COLERIDGE (1772–1834), "Dejection: An Ode"
A grief without a pang, void, dark, and drear,
 A stifled, drowsy, unimpassioned grief,
 Which finds no natural outlet, no relief
  In word, or sigh, or tear—
O Lady! in this wan and heartless mood,
To other thoughts by yonder throstle wooed,
 All this long eve, so balmy and serene,
Have I been gazing on the western sky,
 And its peculiar tint of yellow green:
And still I gaze—and with how blank an eye!
And those thin clouds above, in flakes and bars,

That give away their motion to the stars;
Those stars, that glide behind them or between,
Now sparkling, now bedimmed, but always seen:
Yon crescent Moon, as fixed as if it grew
In its own cloudless, starless lake of blue;
I see them all so excellently fair,
I see, not feel, how beautiful they are!

STENDHAL (1783–1842), *Love*
Boredom strips away everything, even the courage to kill oneself.

IVAN GONCHAROV (1812–1891), *Oblomov*
He was painfully aware that something good and fine lay buried
in him as in a grave, that it was perhaps already dead or lay hidden
like gold in the heart of a mountain, and that it was high time that
gold was put into circulation. But the treasure was deeply buried
under a heap of rubbish and silt. It was as though he himself had
stolen and buried in his own soul the treasures bestowed on him
as a gift by the world and life. Something prevented him from
launching out into the ocean of life. . . . Some secret enemy
seemed to have laid a heavy hand upon him at the very start of
his journey. . . . His mind and will had long been paralyzed and,
it seemed, irretrievably.

SØREN KIERKEGAARD (1813–1855), *Either/Or*
Since boredom advances and boredom is the root of all evil, no
wonder, then, that the world goes backwards, that evil spreads. This
can be traced back to the very beginning of the world. The gods were

bored; therefore they created human beings. Adam was bored because he was alone; therefore Eve was created. [Thus] boredom entered the world and grew in quantity in exact proportion to the growth of population. Adam was bored alone; then Adam and Eve were bored together; then Adam and Eve and Cain and Abel were bored *en famille*; [then] the population of the world increased, and the nations were bored *en masse*.

CHARLES BAUDELAIRE (1821–1867), letter to his mother, 1860
Oh, how weary I am, how weary I've been for many years already, of this need to live twenty-four hours every day!

GUSTAVE FLAUBERT (1821–1880), *November*
Aren't you tired, as I am, of waking up every morning and seeing the sun again? Tired of living the same life, of suffering the same pain? Tired of desiring and tired of being disgusted? Tired of waiting and tired of possessing?

EMILY DICKINSON (1830–1886), Poem 1194
Somehow myself survived the Night
And entered with the Day—
That it be saved the Saved suffice
Without the Formula.

Henceforth I take my living place
As one commuted led—
A Candidate for Morning Chance
But dated with the Dead.

STÉPHANE MALLARMÉ (1842–1898), "Renewal"
Lucid winter, season of art serene,
Is sadly driven out by sickly spring,
And where pure blood presides within my being
Impotence stretches itself in a drawn-out yawn.

White twilights glow lukewarm beneath my skull
Squeezed by an iron band like an ancient tomb,
As, following a vague, sweet dream, I sadly roam
Through fields whose sap is flaunted to the full

—Then, fall, enfeebled by the trees' perfume,
And hollowing my face with a grave for my own dream,
Biting warm earth in which the lilacs push,

I wait, engulfed in rising ennui . . .
—Meanwhile the Azure laughs on every bush
And wakened birds bloom twittering in the sun.

BISHOP FRANCIS PAGET (1851–1911), *The Spirit of Discipline*
[To] look too attentively for signs of fatigue, which come to
command an ever increasing deference encroaching more and more
upon the realm of will, [discourages] a man from ventures he might
safely make, filching from him all his fortitude, the prophylactic and
antidote to accidie.

AGNES REPPLIER (1855–1950), "Ennui"

When we come to think of it, conversation between [Adam and Eve] must have been difficult . . . because they had nobody to talk about. If we exiled our neighbors permanently from our discussions, we should soon be reduced to silence; and if we confined ourselves even to laudatory remarks, we should probably say but little. . . . Here, indeed, is the very soul and essence of ennui; not the virtuous sentiment which revolts at the disclosure of another's faults, but that deep and deadly ennui of life which welcomes evil as a distraction. The same selfish lassitude which made the gladiatorial combats a pleasant sight for the jaded eyes that witnessed them finds relief for its tediousness today in the swift destruction of confidence and reputation.

WILLIAM R. INGE (1860–1954), *Outspoken Essays*

We are reminded that the medieval casuists classified acedia . . . among the seven deadly sins. We had almost forgotten acedia . . . but it is at the bottom of the diseases from which we are suffering.

IRVING BABBITT (1865–1933), *Rousseau and Romanticism*

[Christianity] has perceived clearly . . . the supreme importance of spiritual effort and the supreme danger of spiritual sloth. The man who looked on himself as cut off from God . . . was according to the medieval Christian the victim of *acedia*. . . . It would not be hard to show that what was taken by [the Romantic] to be the badge of spiritual distinction was held by the medieval Christian to be the chief of all the deadly sins. The victim of *acedia* often looked upon himself . . . as foredoomed. But though the idea of fate enters at times into medieval melancholy, the man of the Middle Ages could scarcely so detach himself from the community as to suffer that sense of loneliness which is the main symptom of romantic melancholy.

H. G. WELLS (1866–1946), *The Anatomy of Frustration*
If you cannot lift yourself to be Life invincible and immortal, then you must accept frustration. You must live in a succession of stimulations and new excitements, live for the day, and when these sustaining accidents begin to fail you or you yourself fail to respond to them, then there is nothing before you but sloth and apathy, accidie, which is a lingering suicide.

BERTRAND RUSSELL (1872–1970), *The Conquest of Happiness*
A generation that cannot endure boredom will be a generation of little men, of men unduly divorced from the slow processes of nature, of men in whom every vital impulse slowly withers, as though they were cut flowers in a vase.

G. K. CHESTERTON (1874–1936), *Orthodoxy*
Perhaps God is strong enough to exult in monotony. It is possible that God says every morning "Do it again" to the sun; and every evening "Do it again" to the moon. It may not be automatic necessity that makes all daisies alike; it may be that God makes every daisy separately, but has never gotten tired of making them.

EVELYN UNDERHILL (1875–1941), *Practical Mysticism*

If the doors of perception were cleansed, said Blake, everything
would appear to man as it is—Infinite. But the doors of perception
are hung with the cobwebs of thought; prejudice, cowardice,
sloth. Eternity is with us, inviting our contemplation perpetually,
but we are too frightened, lazy, and suspicious to respond: too
arrogant to still our thought, and let divine sensation have its way.
It needs industry and goodwill if we would make that transition:
for the process involves a veritable spring-cleaning of the soul,
a turning-out and rearrangement of our mental furniture, a wide
opening of closed windows, that the notes of the wild birds beyond
our garden may come to us fully charged with wonder and
freshness, and drown with their music the noise of the gramophone
within.

MIKHAIL ARTZYBASHEV (1878–1927), *Breaking-Point*

"Yes, I'm going to shoot myself in a minute," he said, with perfect
composure. . . . "I was waiting for a moment when it wouldn't seem
particularly dreadful, but at the most ridiculous and futile. . . . Let
others live, if they can. . . . For my part, I won't, because to me it's
simply uninteresting. That's all. . . . Nature and beauty are so trivial,
one gets so tired of them . . . love is so petty . . . humanity—simply
foolish. The mysteries of the universe are impenetrable, and even
should one fathom them it would be just as dull as before.
Everything is as uninteresting as what we know already. In eternity
there is nothing either small or large. . . . And it's the same with
everything. Why have a God at all? It's superfluous."

FRANZ KAFKA (1883–1924), *Diaries 1914–1923*
May 3, 1915. Completely indifferent and apathetic. A well gone dry, water at an unattainable depth and no certainty is there. Nothing, nothing . . . What is there to tie me to a past or a future? The present is a phantom state for me; I don't sit at the table but hover round it. Nothing, nothing. Emptiness, boredom, no, not boredom, merely emptiness, meaninglessness, weakness.

KARL BARTH (1886–1968), *Church Dogmatics*
[Man] is guilty of falsehood in the pride in which, in contrast to the humility of the Son of God, he seeks to occupy the place of God . . . as also in the sloth in which, in contrast to the majesty of . . . Jesus, he seeks to divest himself of the dignity of his divinely given nature.

ATTRIBUTED TO PAUL TILLICH (1886–1965),
cited in *The Book of Positive Quotations*
Boredom is rage spread thin.

GEORGES BERNANOS (1888–1948), *The Diary of a Country Priest*
The world is eaten up by boredom. . . . You can't see it all at once. It is like dust. You go about and never notice. . . . But stand still for an instant and there it is, coating your face and hands. To shake off this drizzle of ashes you must be forever on the go. And so people are always "on the go."

FERNANDO PESSOA (1888–1935), *The Book of Disquiet*

Nothing is worse than the contrast between the natural splendour of the inner life, with its . . . unexplored lands, and the squalor . . . of life's daily routine. And tedium is more oppressive when there's not the excuse of idleness. The tedium of those who strive hard is the worst of all. Tedium is not the disease of being bored because there's nothing to do, but the more serious disease of feeling that there's nothing worth doing.

HENRI MICHAUX (1889–1984), *Miserable Miracle*

I would like. I would like anything at all, but fast. I would like to get out of here. I would like to be rid of all this. I would like to start all over again. I would like to leave all this. Not to leave through an exit. I would like a multiple leaving, a whole spread of them. An endless leaving, an ideal leaving so that once I've left I begin leaving again right away.

I would like to get up. No, I would like to lie down, no, I'd like to get up, right away, no, I'd like to lie down this very second, I want to get up, I'm going to make a phone call, no, I won't call. Yes, I have to. No, I'm absolutely not going to call. Yes, I'll call. No, I'll lie down. So ten times, twenty times, fifty times in a few minutes I decide something, decide the contrary, come back to the first decision, come back to the second decision, make my first resolution again, completely, fanatically carried away as if on a crusade, but the next second totally indifferent, uninterested, perfectly relaxed.

IRÉNÉE HAUSHERR (1891–1978),
Spiritual Direction in the Early Christian East
Akēdia (*acedia*), etymologically, lack of care, of interest; negligence. . . .
Mental or spiritual torpor, a general uneasiness of soul, for no
particular reason. If one gives in to it, it has lamentable results,
mainly inconstancy; if one overcomes it, this gives rise to deep peace.

KARL MENNINGER (1893–1990), *Whatever Became of Sin?*
Let it stand that there is a sin of not doing, of not knowing, of not
finding out what one must do—in short, of not caring. This is the
literal meaning of acedia, recognized as a sin for so many centuries
and plaguing us still.

DOROTHY SAYERS (1893–1957), "The Other Six Deadly Sins"
[Sloth] is the sin that believes nothing, cares to know nothing, seeks
to know nothing, loves nothing, hates nothing, finds purpose in
nothing . . . and remains alive because there is nothing for which it
will die.

ALDOUS HUXLEY (1894–1963), "Accidie"
The cenobites of the Thebaid [the desert monastics] were subjected
to the assaults of many demons. Most of these evil spirits came
furtively with the coming of night. But there was one, a fiend of
deadly subtlety, who was not afraid to walk by day. . . . Inaccurate
psychologists of evil are wont to speak of accidie as though it were
plain sloth. But sloth is only one of the numerous manifestations
of the subtle and complicated vice of accidie. . . . It paralyzes
human will.

F. SCOTT FITZGERALD (1896–1940), "Sleeping and Waking"
The horror has come now like a storm—what if this night prefigured
the night after death—what if all thereafter was an eternal quivering
at the edge of an abyss, with everything base and vicious in oneself
urging one forward and the baseness and viciousness of the world
just ahead. No choice, no road, no hope—only the endless repetition
of the sordid and the semi-tragic. Or to stand forever, perhaps, on
the threshold of life unable to pass it and return to it.

JORGE LUIS BORGES (1899–1986), "The Duration of Hell"
I dreamed that I was awakening from another dream—an uproar
of chaos and cataclysms—into an unrecognizable room. Day was
dawning, light suffused the room, outlining the foot of the wrought-
iron bed, the upright chair, the closed door and windows, the bare
table. I thought fearfully, "Where am I?" and I realized I didn't know.
I thought, "Who am I?" and I couldn't recognize myself. My fear
grew. I thought: This desolate awakening is in Hell, this eternal vigil
will be my destiny. Then I really woke up, trembling.

ERICH FROMM (1900–1980), *The Dogma of Christ*
I am convinced that boredom is one of the greatest tortures. If I were
to imagine Hell, it would be the place where you were continually
bored.

BRIAN AHERNE (1902–1986), *A Dreadful Man*
How is it possible, one may ask, that a man still not old by modern
standards, still successful in his profession, in fair physical health,
possessed of adequate means, well educated, highly intelligent and

brilliantly talented in many ways, should so lack courage, so lack interest in all that life has to offer, that he could find no other course open to him but death? . . . Could he find nothing to enjoy? Was he unmoved by the glories of the sky, the dawn and the sunset, the recurrent miracle of the changing seasons, the interest and beauty of a garden and the silent mystery of wild life? Was he blind to art and literature, deaf to the music created . . . through the ages? Did he derive no comfort from his family and friends? Is it possible that such a man could tamely succumb to the ignominy of boredom? Yes, it is possible. In fact, it was inevitable.

EVELYN WAUGH (1903–1966), "Acedia"
The malice of Sloth lies not merely in the neglect of duty (though that can be a symptom of it) but in the refusal of joy. It is allied to despair.

JOSEF PIEPER (1904–1997), *Leisure: The Basis of Culture*
At the zenith of the Middle Ages . . . it was held that sloth and restlessness, [and] the incapacity to enjoy leisure, were all closely connected; sloth was held to be the source of restlessness, and the ultimate cause of "work for work's sake." It may well seem paradoxical to maintain that the restlessness at the bottom of a fanatical and suicidal activity should come from the lack of a will to action; a surprising thought, that we shall only be able to decipher with effort. But it is a worth-while effort, and we should do well to . . . enquire into the philosophy of life attached to the word *acedia*.

In the first place, *acedia* does not signify . . . idleness [as it is currently understood]. Idleness, in the medieval view, means that a man renounces the claim implicit in his human dignity. . . . He does not want to be as God wants him to be, and that ultimately means that he does not wish to be what he really, fundamentally, *is*. . . . The contrary of *acedia* is not the spirit of work in the sense of the work of every day, of earning one's living; it is man's . . . affirmation of his own being, his acquiescence in the world and in God—which is to say love.

KARL RAHNER (1904–1984), *The Need and the Blessing of Prayer*
You do not despair . . . when you doubt yourself, your wisdom, your strength, your ability to help yourself to life and the freedom of happiness; rather you are with [God] suddenly as a miracle that daily has to happen anew and never can become a routine. Suddenly you will [know] that the petrifying visage of hopelessness is only God's rising in your soul, that the darkness of the world is nothing but God's radiance, which has no shadow, that the apparent waylessness is only the immensity of God, who does not need any ways because he is already there.

SAMUEL BECKETT (1906–1989), *The Unnamable*
Keep going, going on, call that going, call that on. Can it be that one day, off it goes on, that one day I simply stayed in, in where, instead of going out, in the old way, out to spend day and night as far away as possible, it wasn't far. Perhaps that is how it began. You think you are simply resting, the better to act when the time comes, or for no reason, and you soon find yourself powerless ever to do anything again.

ALBERTO MORAVIA (1907–1990), *Boredom*

My life was dominated by a feeling of extraordinary impatience. Nothing that I did pleased me or seemed worth doing; furthermore, I was unable to imagine anything that could please me, or that could occupy me in any lasting manner. I was constantly going in and out of my studio on any sort of futile pretext—pretexts which I invented for myself with the sole object of not remaining there: to buy cigarettes I didn't need, to have a cup of coffee I didn't want. . . . I felt, moreover, that these occupations were nothing more than crazy disguises of boredom itself, so much so that sometimes I did not complete the errands I undertook. . . . After taking a few steps I would return to the studio which I had left in such a hurry only a few minutes before. Back in the studio boredom, of course, awaited me and the whole process would begin over again.

IAN FLEMING (1908–1964), *From Russia with Love*

Just as, at least in one religion, *accidie* is the first of the cardinal sins, so boredom, and particularly the incredible circumstance of waking up bored, was the only vice Bond utterly condemned.

WILLIAM F. LYNCH (1908–1987), *Images of Faith*

[Boredom] is one of the great forms of irony. It is, but in reverse, as great a force as faith. Where faith, for good or bad, is a tremendous drive toward relationship and contains all the energies that we associate with the life of wishing and longing, boredom moves in just the opposite way. . . . I think we give part of [boredom's] secret away when we reveal it as a force for not wishing. The bored man is acting, within faith, in an intense way which says: I do not wish; I do not

want this, I do not want that, unto infinity. I am not impressed. . . .
Mention any event and I shall wipe it out. Do not try to impress me
for I am not vulnerable. . . . I do not wish to be impressed.

CESARE PAVESE (1908–1950), *The Business of Living: Diary, 1935–1950*
Suffering is . . . intangible. . . . It dwells in time. . . . If it comes in fits
and starts, that is only so as to leave the sufferer more defenceless
during . . . those long moments when one re-lives the last bout of
torture and waits for the next. . . . The sufferer is always in a state of
waiting for the next attack, and the next. The moment comes when
he screams needlessly, just to break the flow of time, to feel that
something is happening. . . . Oh! the power of indifference! That is
what has enabled stones to endure, unchanged, for millions of years.

STEPHEN SPENDER (1909–1995),
introduction to Malcolm Lowry's *Under the Volcano*
The Consul's despair is really acedia, the spiritual apathy of the
religious who have become, as it were, hermetically sealed off from
the source of their religion. His errors are theological: refusal to love
or be loved. Ultimately his sin is pride.

CATECHISM OF THE CATHOLIC CHURCH, Number 2733
[A] temptation, to which presumption opens the gate, is acedia. The
spiritual writers understand by this a form of depression due to lax
ascetical practice, decreasing vigilance, carelessness of heart. The
spirit indeed is willing, but the flesh is weak. The greater the height,
the harder the fall.

SIMONE WEIL (1909–1943), "The Power of Words"
Sameness is both the most beautiful and repulsive thing that exists.
The most beautiful if it reflects eternity. The ugliest if it is a sign of
something endless and unchangeable. Conquered time or infertile
time. The symbol of beautiful sameness is the circle. The symbol of
cruel sameness is the ticking of a pendulum.

E. M. CIORAN (1911–1995), *A Short History of Decay*
Among the Dregs. To console myself for the remorse of sloth, I take
the path to the lower depths, impatient to degrade myself and
identify with the gutter. . . . Behold then, I tell myself, man's negative
lineage, pathetic counterfeiter of the absolute. . . . Here is where he
was to end, in this spitting image of himself, mud God never laid a
hand on, beast no angel had a part in, infinity begotten in moans,
soul risen out of a spasm. . . . I contemplate that dim despair of
spermatazoa that have reached their end, these funeral countenances
of the race.

CZESLAW MILOSZ (1911–2004), "The Garden of Knowledge"
No one can call this failing simply laziness any longer; whatever
it may once have been, nowadays it has returned to its original
meaning: terror in the face of emptiness, apathy, depression. It's not
isolated hermits, however, who are experiencing its sting, but the
masses in their millions.

EUGÈNE IONESCO (1912–1994), *Fragments of a Journal*
Boredom flourishes . . . when you feel safe. It's a symptom of
security.

ROBERTSON DAVIES (1913–1995), "The Deadliest of the Sins"
What is it like, this failure in the art of life? It is the failure which
manifests itself in a loss of interest in really important things. . . .
There is nothing dramatic about it, and thus it works with a dreadful
advantage; it creeps up on us, and once it has us in its grip, it is hard
for us to recognize what ails us. . . . But if . . . your feelings and
sensibilities are withering, if your relationships with people near to
you are becoming more and more superficial, if you are losing touch
even with yourself, it is Acedia which has claimed you for its own.

ROBERT NISBET (1913–1996), *Prejudices: A Philosophical Dictionary*
There is a history as well as a sociology of boredom. It must surely
have been first felt by man where he made the transition some
twenty thousand years ago from a hunting or pastoral existence to
village life and the tyrannies of soil and season. It was something
else to face the sheer drudgery of tilling and harvesting and the
monotony of life in the village. The word *paradise* comes from the
Persian, where originally it meant "wilderness," and there is no doubt
a lesson there.

FRANK LAKE (1914–1982), *Clinical Theology: A Theological and
Psychiatric Basis to Clinical Pastoral Care*
This is the climate of depression, a world in which, as Epictetus said,
men were seeking a peace, "not of Caesar's proclamation, but of
God's." Bread and circuses were symptomatic treatments for a
depression of epidemic proportions, such as we have again in our
own day.

SAUL BELLOW (1915–2005), *Humboldt's Gift*
I had a lively time in the vast jurors' hall going over my boredom
notes. I saw that I had stayed away from problems of definition. Good
for me. I didn't want to get mixed up with theological questions
about *accidia* and *tedium vitae*. I found it necessary to say only that
from the beginning mankind experienced states of boredom but that
no one had ever approached the matter front and center as a subject
in its own right. . . . It seemed to me . . . that one might begin with
this belief of the modern world—either you burn or you rot.

ORRIN E. KLAPP (b. 1915), *Overload and Boredom*
It is not at all clear that these three features of modern society—fun
industries, fashions, and celebrity cult—banish boredom. Analogy
with aspirin is appropriate: high dosage means not the absence but
the presence of pain.

THOMAS MERTON (1915–1968), *Cassian and the Fathers*
Tristitia seems to be a sadness caused by adversity and trial in social life.
It comes from lack of peace *with others*. *Acedia* is rather the sadness,
the disgust with life, which comes from a much deeper source—our
inability to get along *with ourselves*, and our disunion *with God*.

WALKER PERCY (1916–1990), *The Message in the Bottle*
Why does man feel so bad in the very age when, more than in any
other age, he has succeeded in satisfying his needs and making over
the world for his own use?

    Why has man entered on an orgy of war, murder, torture, and
self-destruction unparalleled in history?

Why is the good life which men have achieved in the twentieth century so bad that only news of world catastrophes, assassinations, plane crashes, mass murders, can divert one from the sadness of ordinary mornings?

MORRIS L. WEST (1916–1999), *The Ambassador*
But is it ended there—the traveler motionless, without tears, lacking light, refusing compassion? There is a word for that in the West: *accidie,* it signifies the false and terrible *Nirvana* which is founded not on union but [on] separation, not on the extinction of desire, but on the contempt of it.

RUTH BURROWS (b. 1920s?), *Guidelines for Mystical Prayer*
Pride and sloth form the taproot from which the other sins branch out. They pervade them all. Respectively they pervert two complementary aspects of reality, that we are very small before the great God, but on the other hand, we are made in his image and therefore of infinite value.

WAYNE C. BOOTH (1921–2005), *The Vocation of a Teacher*
Before the romantic individual was invented, people suffered from things like *tedium vitae,* melancholia, the spleen, or ennui, all of them internal conditions. The Copernican Revolution occurred when people began blaming everybody but themselves for their condition. The first Englishman recorded as using "bore" as a transitive verb was apparently Earl Carlisle, in 1768, and as you would expect, he . . . blamed it all on the French.

ALEXANDER SCHMEMANN (1921–1983), *Great Lent*

The basic disease is *sloth*. It is that strange laziness and passivity
of our entire being . . . which constantly convinces us that no
change is possible and therefore desirable. It is in fact a deeply
rooted cynicism which to every spiritual challenge responds "What
for?" and makes our life one tremendous spiritual waste. It is the
root of all sin because it poisons the spiritual energy at its
very source.

URBAN VOLL, O.P. (b. 1922), *The Vice of Acedia*

Acedia as a phenomenon is probably as old as humanity itself, but
speaking properly of its history as an idea, it begins in the fourth
century of the Christian era. It was then that the monks of the
Egyptian desert sketched its outlines as one of a group of
particularly dangerous obstacles to their pursuit of holiness.

EVAN S. CONNELL (b. 1924), "Acedia"

I couldn't imagine going to a party. Something's wrong with me,
I said. I believe I have Acedia.

Pax took a little step backward. You have what?

It was a medieval illness, I said, I've forgotten exactly what it
means. Sloth. Weariness. Torpor. It's much worse than boredom.
I can't seem to get over it.

My goodness, Pax said. She tried to sound sympathetic but
I knew she was wondering if it might be contagious. Roscoe looked
at me suspiciously.

HENRY FAIRLIE (1924–1990), *The Seven Deadly Sins Today*
We may say this of the face of Sloth: that at any age it is the face of
those who are already old beyond their years, who seem never to
have known any springtime, whether in their own lives or around
them each year, in whom the sap seems never to have risen.

CLAUDE J. PEIFER, OSB (b. 1927), *Monastic Spirituality*
Acedia is a formidable adversary because on purely natural grounds
its arguments are unassailable.

ANITA BROOKNER (b. 1928), *Brief Lives*
They shared a vast boredom; they were terrified of nothing
happening. Vinnie's haplessness came from a sort of despair, a
conviction that no one would care for her . . . while Owen's case was
perhaps more serious. In the absence of distractions he foundered. . . .
That was why he put up with a way of life that would have exhausted
many men of his age, why he pursued this fantasy of endless mobility,
endless availability. . . . He had the fullest diary of anyone I have ever
known. . . . He feared permanence.

MARTIN MARTY (b. 1928), "Glittering Vices"
"Sloth" is a bad translation of acedia, or accidie, the "noonday
demon," what Aquinas defined as sadness in the face of spiritual
good. Deadly sloth demands spiritual therapy and the grace of God,
not downgrading.

MAURICE SENDAK (b. 1928),
Pierre: A Cautionary Tale in Five Chapters and a Prologue
"If only you would say, I CARE."
"I don't care!"

MILAN KUNDERA (b. 1929), *Identity*
I'd say that the quantity of boredom, if boredom is measurable, is
much greater today than it once was. Because the old occupations,
at least most of them, were unthinkable without a passionate
involvement: the peasants in love with their land . . . the shoemakers
who knew every villager's feet by heart; the woodsmen; the
gardeners . . . The meaning of life wasn't an issue, it was there with
them, quite naturally, in their workshops, in their fields. . . . Today
we're all alike, all of us bound together by our shared apathy . . .
[which] has become a passion. The one great collective passion of
our time.

S. GIORA SHOHAM (b. 1929), *Society and the Absurd*
The processes leading to accidia are dynamic . . . existential and not
abstract. Nobody becomes accidic by proxy.

DOROTHEE SOELLE (1929–2003), *Suffering*
In the depth of suffering, people see themselves as abandoned and
forsaken by everyone. That which gave life its meaning has become
empty and void: it turned out to be an error, an illusion that is
shattered, a guilt that cannot be rectified, a void. The paths that lead
to this experience of nothingness are diverse, but the experience of
annihilation that occurs in unremitting suffering is the same.

PATRICIA SPACKS (b. 1929), *Boredom*
Boredom . . . is not the same as ennui, more closely related to
acedia. Ennui implies a judgment of the universe; boredom a
response to the immediate. Ennui belongs to those with a sense
of sublime potential, those who feel themselves superior to their
environment. . . . If only because it seems more dignified, many
people would rather suffer ennui than boredom, despite its
presumably greater misery.

MICHAEL CASEY, OCSO (b. 1930s?),
Fully Human, Fully Divine: An Interactive Christology
The vice of noninvolvement is said to be endemic in the Western
world. The acediac is a person without commitment, who lives
in a world characterized by mobility, passive entertainment,
self-indulgence, and the effective denial of the validity of any
external claim. . . . Sometimes [acedia] is identified with sloth or
idleness, but that is only the external face of an attitude marked by
chronic withdrawal from reality into the more comfortable zone of
uncommitted and free-floating fantasy. The temptation to acedia is
an invitation to abandon involvement and leave the pangs of
creativity to others.

MELVIN MADDOCKS (b. 1930s?), cited in *The American Heritage
Dictionary of the English Language*, 3rd edition, 1992
There is a name for the generic shoulder shrug—the buzzing
indifference, as if it's always 90 degrees in the shade after a large
lunch. The word is acedia. It is the weariness of effort that extends
to the heart and becomes a weariness of caring.

DONALD BARTHELME (1931–1989), "January"
Acedia is often conceived of as a kind of sullenness in the face of existence; I tried to locate its positive features. For example, it precludes certain kinds of madness, crowd mania, it precludes a certain type of error. You're not an enthusiast and therefore you don't go out and join a lynch mob—rather you languish on a couch with your head in your hands.

STANFORD M. LYMAN (1933–2003), *Deadly Sins: Society and Evil*
Acedia has a number of distinct components of which the most important is affectlessness, a lack of any feeling about self or other, a mind-state that gives rise to boredom, rancor, apathy, and a passive, inert, or sluggish mentation.

GODFRIED DANNEELS (b. 1933),
Speech at the Sixth Symposium of Bishops of Europe, Rome, 1985
Everywhere we are witnessing the fall of idols—science, progress—that have lost their halo. They have become—what they never should have ceased to be—tools in the hands of men . . . [but] all this has led among many people to a feeling of disenchantment and disillusion, boredom, unhappiness. . . . Our era is marked by a great spiritual "void," the *"taedium vitae"* and "acedia". . . found among many of our contemporaries.

ANDREI VOZNESENSKY (b. 1933), "An Ironic Treatise on Boredom"
Boredom is a fast of the spirit,
It is a solitary supper.

MIHALY CSIKSZENTMIHALYI (b. 1934), *Finding Flow*

Just as the excellence of an individual life depends to a large extent on how free time is used, so the quality of a society hinges on what its members do in their leisure time. . . . We have seen that at the social as well as the individual level habits of leisure act as both effects and . . . causes. . . . When work turns into a boring routine and community responsibilities lose their meaning, it is likely that leisure will become increasingly more important. And if a society becomes too dependent on entertainment, it is likely that there will be less psychic energy left to cope creatively with the technological and economic challenges that will inevitably arise.

JOAN DIDION (b. 1934), *Slouching Towards Bethlehem*

To have that sense of one's intrinsic worth which constitutes self-respect is potentially to have everything: the ability to discriminate, to love and to remain indifferent. To lack it is to be locked within oneself, paradoxically incapable of either love or indifference. . . . It is the phenomenon sometimes called "alienation from self." In its advanced stages, we no longer answer the telephone, because someone might want something. . . . Every encounter demands too much, tears the nerves, drains the will, and the specter of something as small as an unanswered letter arouses such disproportionate guilt that answering it becomes out of the question. To assign unanswered letters their proper weight . . . to give us back to ourselves—there lies the great, the singular power of self-respect. Without it, one eventually discovers the final turn of the screw: one runs away to find oneself, and finds no one at home.

VÁCLAV HÁVEL (b. 1936), *Letters to Olga: June 1979–September 1982*
The tragedy of modern man is not that he knows less and less about
the meaning of his own life, but that it bothers him less and less.

TERRENCE KARDONG, OSB (b. 1936),
Benedict's Rule: A Translation and Commentary, 48:18
bored (*acediosos*). Boredom is a different problem than laziness. In
fact, a monk with an abundant supply of physical energy may find
lectio [meditative reading] very hard because it requires repose and
concentration. If *acediosus* is closely connected to the classic fault/sin
of *acedia,* then it means disinterest in spiritual things.

THOMAS PYNCHON (b. 1937), "Nearer, My Couch, to Thee"
By the time of [Melville's] "Bartleby the Scrivener: A Story of
Wall-Street" (1853), acedia had lost the last of its religious
reverberations and was now an offense against the economy. . . .
Who is more guilty of Sloth, a person who collaborates with the
root of all evil, accepting things-as-they-are in return for a paycheck
and a hassle-free life, or one who does nothing, finally, but persist
in sorrow?

HUGH FEISS, OSB (b. 1939), "Acedia"
Of all the categories of sin and spiritual difficulty which the ancients
called the eight principal thoughts and the Middle Ages the seven
capital vices or sins none is more fluid and elusive than acedia.

JOSEPH BRODSKY (1940–1996), "In Praise of Boredom"
[Boredom is] life's main medium. . . . In general, a man shooting
heroin into his veins does so largely for the same reason you buy a
video: to dodge the redundancy of time. . . . Boredom speaks the
language of time, and it is to teach you the most valuable lesson in
your life: the lesson of your utter insignificance. . . . For boredom is
an invasion of time into your set of values. It puts your existence
into perspective, the net result of which is . . . humility.

GABRIEL BUNGE, OSB (b. 1940), *Earthen Vessels*
Every man is probably acquainted with [spiritual] "wildness" in the
form of that oppressive state of soul that the Fathers call *acedia,
taedium cordis* (John Cassian), weariness of soul, boredom, empty
indifference. . . . Against this, tears are a powerful antidote.

JEAN BETHKE EISHTAIN (b. 1941), *Who Are We?*
I take sloth to mean not simply inactivity but acquiescence in the
conventions of one's day; a refusal to take up the burden of self-
criticism; a falling into the zeitgeist unthinkingly, and, in so doing,
forgetting that we are made to [citing Karl Barth] "serve God
wittingly, in the tangle of our minds." . . . Pride and sloth may seem
antitheses but there is "profound correspondence" between the
Promethean and the "unheroic and trivial form of sloth." . . . Sloth is
a type of escapism, an evasion of responsibility. It comes down to a
form of "practical atheism." . . . What is at stake [whether in] pride
or slothfulness is a negation of appropriate humility; a denial of
relationality and community; a quest for self-sufficiency that, in

the case of sloth, involves too thoroughgoing an absorption in the views and evaluations of others. . . . One is akin to Kafka's bird in search of a cage.

SOLOMON SCHIMMEL (b. 1941), *The Seven Deadly Sins*
It is ludicrous and pitiful to see "mature" adults flock to every New Age fad. But this is a symptom of the spiritual sloth of our age. These people are searching for something worth living for, and for some way to be at peace with themselves. . . . They are looking in the wrong place. The answers will not be found in magic and witchcraft and shamanism, or even in swimming with dolphins—but in an honest grappling with their own inner natures.

ANGELO SCOLA (b. 1941), *Ospitare il reale: Per una "idea" di Università* (To Host the Real: For an "Idea" of University)
Today's society is characterized by a certain cultural acedia. . . . Being disinclined to be curious about what we are, what happens to us, and what we do, we are too lazy to undertake that "cultural work". . . that human life itself naturally asks of us.

DOM BERNARDO OLIVERA, OCSO (b. 1943),
"The Sadness Corroding Our Desire for God"
The great masters of the spiritual craft [observed] that at the root of bad thoughts are disordered desires . . . and referred [to them] as spirits, demons, thoughts, afflictions, passions, attachments, appetites, wills, vices, capital sins. These masters have taught us to fight them . . . in a special combat [using] self-denial and humility. In the last analysis, it is a question of stripping off the old man so as to put on the new . . . with the help of divine grace. . . . What is

impossible for us is very possible for God, [who] is waiting for us to receive his gift as best we can. So if we feel too small and too weak to fight the devilish scourge of acedia, we can at least begin by accepting the pain killer recommended by Saint Thomas Aquinas: a shower and a good nap [*Summa theologica* I–II, 38, 5].

OWEN EDWARDS (b. 1947), "The Big Squeeze"
Process is a drag, marketers have been telling us for a century or so: delay, drudgery, an exhausting gap between the starter's pistol and the finish line. Process is boring. So out with the tedium, in with joy! As we drift toward our digital dream, process seems eradicable, like smallpox. Thus we are asked to celebrate what could be one of the great hidden disasters of our technological era . . . because process matters as much to human endeavors as results. In our endless quest to eliminate work, to find effortless fulfillment and the grail of One E-Z Step, we deny the ultimate value of the grind.

S. DENNIS FORD (b. 1947),
Sins of Omission: A Primer on Moral Indifference
Psychologically, sloth is described as a sin of arrested childhood: sloth extends into adulthood the passivity, dependency, and egocentricity characteristic of childhood . . . [providing] a context for indifference, a slothful expectation that someone else will do it for us.

KENNETH R. HIMES, OFM (b. 1950s?), "The Formation of Conscience: The Sin of Sloth and the Significance of Spirituality"
When used in the moral sense, the person seized by *acedia* is the affect-less individual, the one incapable of investment or commitment, a person who cannot get deeply involved in any cause

or relationship. . . . Sloth as moral apathy is what hinders a person from pursuing that which is good. It is a refusal to seek the good because it is difficult and demanding.

MICHAEL L. RAPOSA (b. 1950s?),
Boredom and the Religious Imagination
One discovers in the Buddhist concept of *sunyata,* as well as in the world-weariness of Ecclesiastes, a powerful vision of the emptiness of all things, something akin to a deep boredom, but acting to stimulate rather than cloud awareness. Likewise, within Christianity, acedia is to be resisted, but the achievement of a certain kind of disinterestedness is regarded as necessary for real progress in the spiritual life.

WENDY WASSERSTEIN (1950–2006), *Sloth*
When you achieve true slothdom, you have no desire for the world to change. True sloths are not revolutionaries. There is no possible dialectic. . . . Sloths are neither angry nor hopeful. They are not even anarchists. Anarchy takes too much work. Sloths are the lazy guardians at the gate of the status quo. . . . Whether you're a traditional sloth or a New Age übersloth, we are all looking at the possibility of real thought, and rejecting it. Better to fall into line than to question the going ethos.

THOMAS L. FRIEDMAN (b. 1953), "Singapore and Katrina"
There is something troublingly self-indulgent and slothful about America today—something that Katrina highlighted and that people who live in countries where the laws of gravity still apply really noticed. . . . [As Janadas Devan of the *Straits Times* in Singapore

wrote,] "It is not only government that doesn't show up when [it] is starved of resources and leached of all its meaning. Community doesn't show up either, sacrifice doesn't show up, pulling together doesn't show up, 'we're all in this together' doesn't show up."

COLUMBA STEWART, OSB (b. 1957),
"Evagrius Ponticus and the 'Eight Generic *Logismoi*'"
Evagrius is the first writer we know to have provided a systematic analysis of accidie, and his descriptions of monks beset with this affliction are extraordinary vignettes surely drawn from his own experience. Evagrius noted the complex nature of accidie, which creates a black hole that swallows all other thoughts.

R. R. RENO (b. 1959), "Fighting the Noonday Devil"
Most of us want to be safe. We want to find a cocoon, a spiritually, psychologically, economically, and physically gated community in which to live without danger and disturbance. The care-free life, a life *a-cedia*, is our cultural ideal.

ANDREW CRISLIP (b. 1970s?),
"The Sin of Sloth or the Illness of the Demons"
The semantics of acedia are so broad that there is no proper modern equivalent. . . . Yet given the diversity of its descriptions, acedia may be coherently understood as a constellation of behaviors, all of which entail deviant or culturally illegitimate adaptations to anomie. . . . Early monastic writers clearly felt no sense of contradiction when attributing widely diverse psychological and somatic symptoms to acedia—which is a testament to both the

depth of insight and the practical utility of the monastic traditions of psychological and spiritual guidance.

JEAN-CHARLES NAULT, OSB (b. 1970),
"Acedia: Enemy of Spiritual Joy"
Acedia . . . is a profound withdrawal into self. Action is no longer perceived as a gift of oneself, as the response to a prior love that calls us. . . . It is seen instead as an uninhibited seeking of personal satisfaction in the fear of "losing" something. The desire to save one's "freedom" at any price reveals, in reality, a deeper enslavement to the "self." There is no longer any room for an abandonment . . . to the other or for the joy of gift; what remains is sadness or bitterness within the one who distances himself from the community and who, being separated from others, finds himself likewise separated from God.

LARS SVENDSEN (b. 1970), *A Philosophy of Boredom*
In a world of emptiness, extremism will stand out as an attractive alternative to boredom.

A. J. SCHEMADOVITS-NORRIS (b. 1989), "Hobs the Hobo"
Hobs lacked desire. However, Hobs was not ordinary. . . . [He] was blessed with a special gift like no one in the history of the world has ever seen. . . . Hobs could do anything. There was no boundary to his infinite power. He could fly, teleport, heal, seduce, corrupt, and even destroy. . . . However, he referred to his "gift" as his "curse." The entire world in all of its glory and wonder lay in front of Hobs to discover yet he had no desire to explore it.

WEBSTER'S 1913 DICTIONARY

(as edited from www.webster-dictionary.net/definition/acedia)

acedia: n. 1. apathy and inactivity in the practice of virtue
(personified as one of the deadly sins)

Related Words: accidia, aloofness, anger, apathy, ataraxia, ataraxy,
avarice, avaritia, benumbedness, blah, blahs, boredom, carelessness,
casualness, cave of despair, cave of Trophonius, comatoseness, deadly
sin, despair, desperateness, desperation, despondency, detachment,
disconsolateness, disinterest, dispassion, disregard, disregardfulness,
drowsiness, dullness, easygoingness, enervation, ennui, envy, fatigue,
forlornness, gluttony, greed, gula, heartlessness, heaviness, hebetude,
heedlessness, hopelessness, inanimation, inappetence, inattention,
incuriosity, indifference, indiscrimination, inexcitability, insouciance,
invidia, ira, jadedness, lack of affect, lack of appetite, lackadaisicalness,
languidness, languishment, languor, languorousness, lassitude,
lenitude, lentor, lethargicalness, lethargy, lifelessness, listlessness, lust,
luxuria, mindlessness, negligence, no exit, no way, no way out,
nonchalance, numbness, oscitancy, passiveness, passivity, phlegm,
phlegmaticalness, phlegmaticness, plucklessness, pococurantism,
pride, recklessness, regardlessness, resignation, resignedness,
satedness, sleepiness, sloth, slothfulness, slowness, sluggishness,
somnolence, sopor, soporiferousness, spiritlessness, spunklessness,
stupefaction, stupor, superbia, supineness, torpidity, torpidness,
torpitude, torpor, unanxiousness, unconcern, unmindfulness,
unsolicitousness, weariness, withdrawnness, world-weariness, wrath

ROLAND BARTHES (1915–1980), *The Pleasure of the Text*
It can't be helped: [ennui] is not simple.

Acknowledgments

I am grateful for the work of the many scholars I have cited in this text, and for the encouragement and assistance of my agent, Lynn Nesbit, and the people at Riverhead, notably my editor, Carolyn Carlson, and Susan Petersen Kennedy, for their patience and kind attention.

I thank the people who read this manuscript in whole, or in part, and offered helpful comments: John Eudes Bamberger, OCSO; Dr. Lynn S. Joy; Terrence Kardong, OSB; Kilian McDonnell, OSB; Paul Philibert, O.P.; Cindy Spiegel; and Dr. Eleonore Stump.

My favorite librarian, Molly O'Hara Ewing, has provided me with invaluable reference services and support, and I also must thank Martin Marty for giving me a book at the right time.

I extend my thanks to my family and David's family; and to Josue Behnen, OSB; Debra Bendis; Renée Branigan, OSB; the Reverend John Buchanan; the Reverend Cynthia Campbell; the Reverend Gail and Sylvia Cross; Jeremy Driscoll, OSB; William Dunn; the late Andrea Dworkin; Warren Farha of Eighth Day Books; Hugh Feiss, OSB; Mary Forman, OSB; Ruth Fox, OSB; the Reverend G. Keith Gunderson; Jeremy Hall, OSB; Patrick Hart, OCSO; Patrick Henry; Kathleen

Hughes, RSCJ; Paul Jasmer, OSB; Aaron Jensen, OSB; Roger Kasprick, OSB, Timothy Kelly, OSB; John Klassen, OSB; Susan Lardy, OSB; James Martin, S.J.; René McGraw, OSB; Dunstan Moorse, OSB; Julian Nix, OSB; Michael Patella, OSB; Fr. Joe Ponessa, SSD; Dietrich Reinhart, OSB; Leo Ryska, OSB; William Skudlarek, OSB; Columba Stewart, OSB; James M. Sullivan; Judith Sutera, OSB; the late Jeanne Tamisiea; Christine Trzcinski; the late Verlyn Weishaar; Robert West, OSB; and Ann and Mike Williams.

Selected Bibliography

ANCIENT SOURCES

Evagrius of Pontus. *The Greek Ascetic Corpus.* Trans. Robert E. Sinkewicz. Oxford University Press, 2003.

————. *The Praktikos & Chapters on Prayer.* Trans. John Eudes Bamberger, OCSO. Cistercian, 1981.

Merton, Thomas. *The Wisdom of the Desert.* New Directions, 1961. Includes a helpful introduction to the lives of the early monks; the translations are by Merton.

RB 1980: The Rule of St. Benedict in English. Ed. Timothy Fry, OSB. Liturgical Press, 1980. With essays on monastic history, commentaries, and a glossary.

Ward, Benedicta, ed. and trans. *The Sayings of the Desert Fathers.* Cistercian, 1975.

CONTEMPORARY SOURCES

The Benedictine Handbook. Liturgical Press, 2003.

de Waal, Esther. *Living with Contradiction: Reflections on the Rule of St. Benedict*. HarperCollins, 1989.

———. *Seeking God: The Way of St. Benedict*. Liturgical Press, 1984.

Driscoll, Jeremy, OSB. *A Monk's Alphabet*. Shambhala, 2006.

Forman, Mary, OSB. *Praying with the Desert Mothers*. Liturgical Press, 2005.

Funk, Mary Margaret, OSB. *Thoughts Matter*. Continuum, 1991.

Hart, Patrick, OCSO, ed. *A Monastic Vision for the 21st Century*. Cistercian, 2006. Authors include John Eudes Bamberger, Michael Casey, Joan Chittister, Gail Fitzpatrick, and Terrence Kardong.

Healy, Seán Desmond. *Boredom, Self, and Culture*. Associated University Presses, 1984.

Jamison, Christopher, OSB. *Finding Sanctuary: Monastic Steps for Everyday Life*. Liturgical Press, 2006.

Kardong, Terrence, OSB. *The Benedictines*. Liturgical Press, 1988.

———. *Benedict's Rule: A Translation and Commentary*. Liturgical Press, 1996.

———. *Day by Day with St. Benedict*. Liturgical Press, 2005.

Kuhn, Reinhard. *The Demon of Noontide: Ennui in Western Literature*. Princeton University Press, 1976.

Nault, Jean-Charles. "Accidie: Enemy of Spiritual Joy." *Communio* 31 (Summer 2004).

Norris, Kathleen. *The Cloister Walk*. Riverhead, 1996.

Olivera, Dom Bernardo, OCSO. "The Sadness Corroding Our Desire for God." osco.org.

Schimmel, Solomon. *The Seven Deadly Sins*. Oxford University Press, 1997.

Solomon, Andrew. *The Noonday Demon: An Atlas of Depression*. Scribner, 2001.

Spacks, Patricia. *Boredom*. University of Chicago Press, 1995.

Stewart, Columba, OSB. *Prayer and Community: The Benedictine Tradition*. Orbis, 1998.

Svendsen, Lars. *A Philosophy of Boredom*. Trans. John Irons. Reaktion, 2005.

Tvedten, Benet, OSB. *How to Be a Monastic and Not Leave Your Day Job*. Paraclete, 2006.

———. *The View from a Monastery*. Paraclete, 2006.

Wasserstein, Wendy. *The Seven Deadly Sins: Sloth*. Oxford University Press, 2005.

Wenzel, Siegfried. *The Sin of Sloth: Acedia in Medieval Thought and Literature*. University of North Carolina Press, 1967.

Credits and Permissions

The author gratefully acknowledges permission to quote from the following:

Charles Baudelaire, "Spleen 76," from *The Flowers of Evil & Paris Spleen*. Translated by William H. Crosby. Translation copyright © 1991 by William H. Crosby. Reprinted with permission of BOA Editions, Ltd. www.boaeditions.org.

John Berryman, "Death Ballad" and "The Fact and Issues," from *Collected Poems: 1937–1971*. Copyright © 1989 by Kate Donahue Berryman. Reprinted by permission of Farrar, Straus and Giroux, LLC. And from *Collected Poems: 1937–1971*. Reprinted by permission of Faber and Faber Ltd.

John Berryman, Dream Song "#14," from *The Dream Songs*. Copyright © 1969 by John Berryman. Copyright renewed 1997 by Kate Donahue Berryman. Reprinted by permission of Farrar, Straus and Giroux, LLC. And from *The Dream Songs*. Copyright © 1969 by John Berryman. Reprinted by permission of Faber and Faber Ltd.

Evagrius Ponticus, *The Praktikos & Chapters on Prayer*. Copyright 1972 by